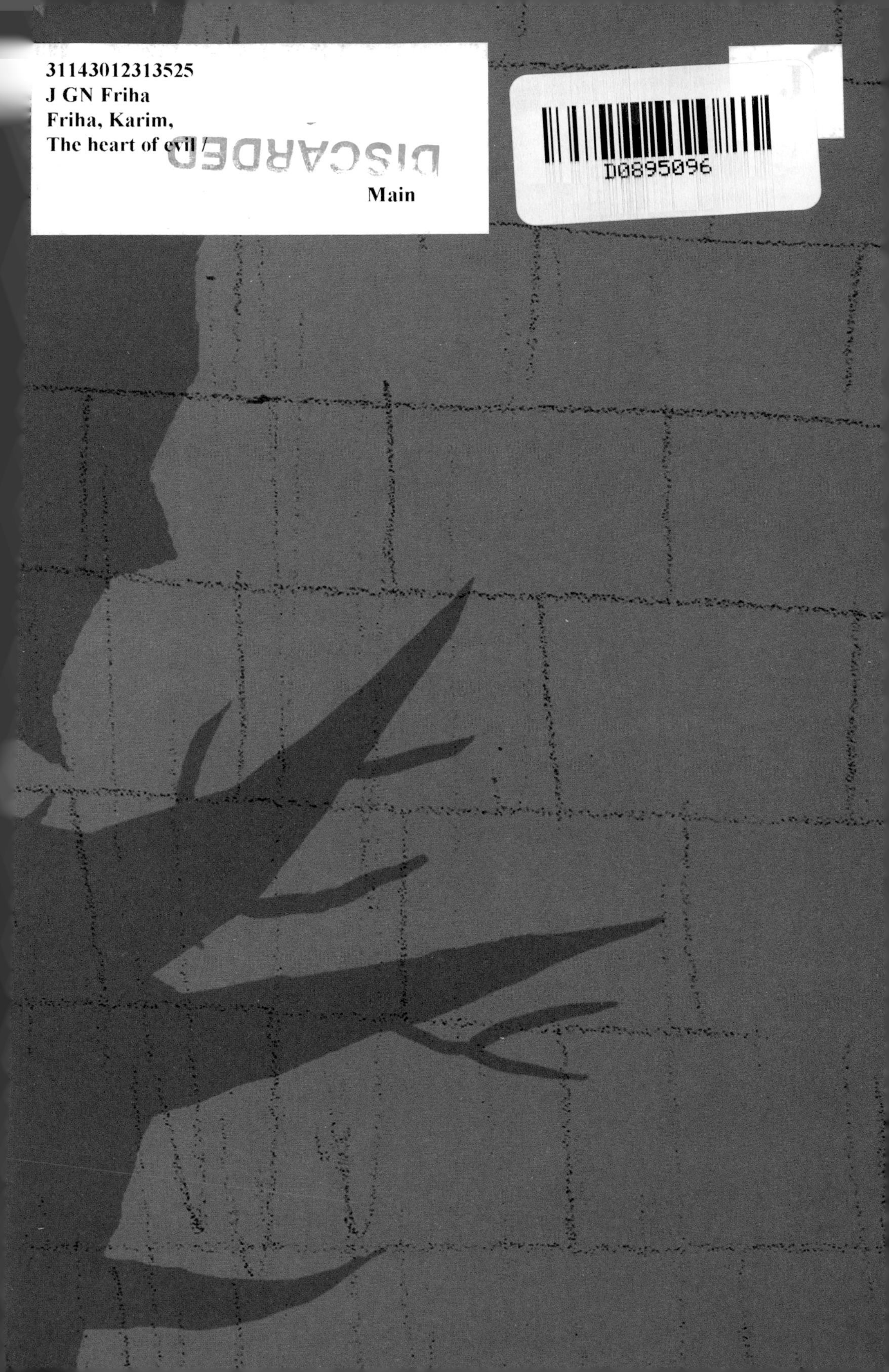

Karim Friha

RISE OF THE ZELPHIRE

Book Three: The Heart of Evil

Written and Illustrated
by
Karim Friha

Translation by Jeremy Melloul
Localization, Layout, and Editing by Mike Kennedy

MAGNETIC™

ISBN: 978-1-942367-90-1

Library of Congress Control Number: 2019917016

Rise of the Zelphire, Volume 3, published 2020 by Magnetic Press, LLC.
Originally published in French under the following title: *Le Réveil du Zelphire, Au Cœur du Mal*
© Gallimard 2012. MAGNETIC™, MAGNETIC PRESS™, and their associated distinctive designs
are trademarks of Magnetic Press, LLC. No similarity between any of the names, characters,
persons, and/or institutions in this book with those of any living or dead person or institution
is intended, and any such similarity which may exist is purely coincidental. All rights reserved.
Printed in China.

10 9 8 7 6 5 4 3 2 1

Thank you
to Joann and Thierry for their trust, and
to Lena, my parents, and friends for their encouragement and precious help.

— Karim Friha

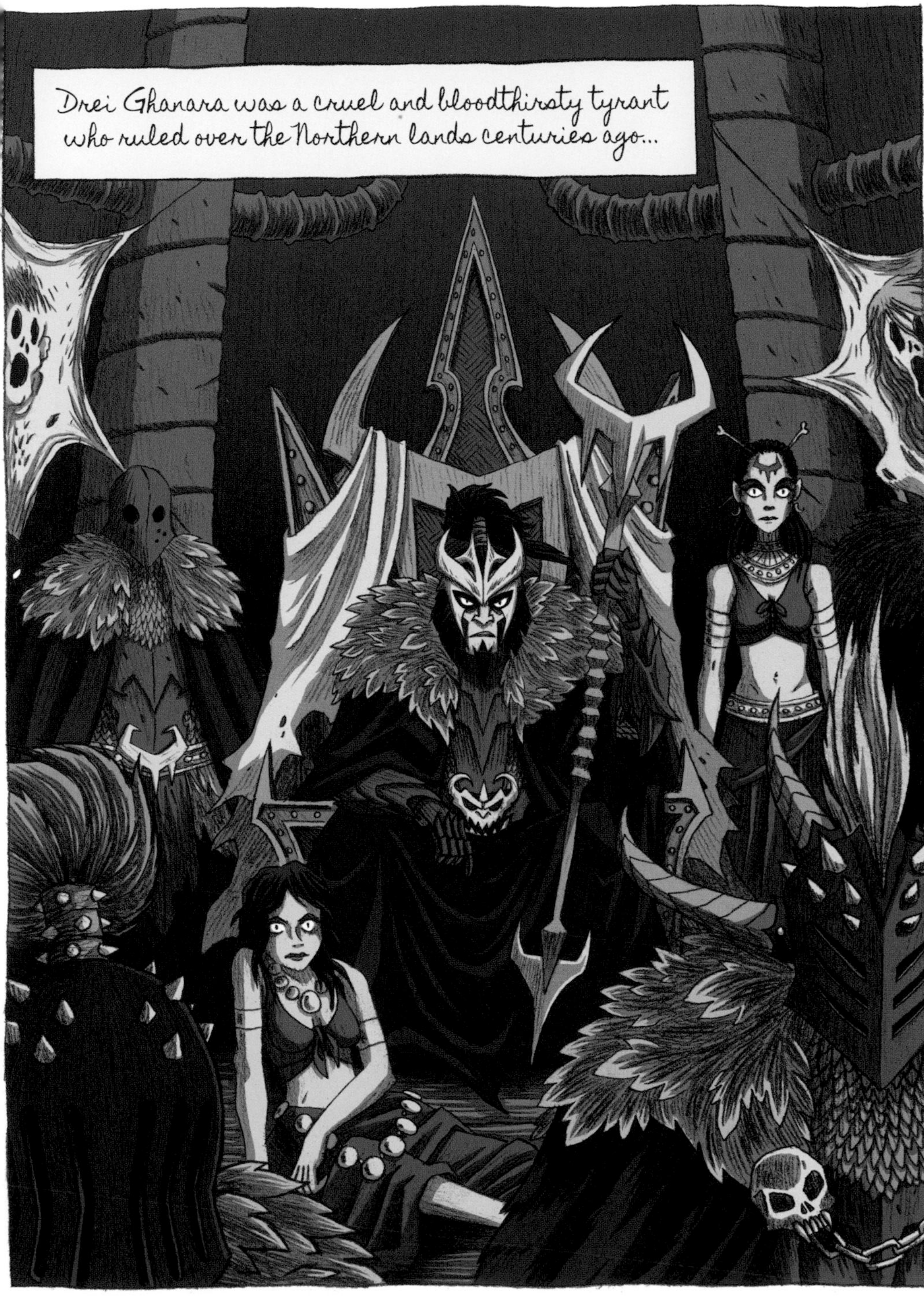
Drei Ghanara was a cruel and bloodthirsty tyrant who ruled over the Northern lands centuries ago...

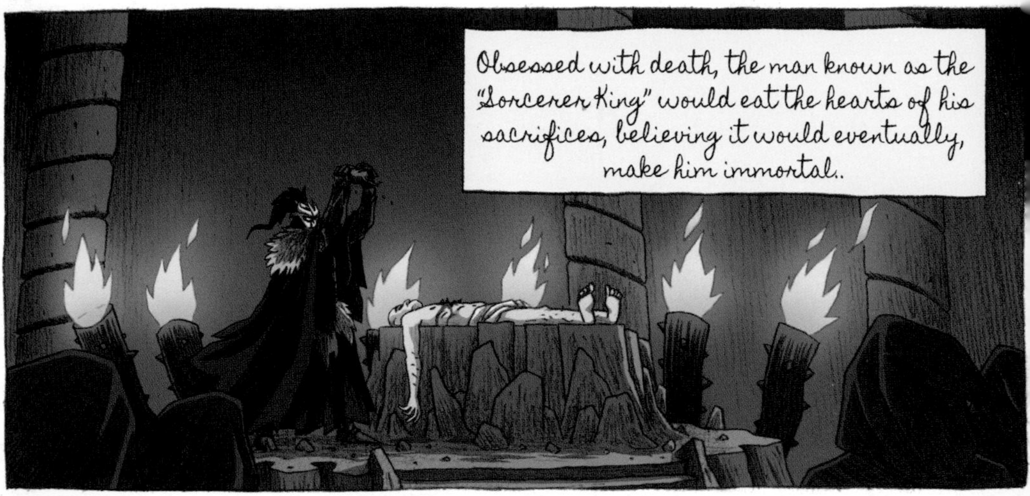
Obsessed with death, the man known as the "Sorcerer King" would eat the hearts of his sacrifices, believing it would eventually make him immortal..

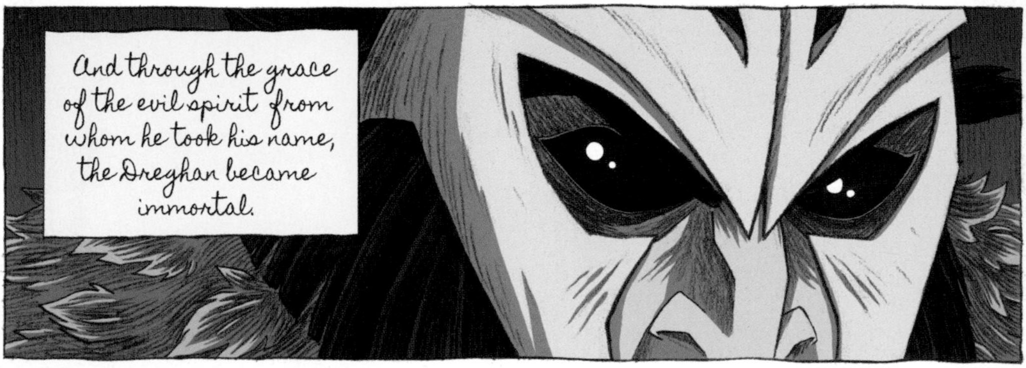
And through the grace of the evil spirit from whom he took his name, the Dreghan became immortal.

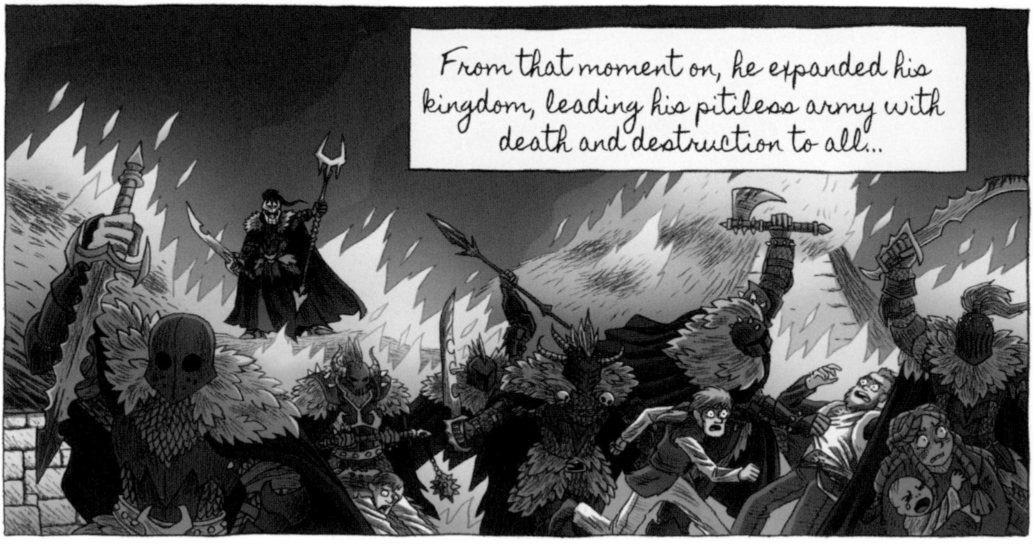
From that moment on, he expanded his kingdom, leading his pitiless army with death and destruction to all...

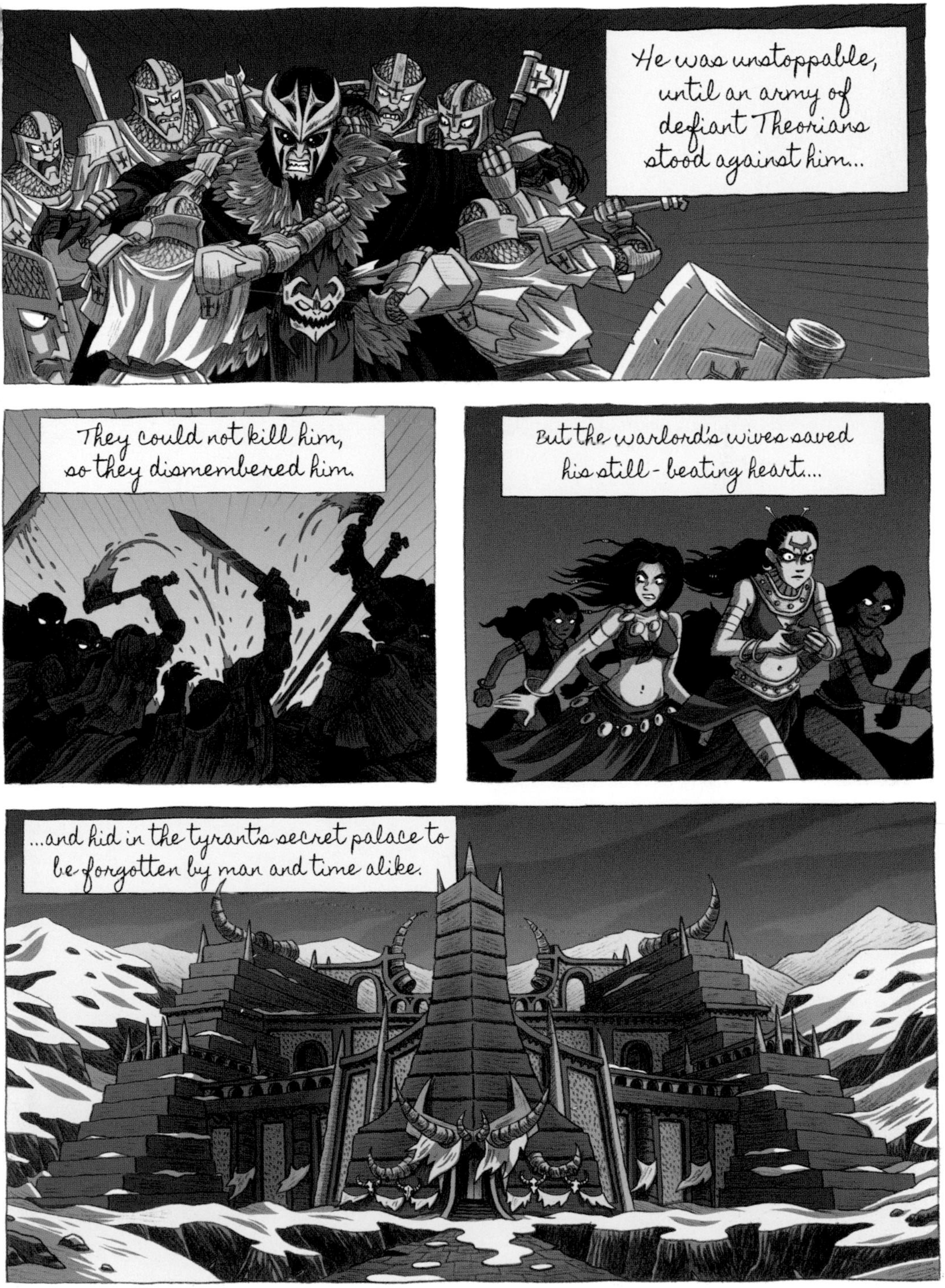
He was unstoppable, until an army of defiant Theorians stood against him...
They could not kill him, so they dismembered him.
But the warlord's wives saved his still-beating heart...
...and hid in the tyrant's secret palace to be forgotten by man and time alike.

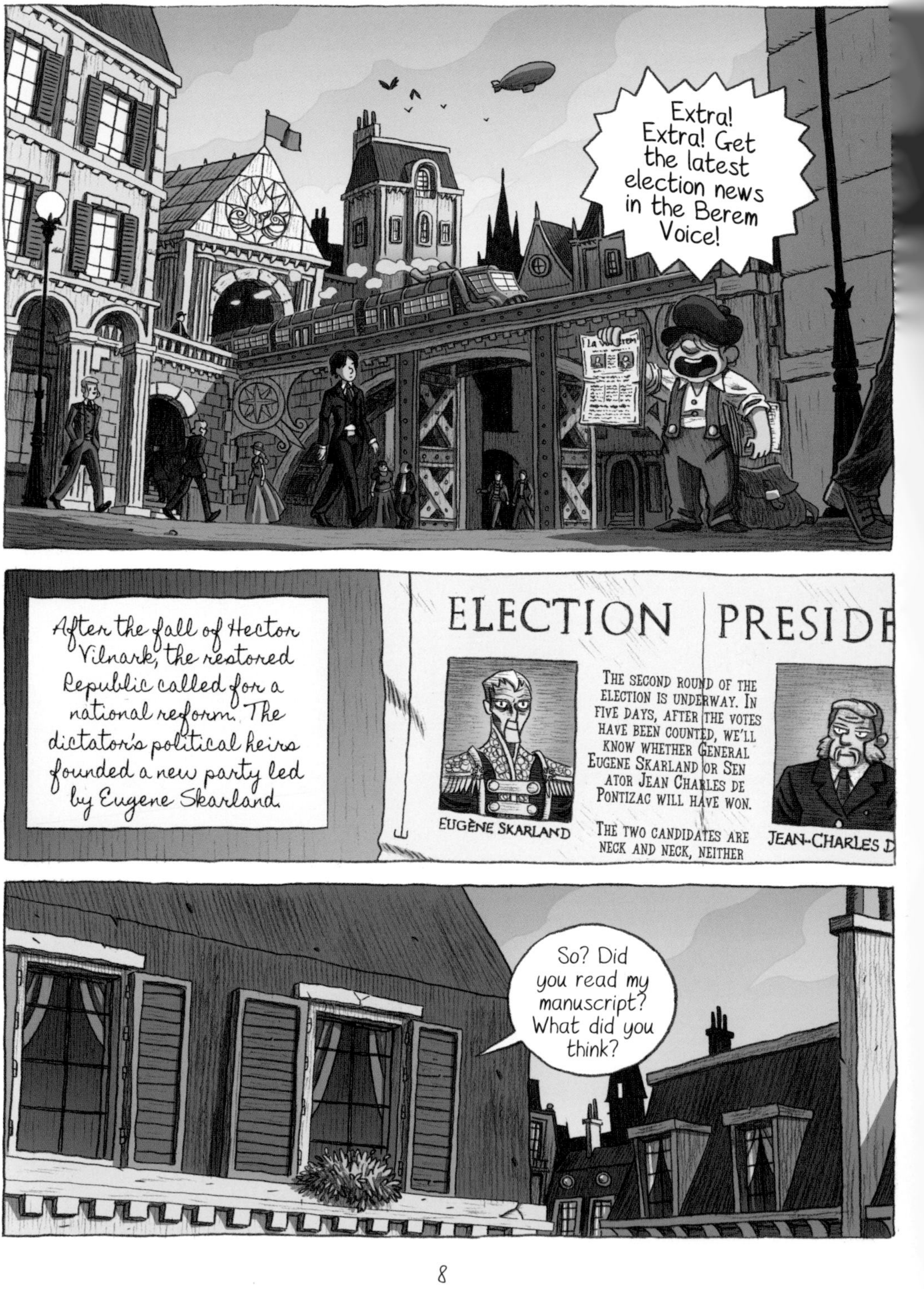
Extra! Extra! Get the latest election news in the Berem Voice!
After the fall of Hector Vilnark, the restored Republic called for a national reform. The dictator's political heirs founded a new party led by Eugene Skarland.
ELECTION PRESIDE
THE SECOND ROUND OF THE ELECTION IS UNDERWAY. IN FIVE DAYS, AFTER THE VOTES HAVE BEEN COUNTED, WE'LL KNOW WHETHER GENERAL EUGENE SKARLAND OR SEN ATOR JEAN CHARLES DE PONTIZAC WILL HAVE WON.
THE TWO CANDIDATES ARE NECK AND NECK, NEITHER
EUGÈNE SKARLAND
JEAN-CHARLES D
So? Did you read my manuscript? What did you think?

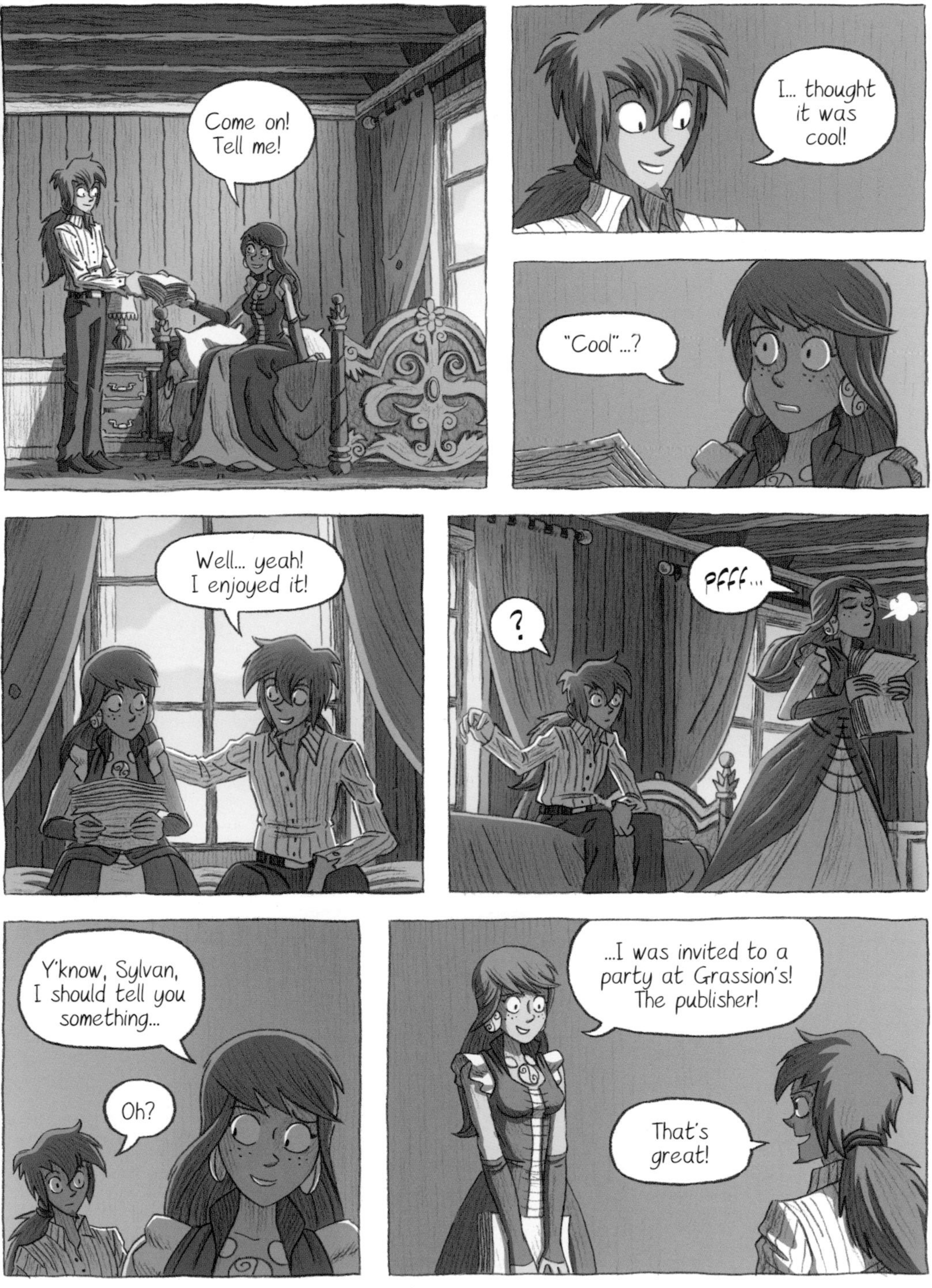
Come on! Tell me!
I... thought it was cool!
"Cool"...?
Well... yeah! I enjoyed it!
?
PFFF...
Y'know, Sylvan, I should tell you something...
Oh?
...I was invited to a party at Grassion's! The publisher!
That's great!

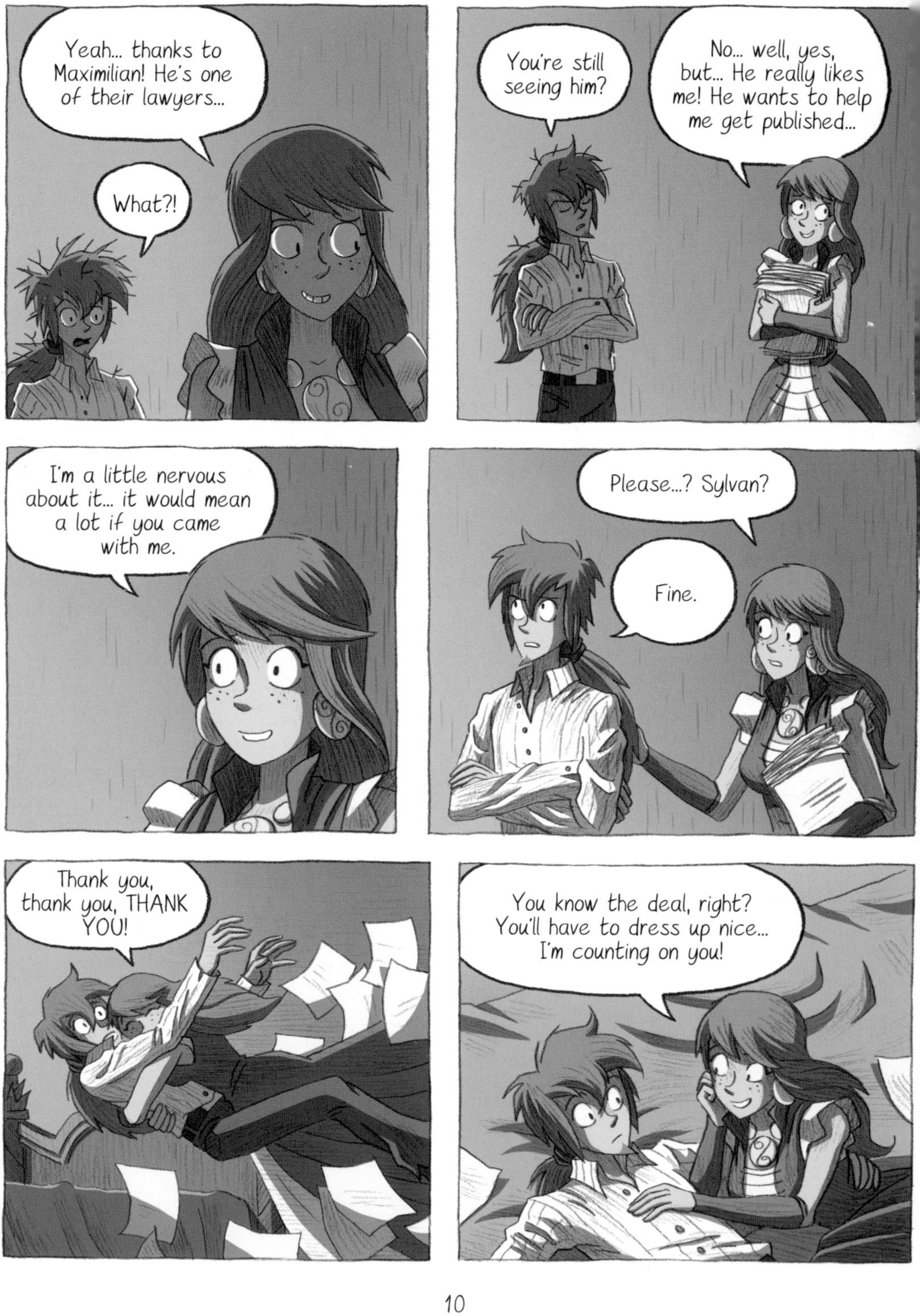
Yeah... thanks to Maximilian! He's one of their lawyers...
What?!
You're still seeing him?
No... well, yes, but... He really likes me! He wants to help me get published...
I'm a little nervous about it... it would mean a lot if you came with me.
Please...? Sylvan?
Fine.
Thank you, thank you, THANK YOU!
You know the deal, right? You'll have to dress up nice... I'm counting on you!

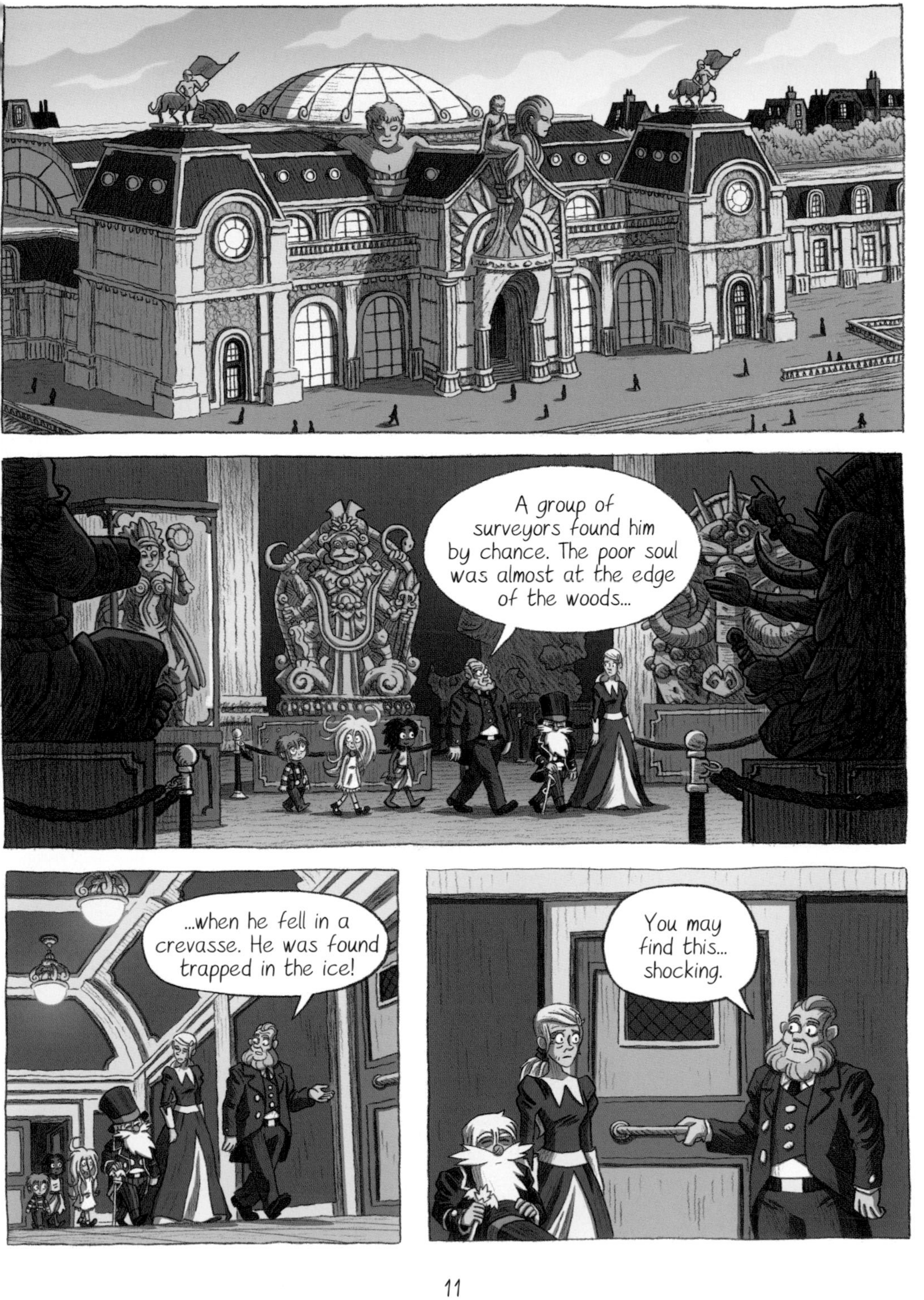
A group of surveyors found him by chance. The poor soul was almost at the edge of the woods...
...when he fell in a crevasse. He was found trapped in the ice!
You may find this... shocking.

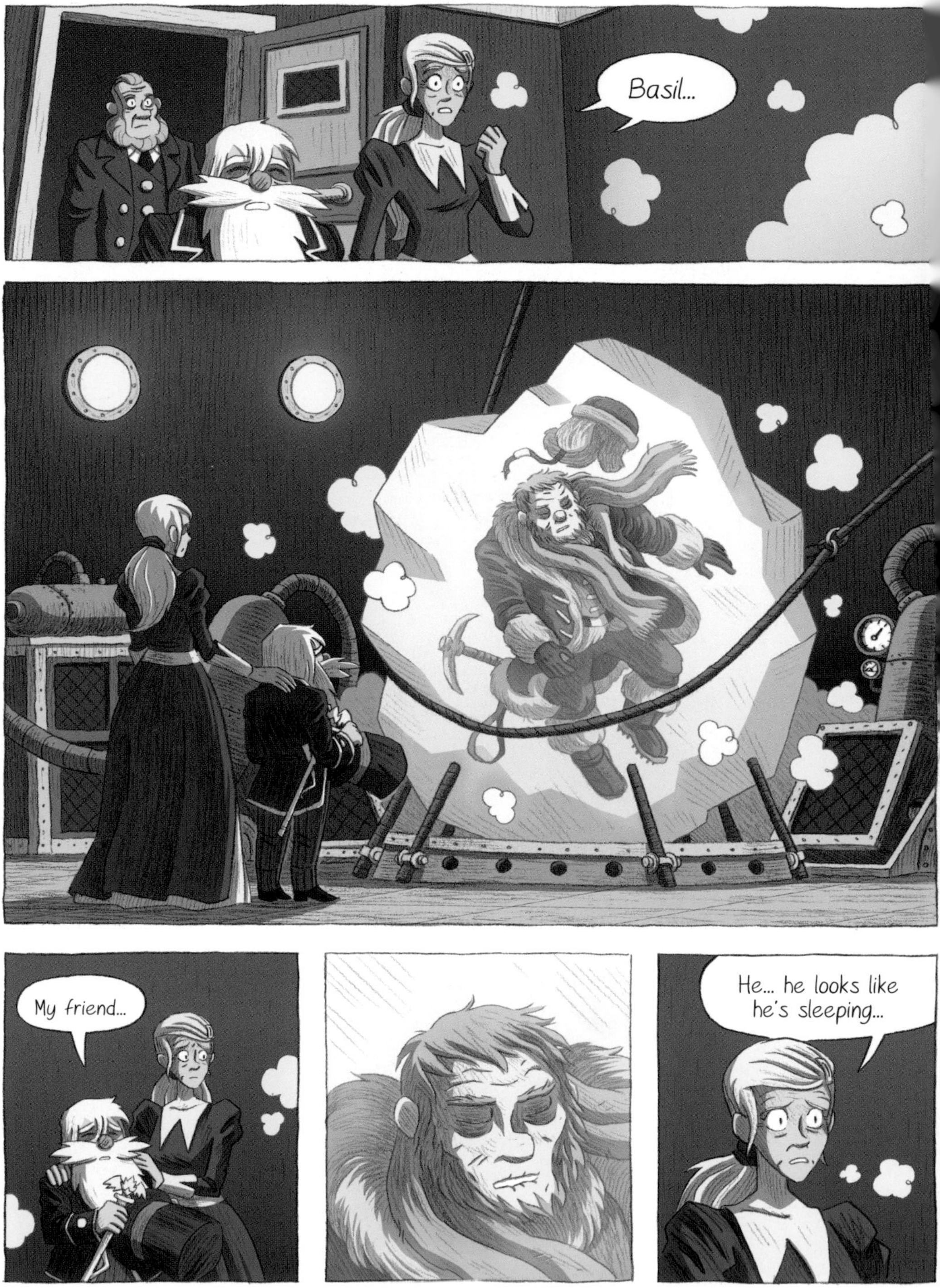
Basil...
My friend...
He... he looks like he's sleeping...

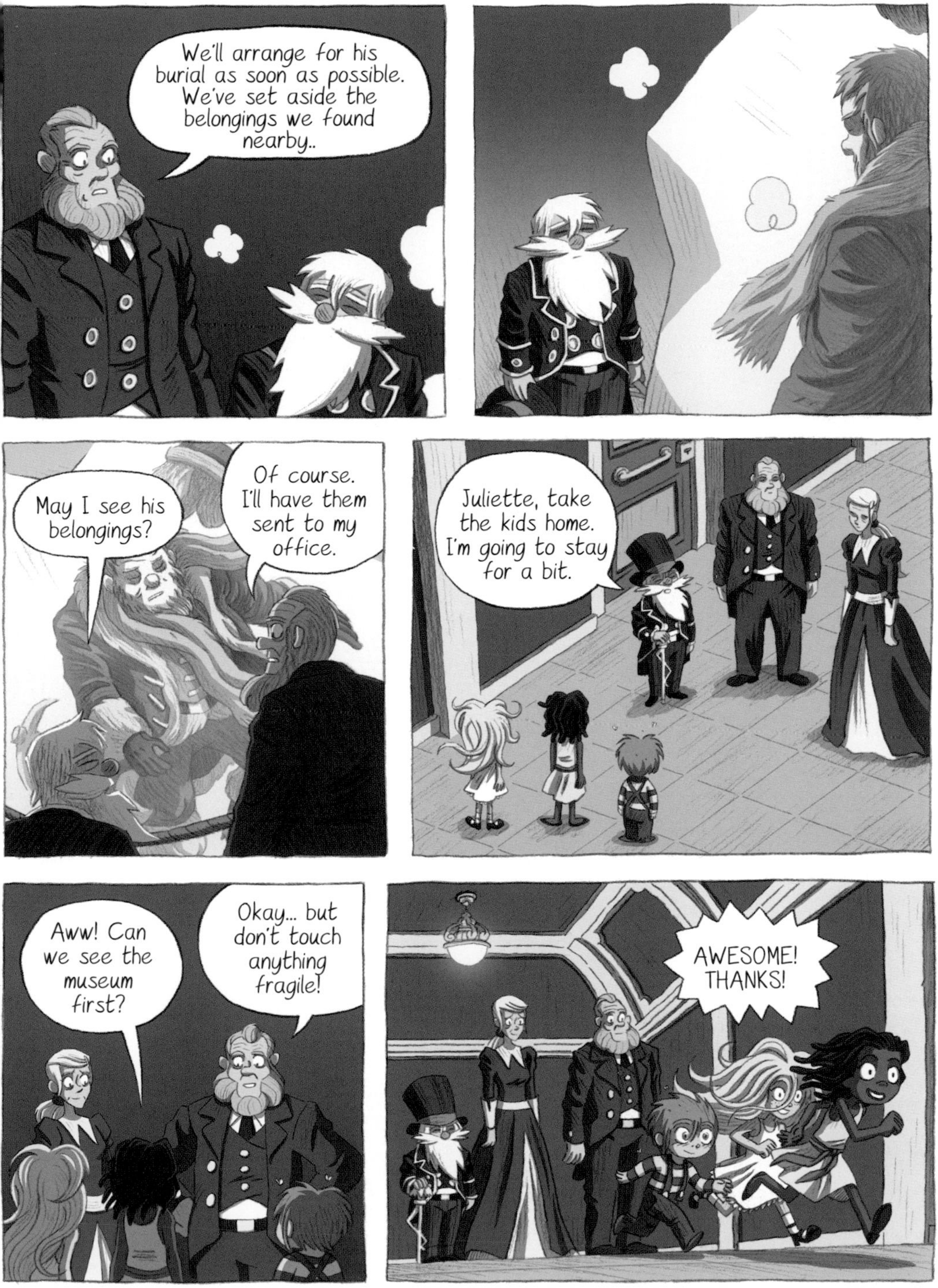
We'll arrange for his burial as soon as possible. We've set aside the belongings we found nearby..
May I see his belongings?
Of course. I'll have them sent to my office.
Juliette, take the kids home. I'm going to stay for a bit.
Aww! Can we see the museum first?
Okay... but don't touch anything fragile!
AWESOME! THANKS!

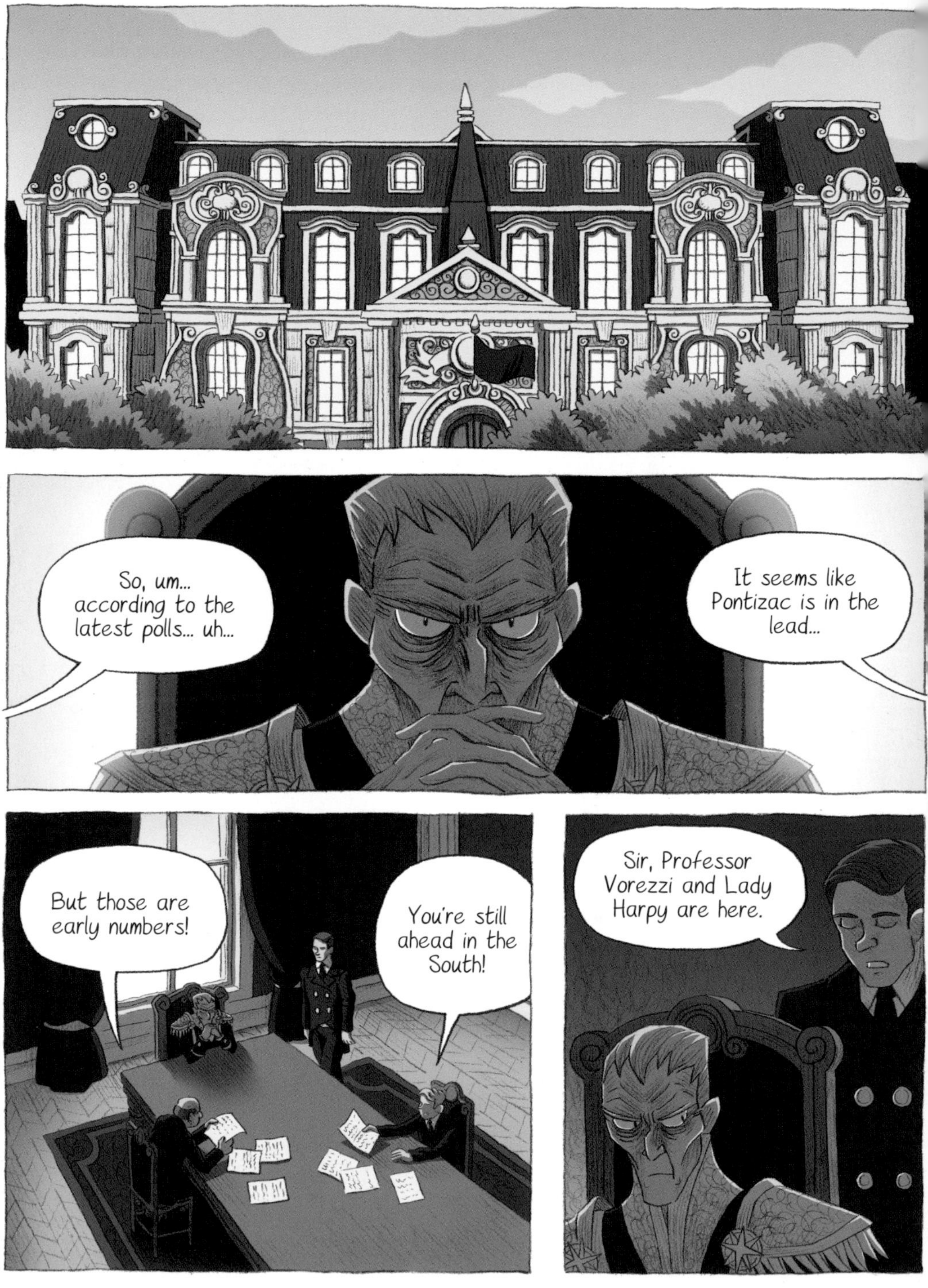
So, um... according to the latest polls... uh...
It seems like Pontizac is in the lead...
But those are early numbers!
You're still ahead in the South!
Sir, Professor Vorezzi and Lady Harpy are here.

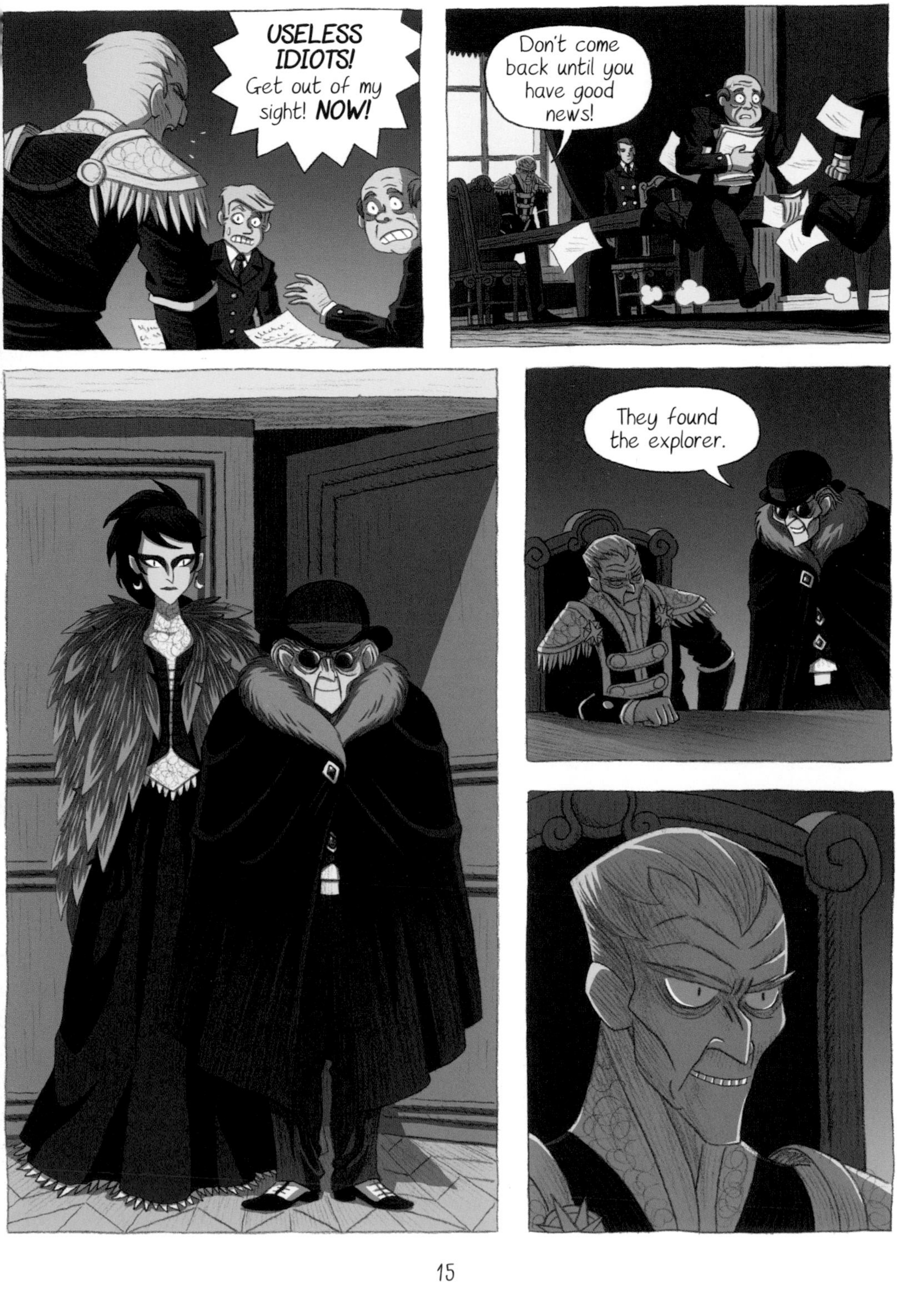
USELESS IDIOTS! Get out of my sight! NOW!
Don't come back until you have good news!
They found the explorer.

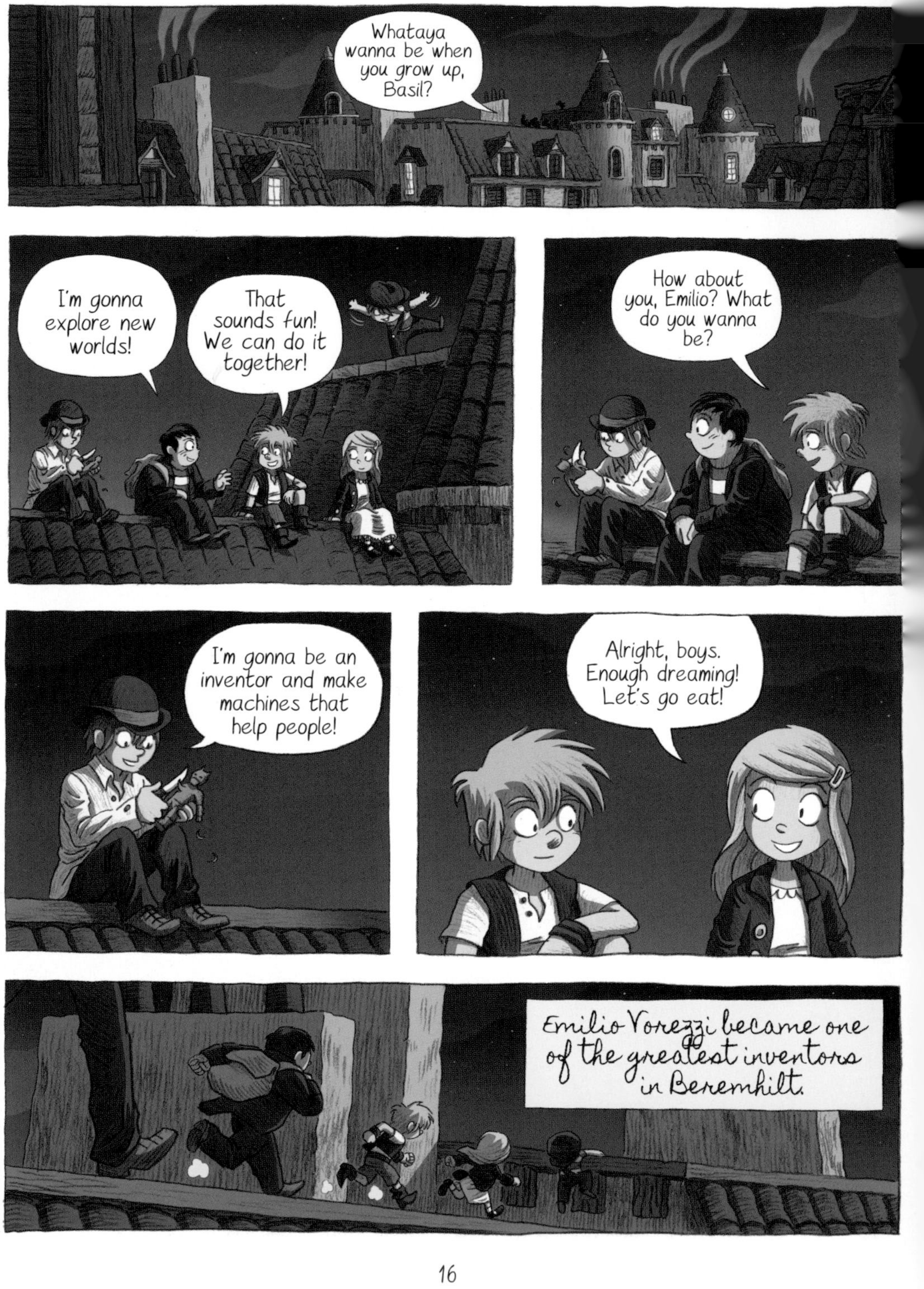
Whataya wanna be when you grow up, Basil?
I'm gonna explore new worlds!
That sounds fun! We can do it together!
How about you, Emilio? What do you wanna be?
I'm gonna be an inventor and make machines that help people!
Alright, boys. Enough dreaming! Let's go eat!
Emilio Vorezzi became one of the greatest inventors in Beremhilt.

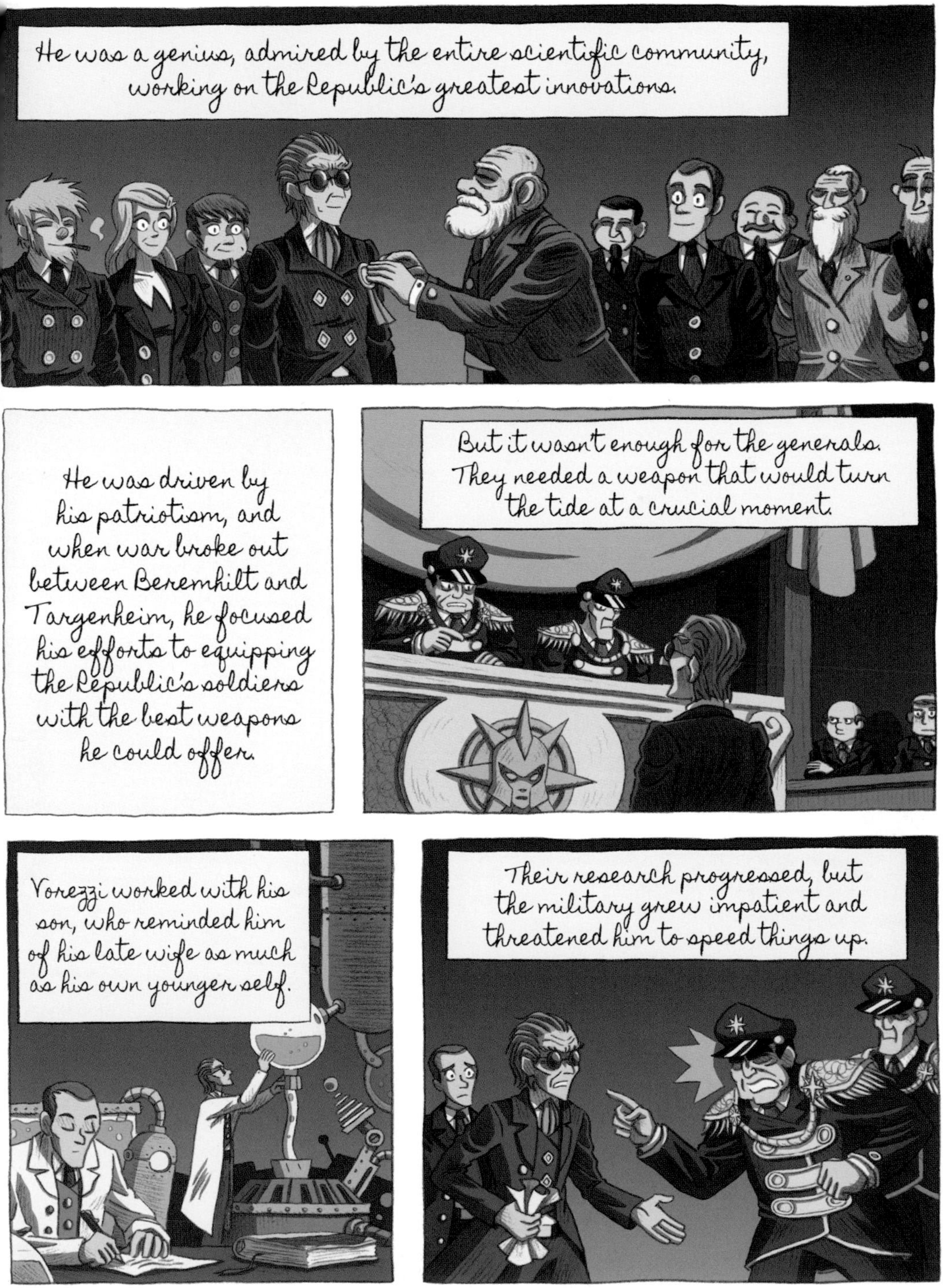
He was a genius, admired by the entire scientific community, working on the Republic's greatest innovations.
He was driven by his patriotism, and when war broke out between Beremhilt and Targenheim, he focused his efforts to equipping the Republic's soldiers with the best weapons he could offer.
But it wasn't enough for the generals. They needed a weapon that would turn the tide at a crucial moment.
Vorezzi worked with his son, who reminded him of his late wife as much as his own younger self.
Their research progressed, but the military grew impatient and threatened him to speed things up.

Despite his warnings, they ordered him to test their latest weapon. His son convinced him to agree.

Vorezzi had designed a chemical formula that could be turned into a devastating bomb.

But he was right to be cautious... the chemical reaction was unstable and the results were terrible...

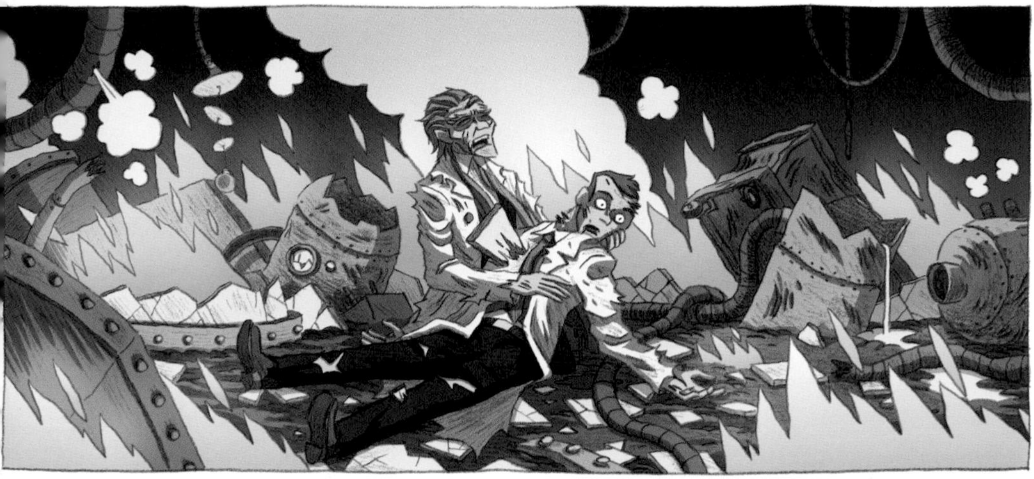

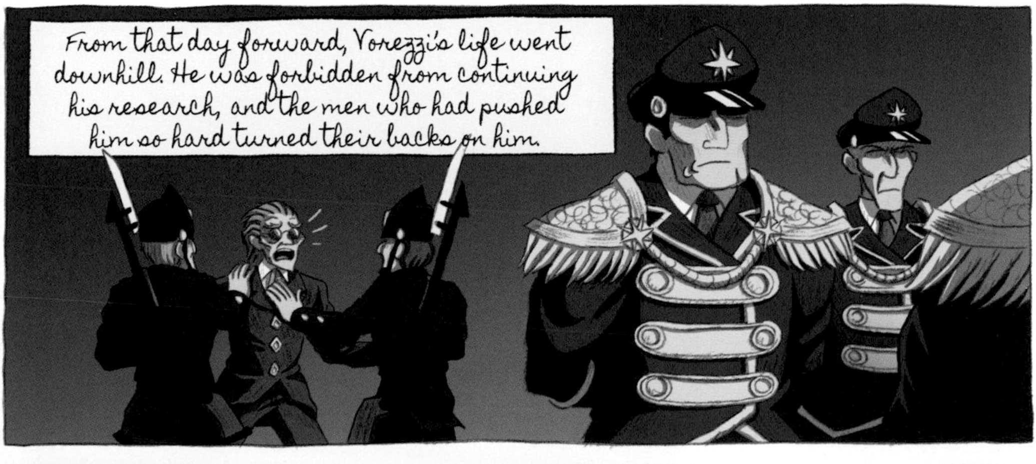
From that day forward, Vorezzi's life went downhill. He was forbidden from continuing his research, and the men who had pushed him so hard turned their backs on him.

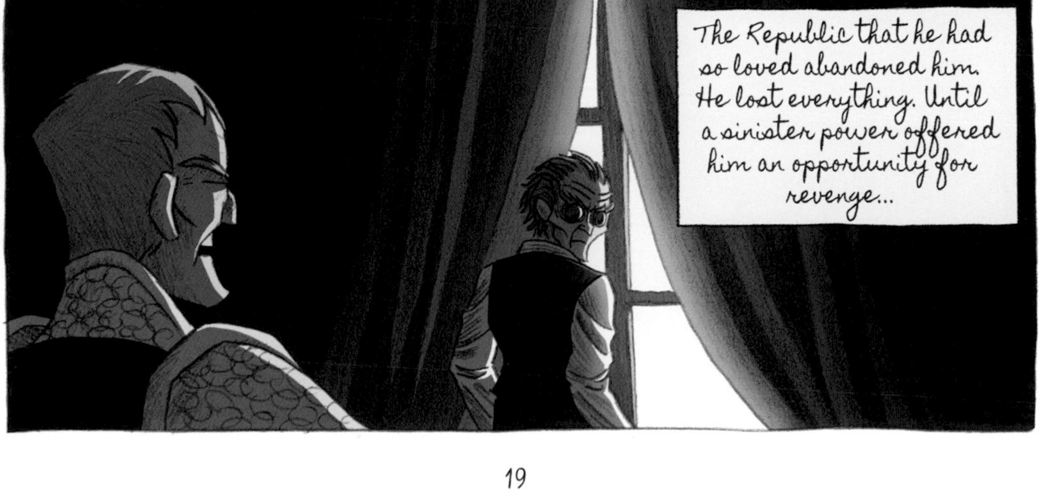
The Republic that he had so loved abandoned him. He lost everything. Until a sinister power offered him an opportunity for revenge...

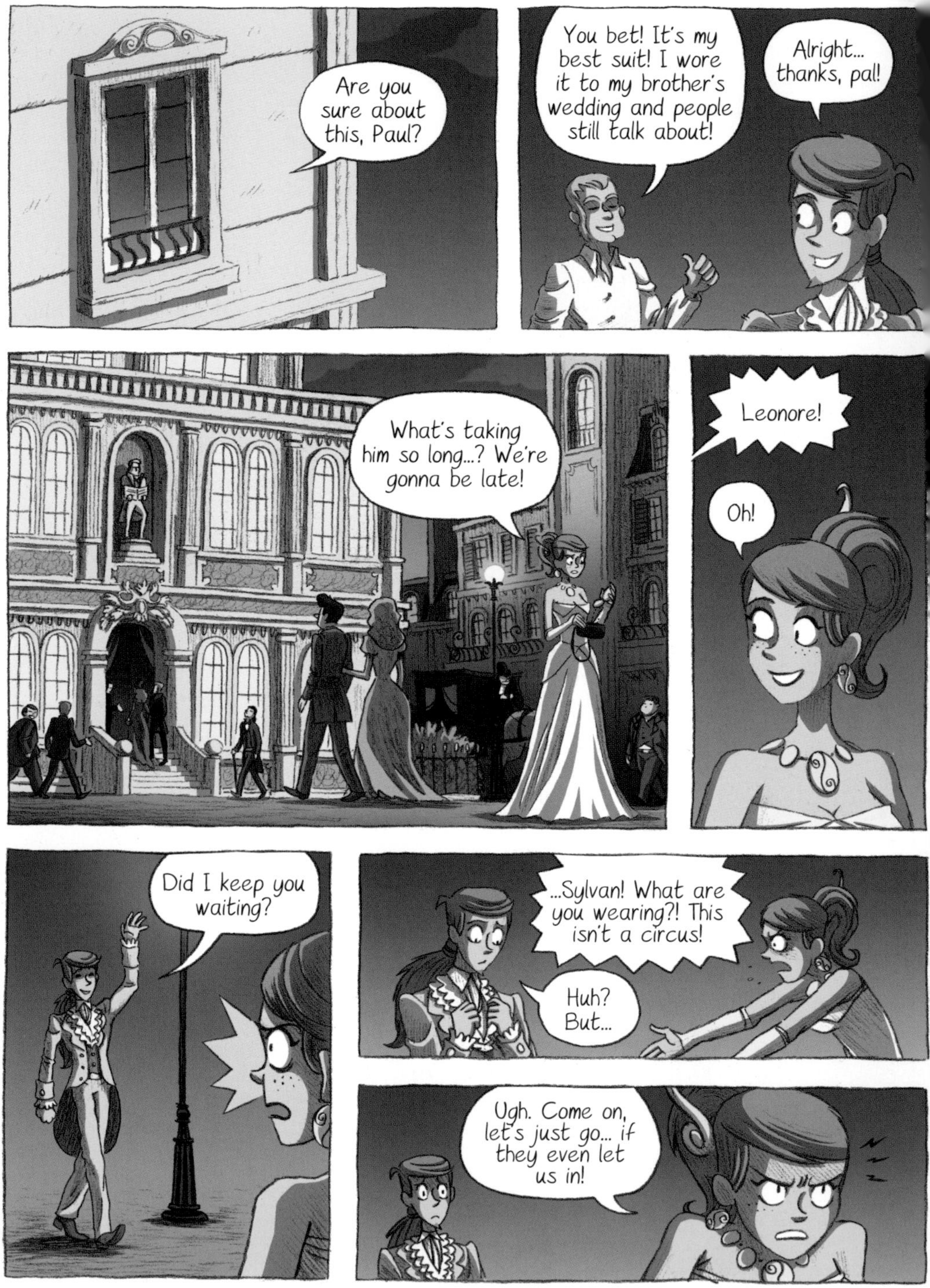
Are you sure about this, Paul?
You bet! It's my best suit! I wore it to my brother's wedding and people still talk about!
Alright... thanks, pal!
What's taking him so long...? We're gonna be late!
Leonore!
Oh!
Did I keep you waiting?
...Sylvan! What are you wearing?! This isn't a circus!
Huh? But...
Ugh. Come on, let's just go... if they even let us in!

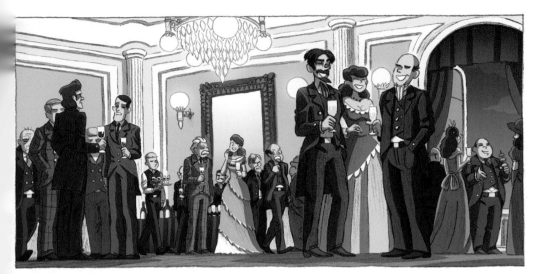

Wow, so many people! The greatest writers are here! Maximilian wasn't kidding!

Look! It's Delestrin and Monterel!

Oh, WOW!

Adrien de Clairmont!

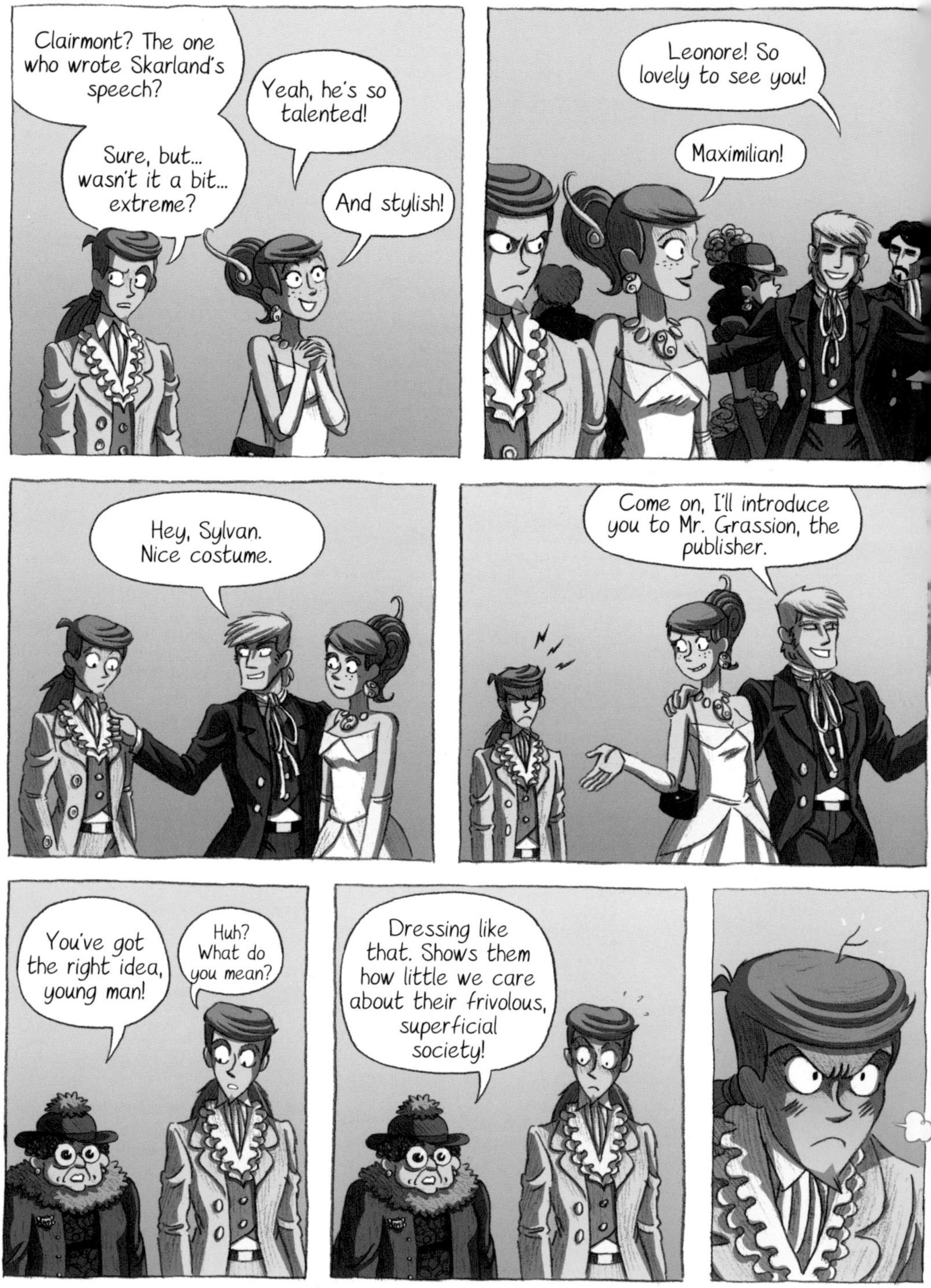
Clairmont? The one who wrote Skarland's speech?
Yeah, he's so talented!
Sure, but... wasn't it a bit... extreme?
And stylish!
Leonore! So lovely to see you!
Maximilian!
Hey, Sylvan. Nice costume.
Come on, I'll introduce you to Mr. Grassion, the publisher.
You've got the right idea, young man!
Huh? What do you mean?
Dressing like that. Shows them how little we care about their frivolous, superficial society!

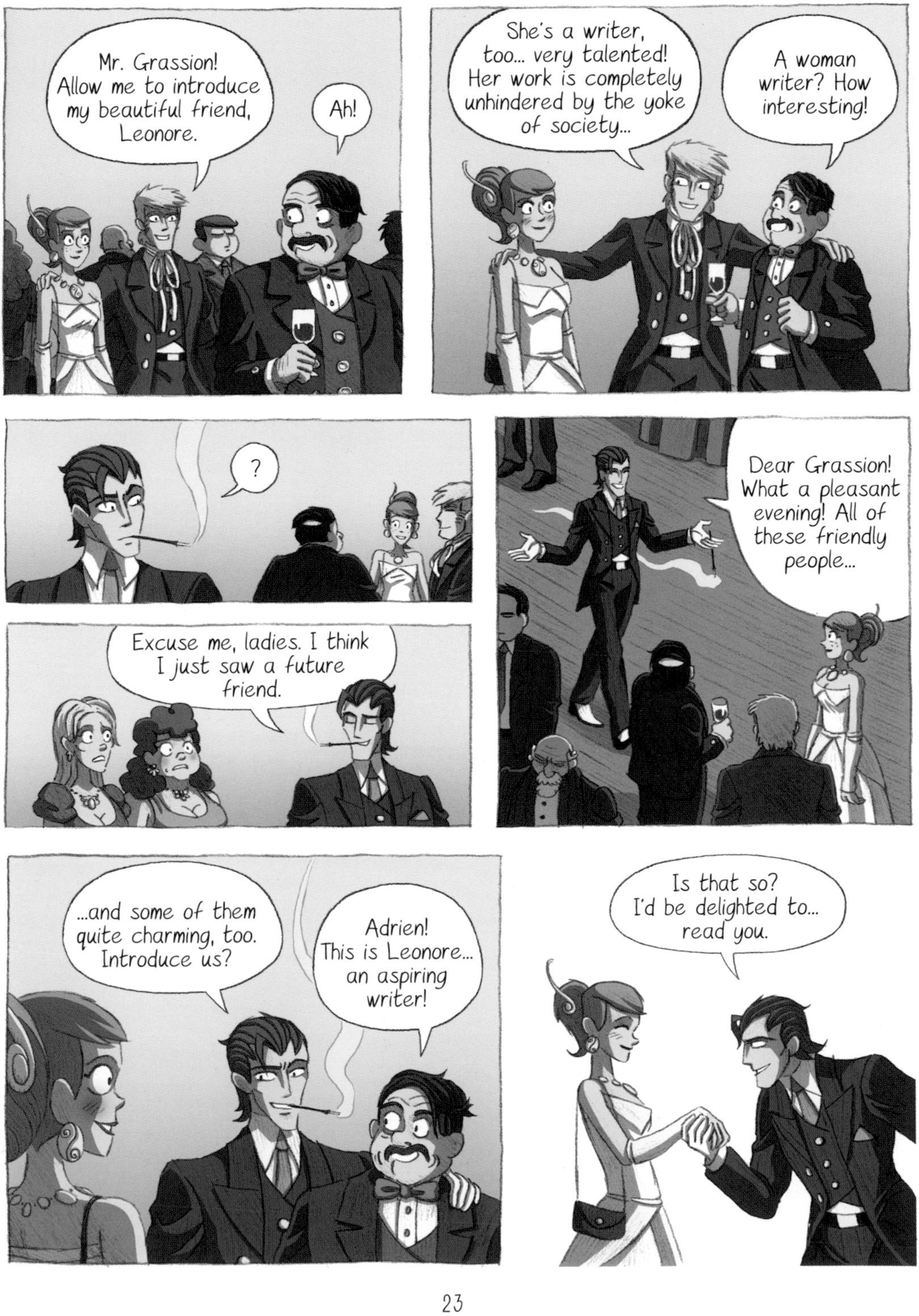
Mr. Grassion! Allow me to introduce my beautiful friend, Leonore.
Ah!
She's a writer, too... very talented! Her work is completely unhindered by the yoke of society...
A woman writer? How interesting!
?
Excuse me, ladies. I think I just saw a future friend.
Dear Grassion! What a pleasant evening! All of these friendly people...
...and some of them quite charming, too. Introduce us?
Adrien! This is Leonore... an aspiring writer!
Is that so? I'd be delighted to... read you.

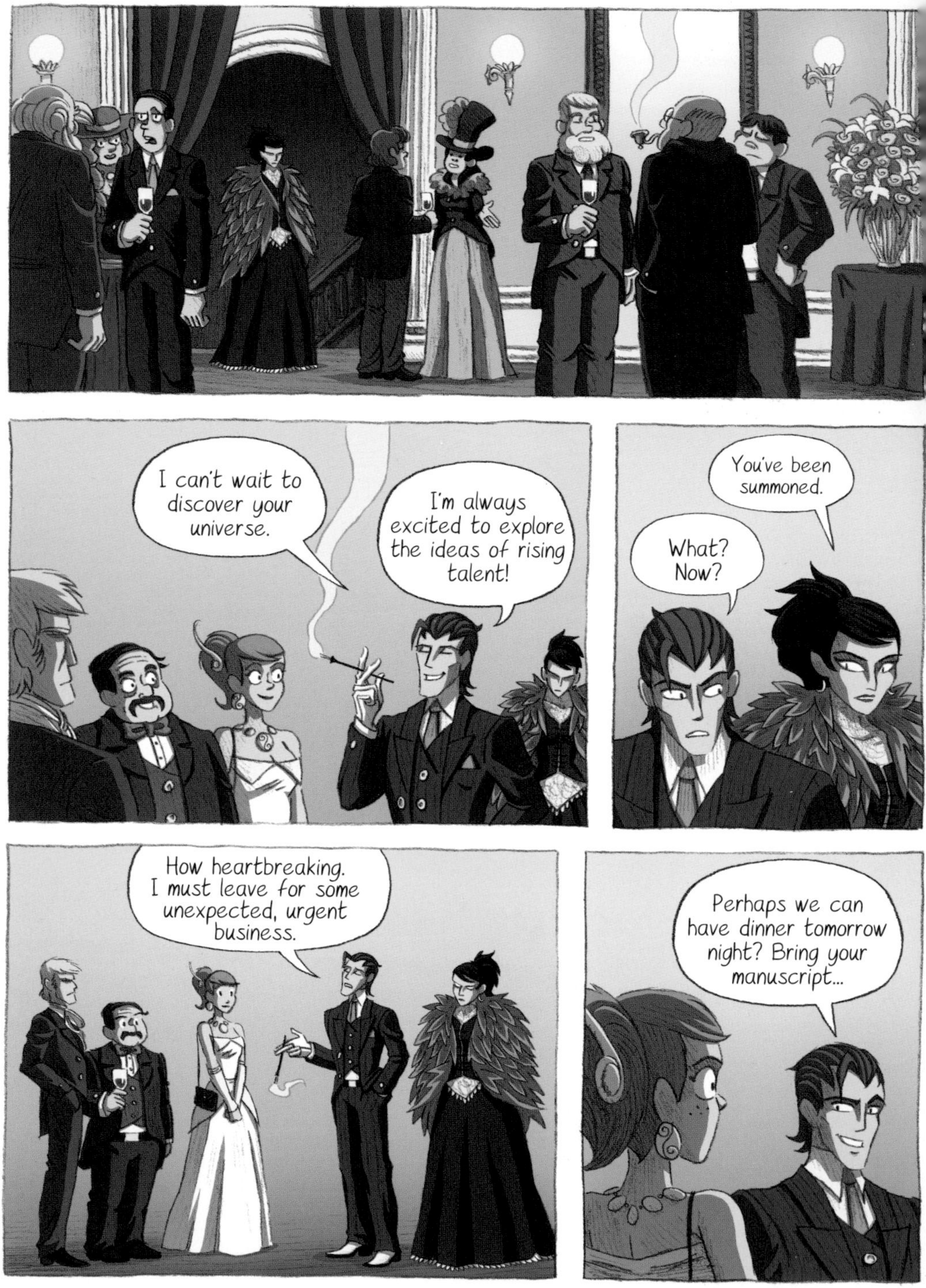
I can't wait to discover your universe.
I'm always excited to explore the ideas of rising talent!
You've been summoned.
What? Now?
How heartbreaking. I must leave for some unexpected, urgent business.
Perhaps we can have dinner tomorrow night? Bring your manuscript...

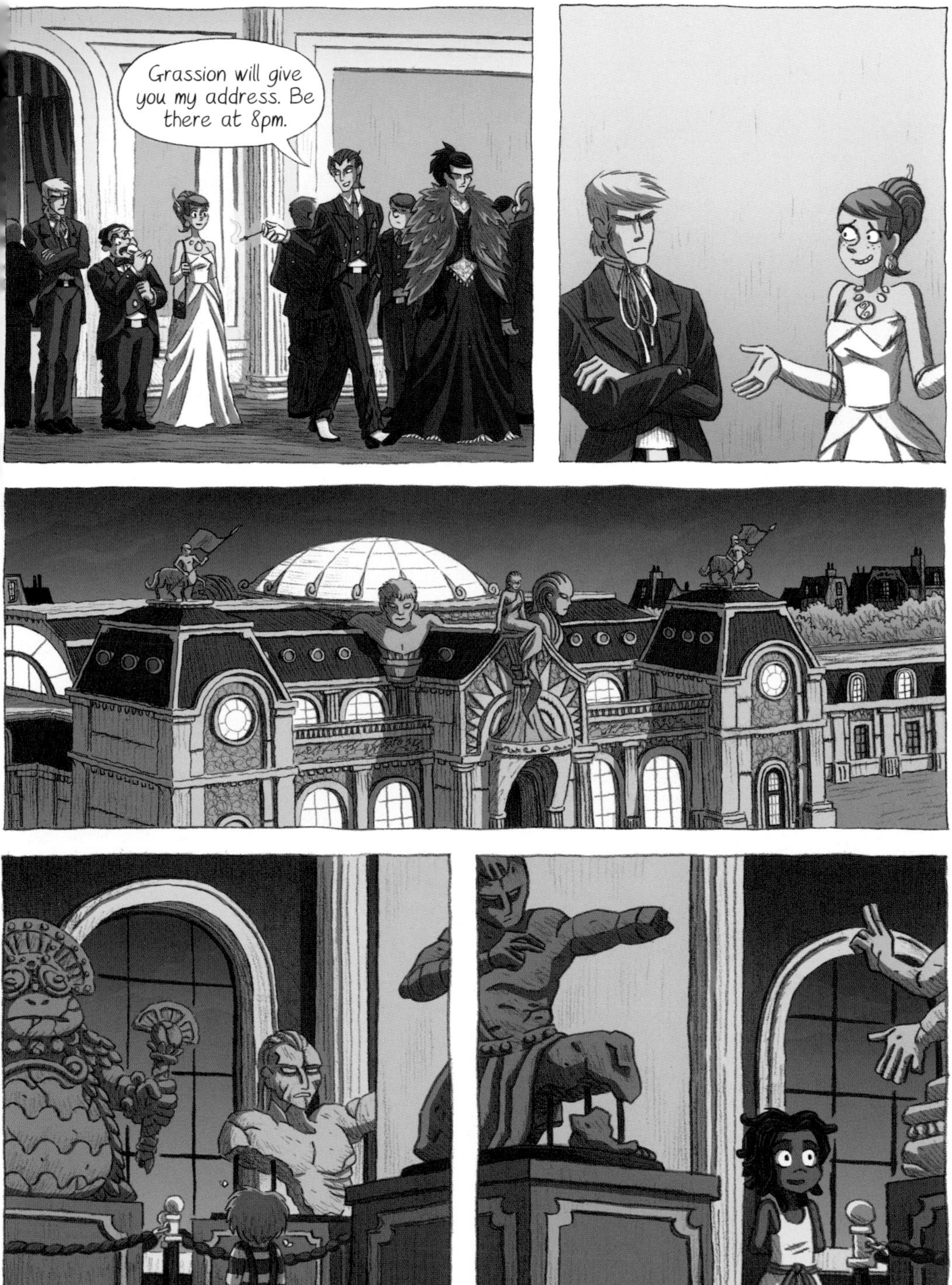
Grassion will give you my address. Be there at 8pm.

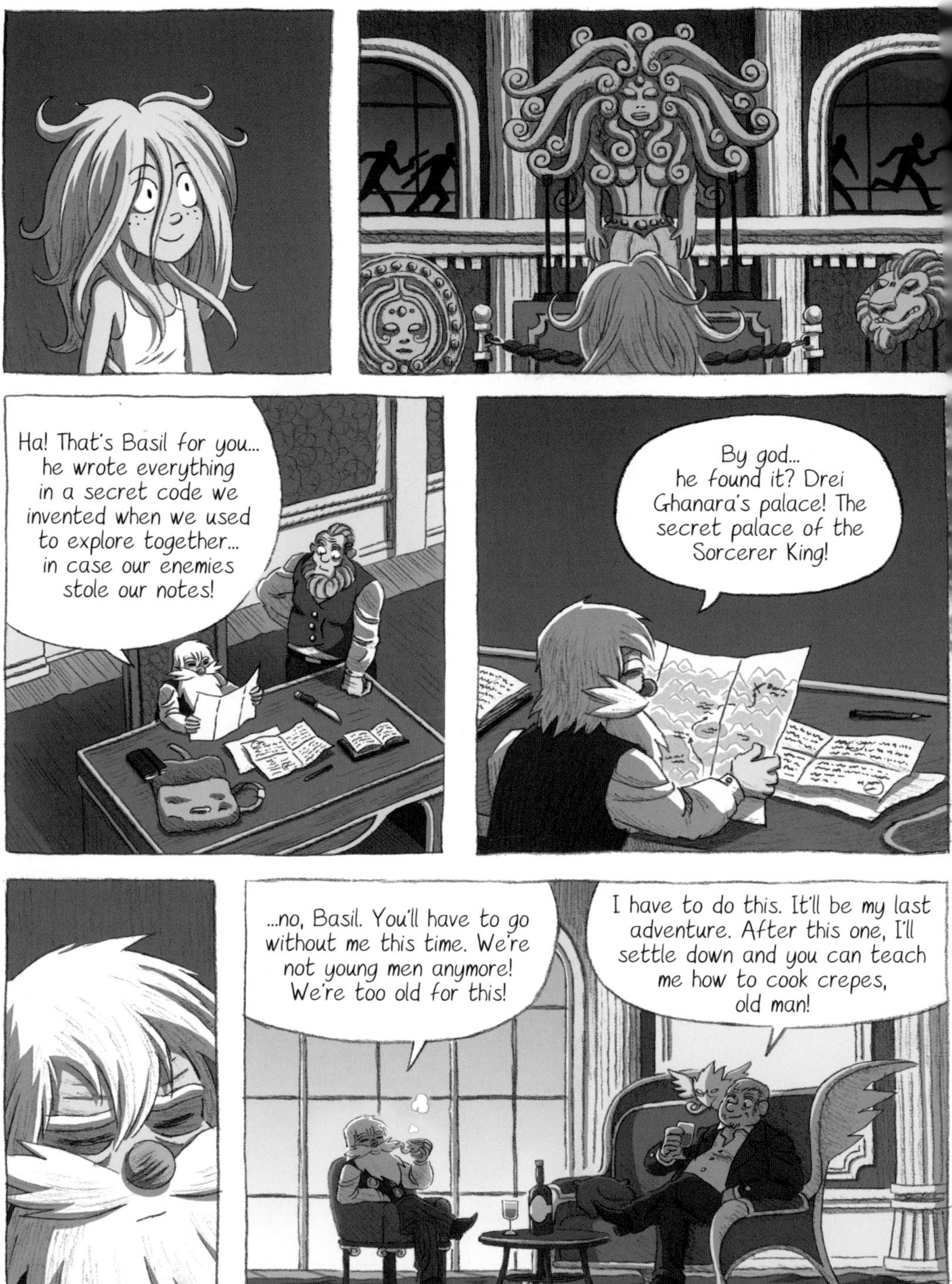
Ha! That's Basil for you... he wrote everything in a secret code we invented when we used to explore together... in case our enemies stole our notes!
By god... he found it? Drei Ghanara's palace! The secret palace of the Sorcerer King!
...no, Basil. You'll have to go without me this time. We're not young men anymore! We're too old for this!
I have to do this. It'll be my last adventure. After this one, I'll settle down and you can teach me how to cook crepes, old man!

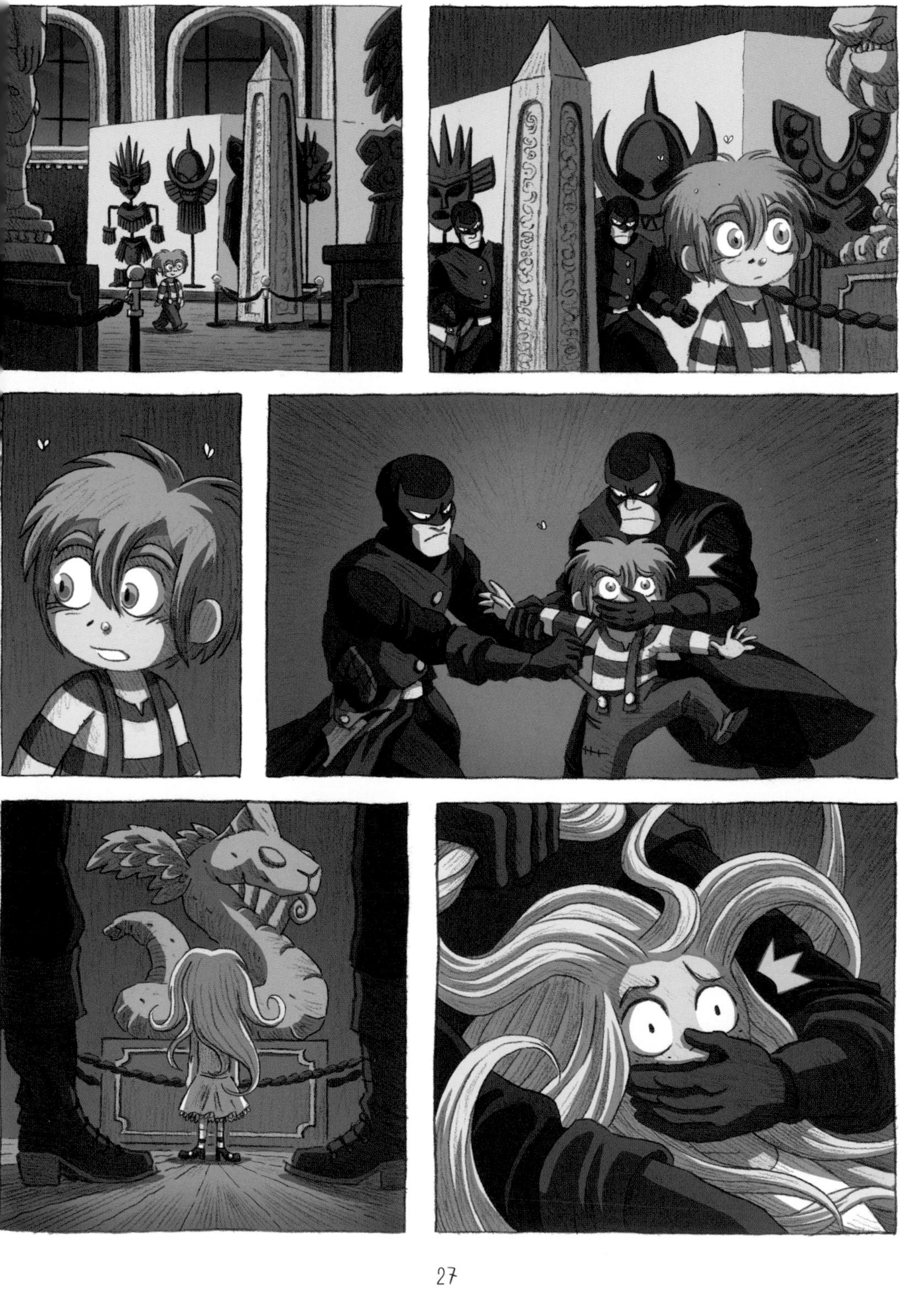

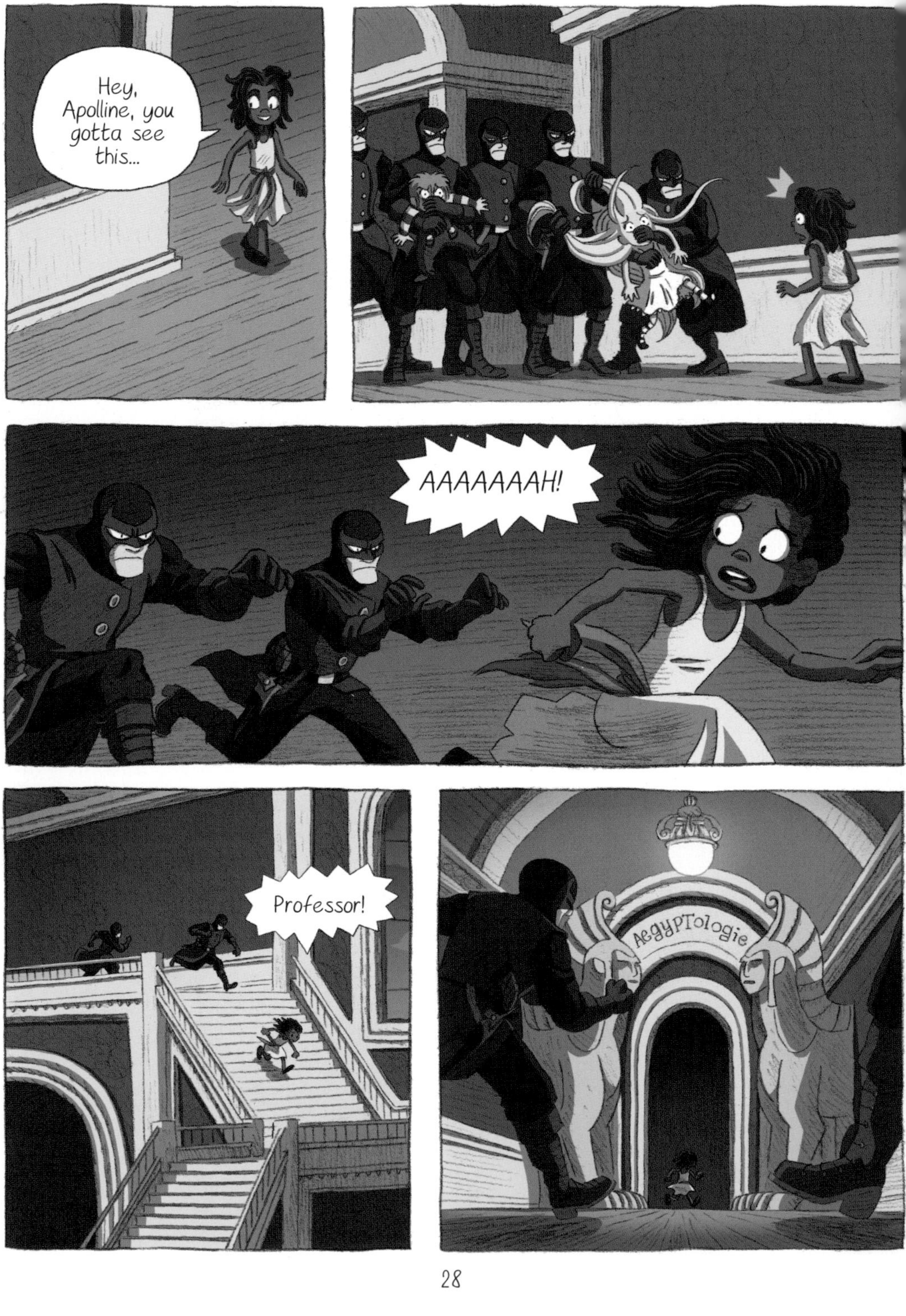
Hey, Apolline, you gotta see this...
AAAAAAAH!
Professor!
AegypTologie

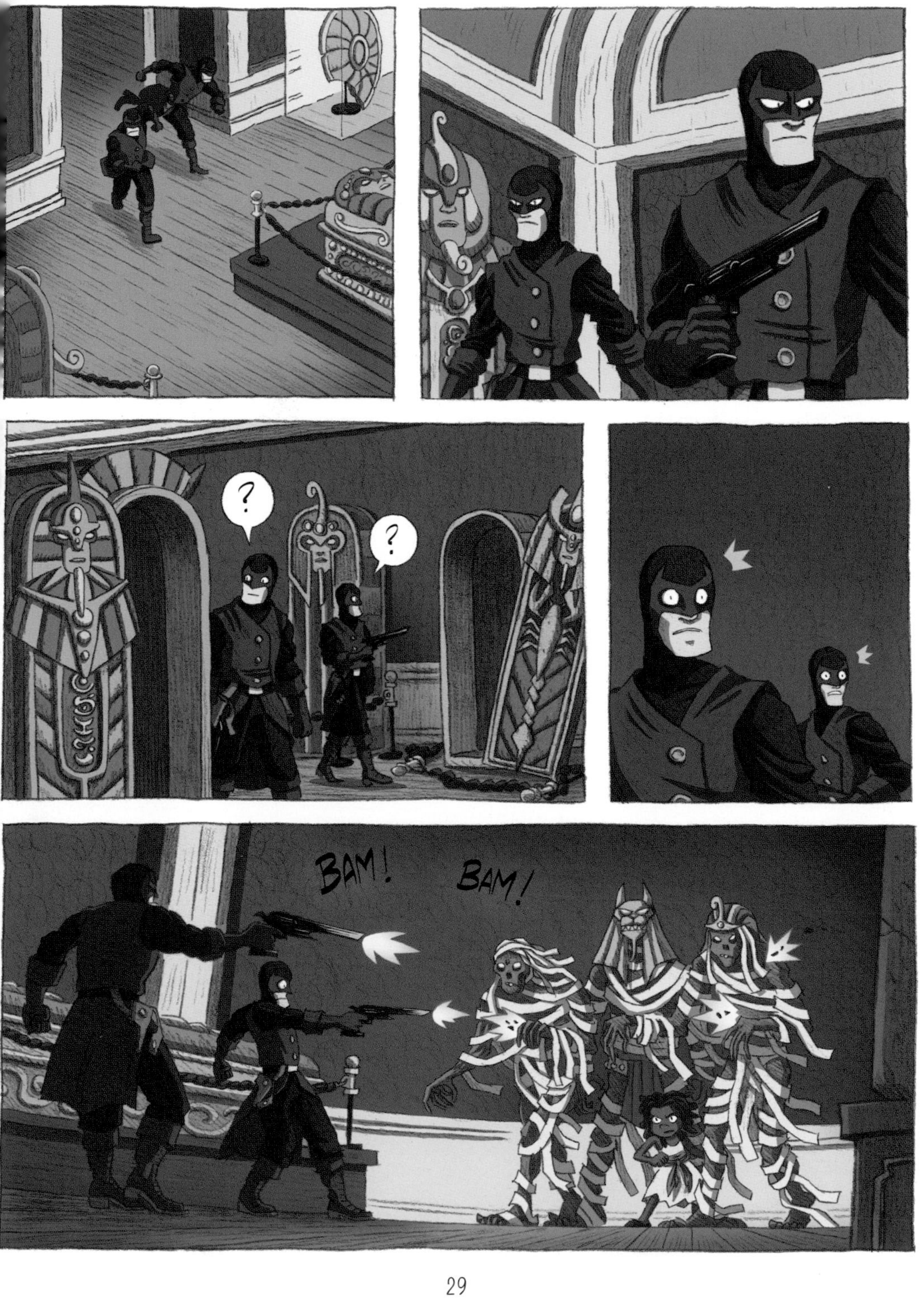
?
?
BAM!
BAM!

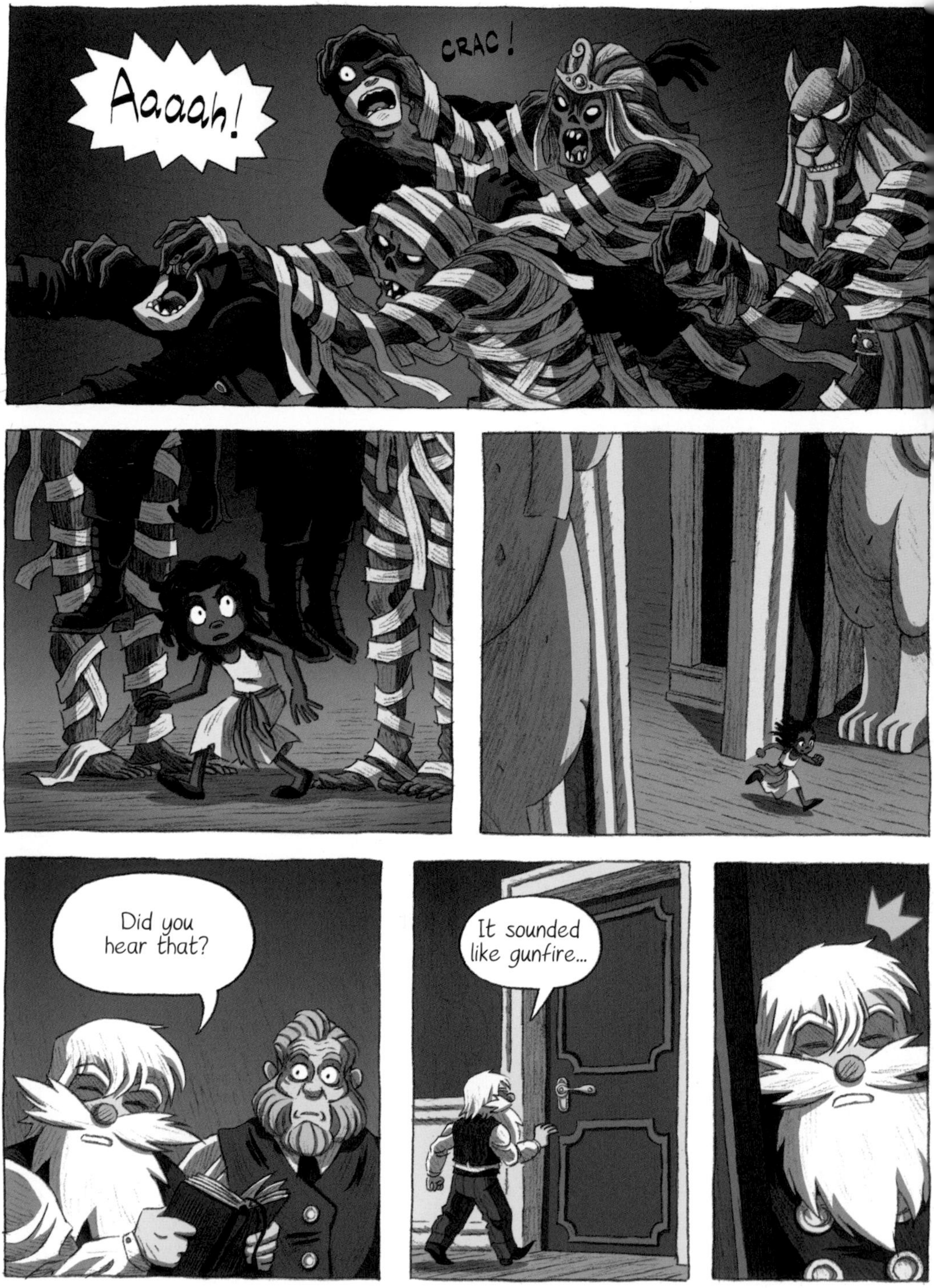
CRAC !
Aaaah!
Did you hear that?
It sounded like gunfire...

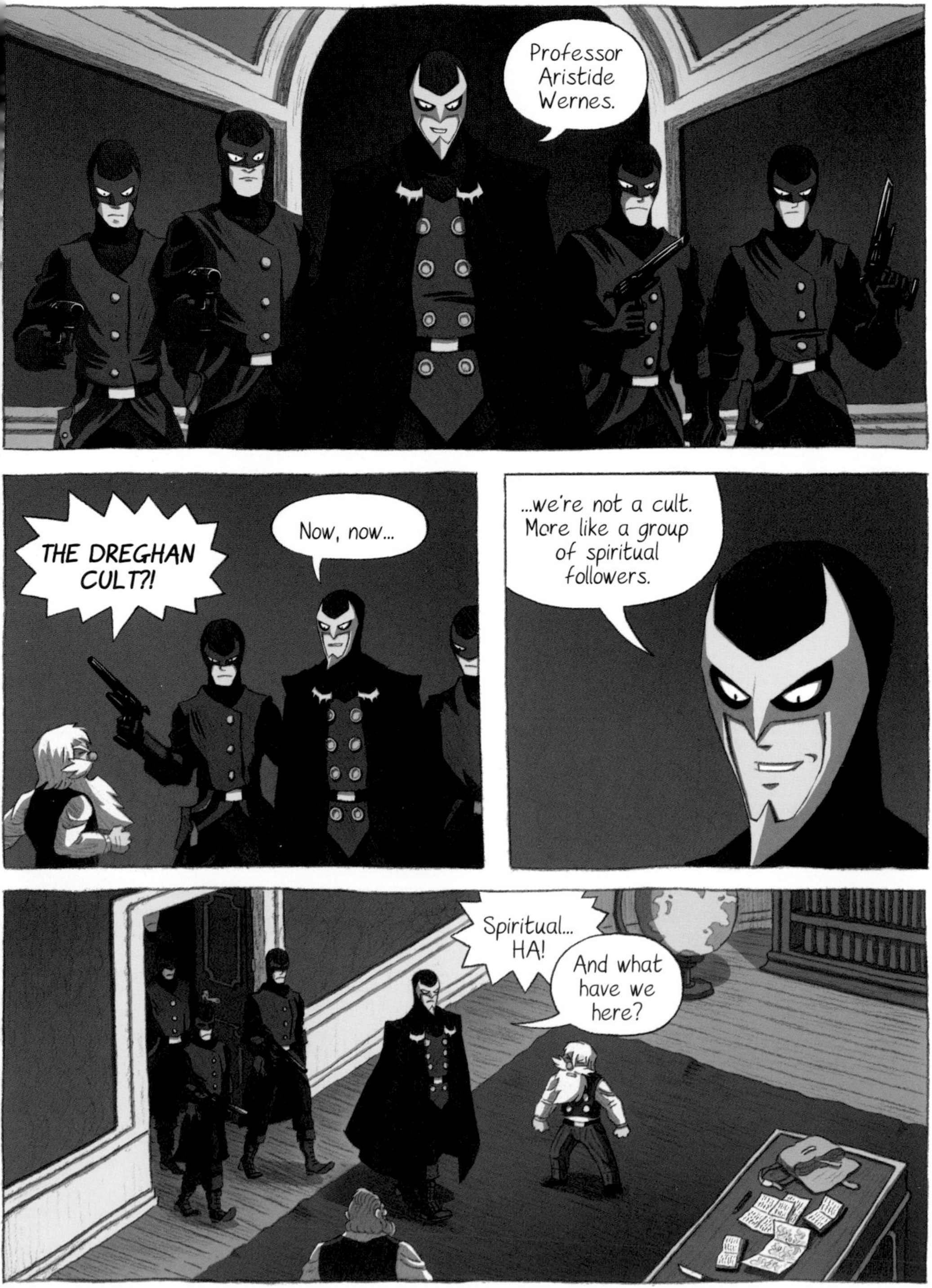
Professor Aristide Wernes.
THE DREGHAN CULT?!
Now, now...
...we're not a cult. More like a group of spiritual followers.
Spiritual... HA!
And what have we here?

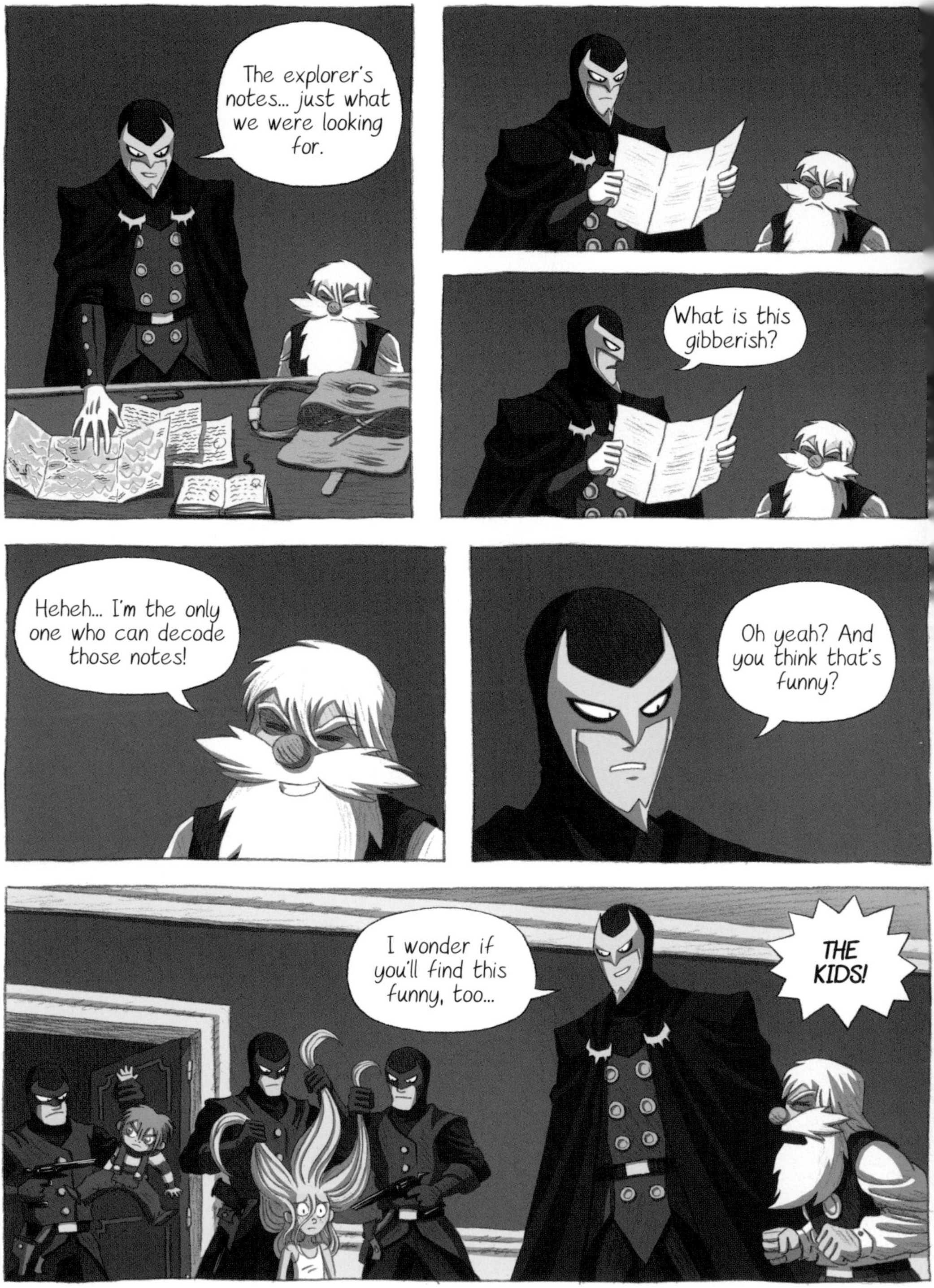
The explorer's notes... just what we were looking for.
What is this gibberish?
Heheh... I'm the only one who can decode those notes!
Oh yeah? And you think that's funny?
I wonder if you'll find this funny, too...
THE KIDS!

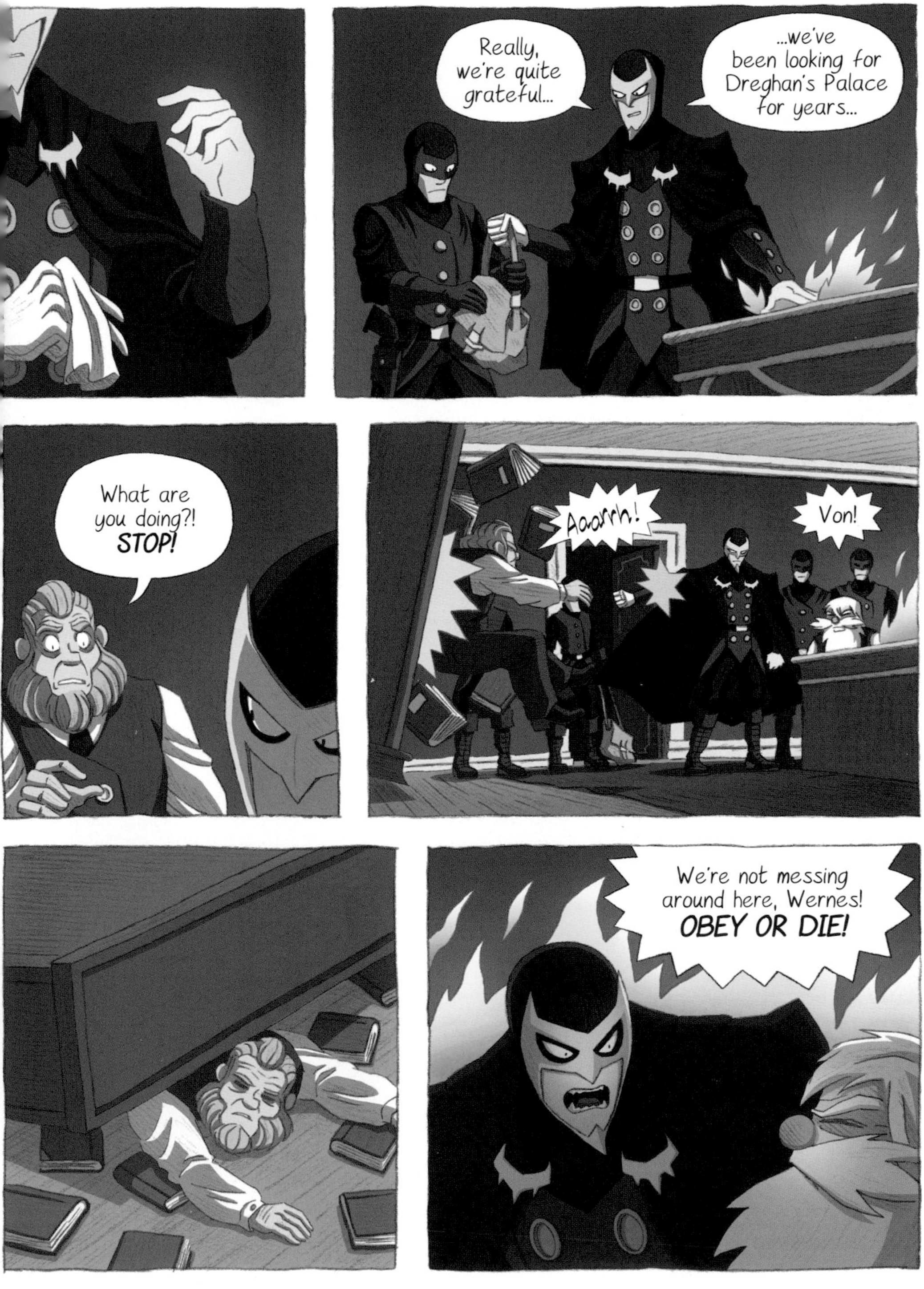
Really, we're quite grateful...
...we've been looking for Dreghan's Palace for years...
What are you doing?! **STOP!**
Aaarrh!
Von!
We're not messing around here, Wernes! **OBEY OR DIE!**

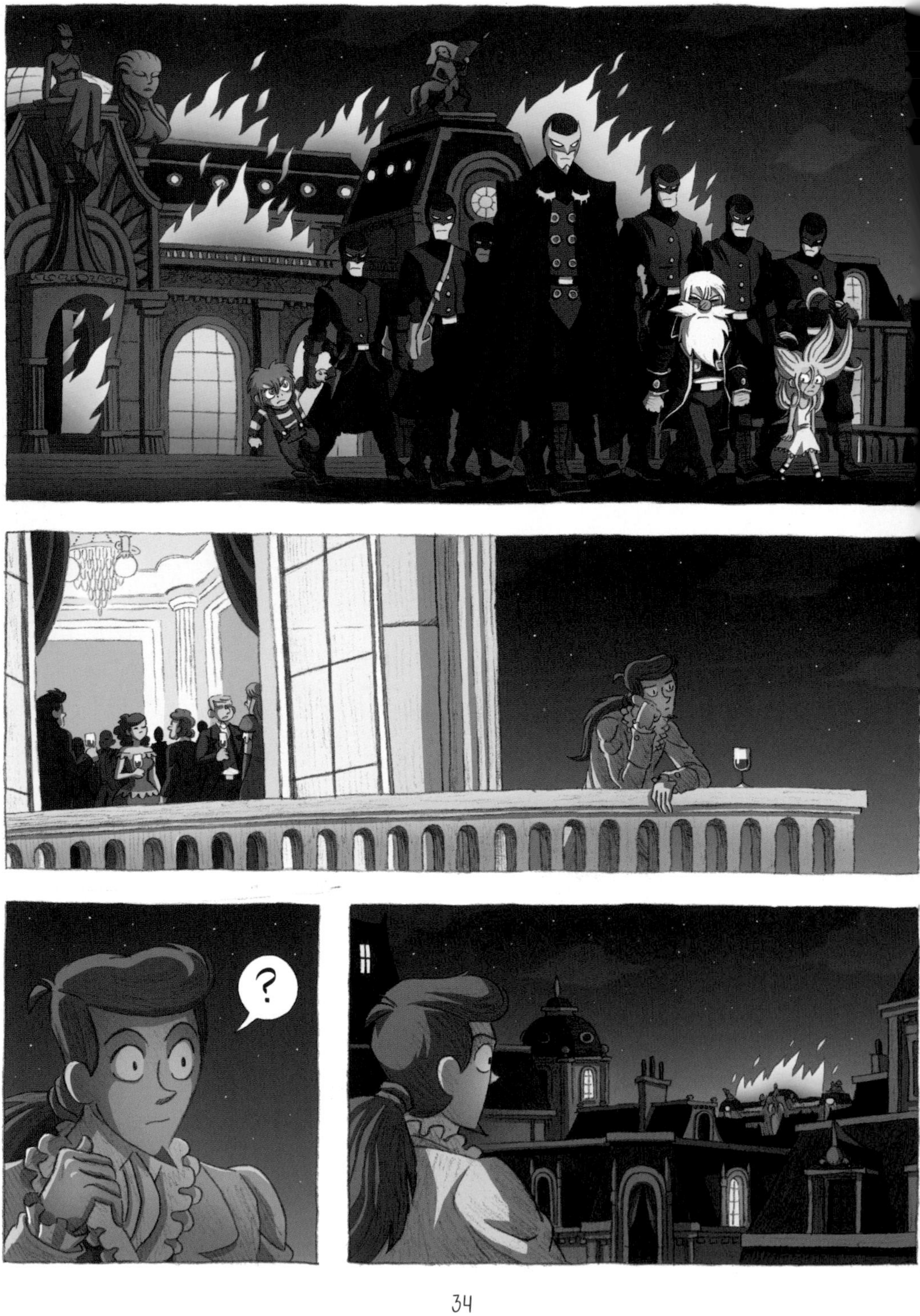
?

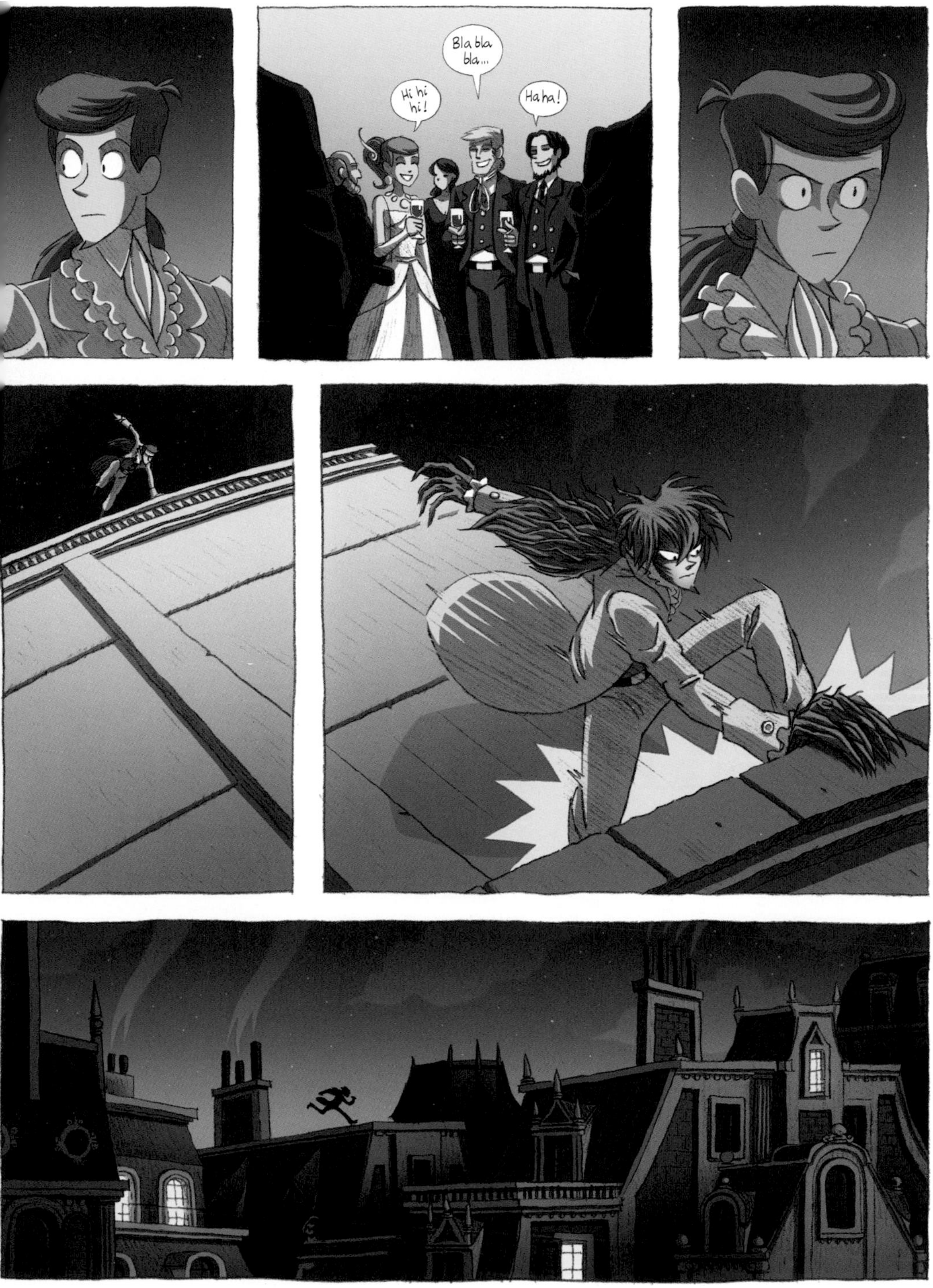
Hi hi hi!
Bla bla bla...
Ha ha!

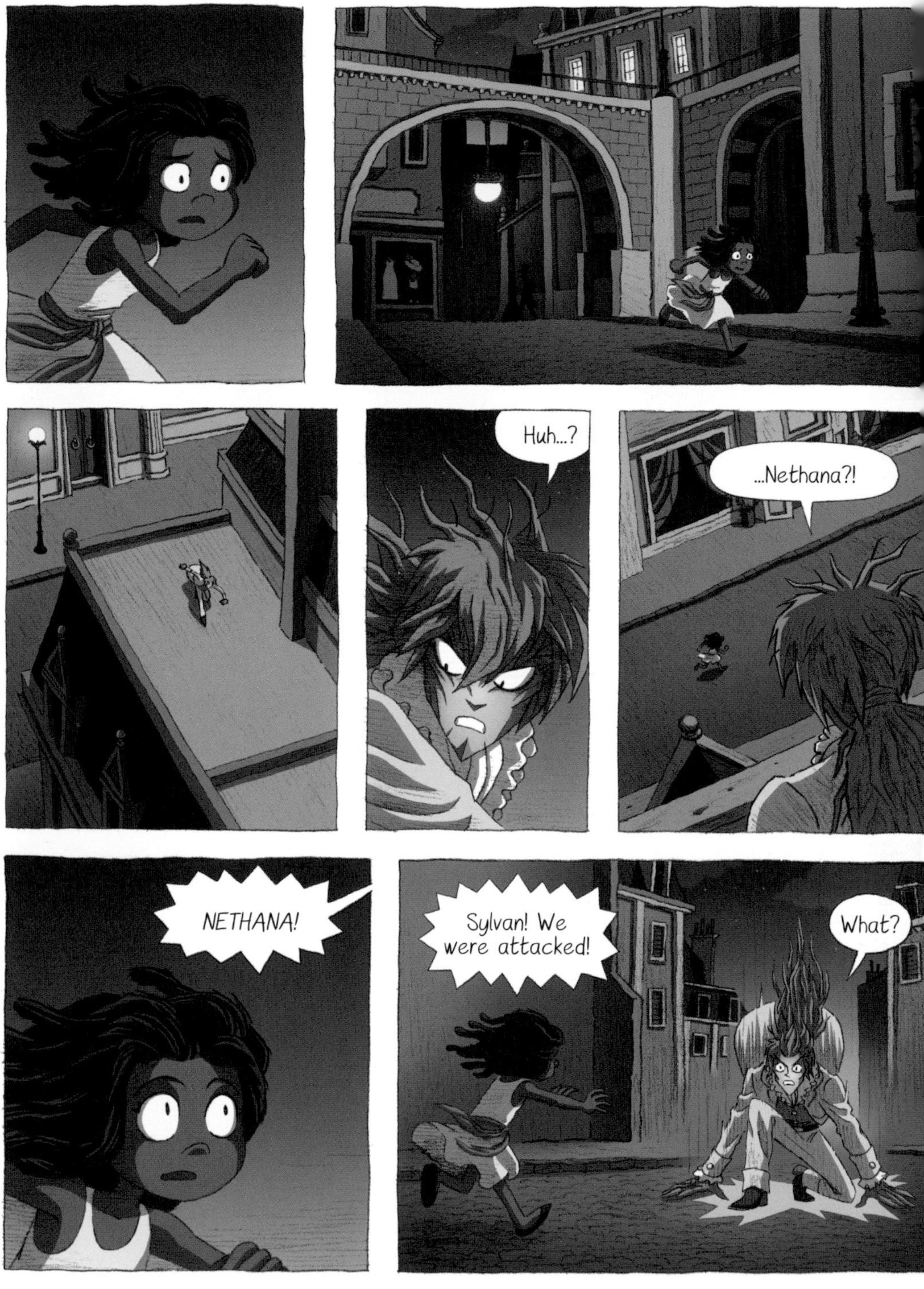
Huh...?
...Nethana?!
NETHANA!
Sylvan! We were attacked!
What?

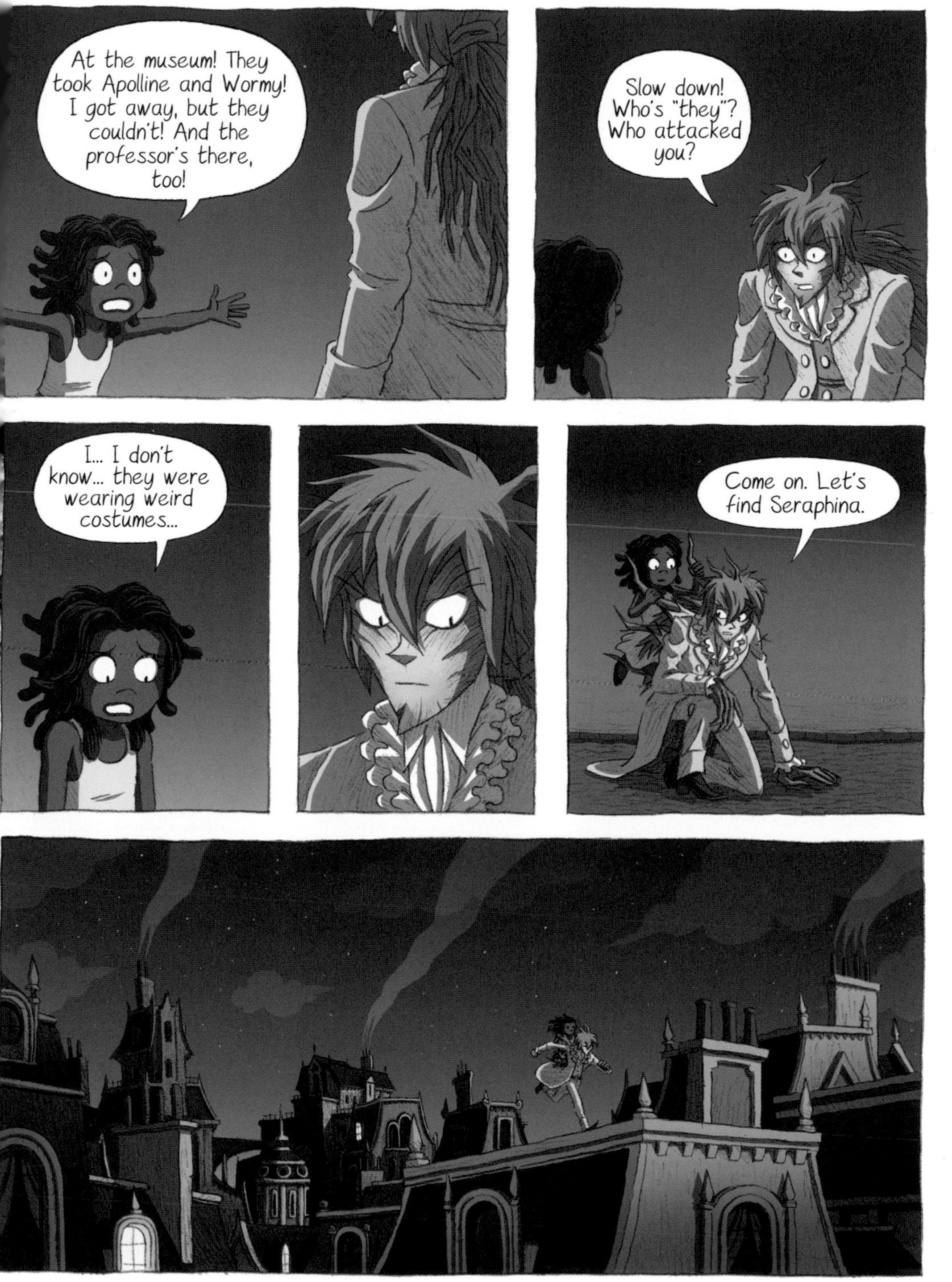
At the museum! They took Apolline and Wormy! I got away, but they couldn't! And the professor's there, too!
Slow down! Who's "they"? Who attacked you?
I... I don't know... they were wearing weird costumes...
Come on. Let's find Seraphina.

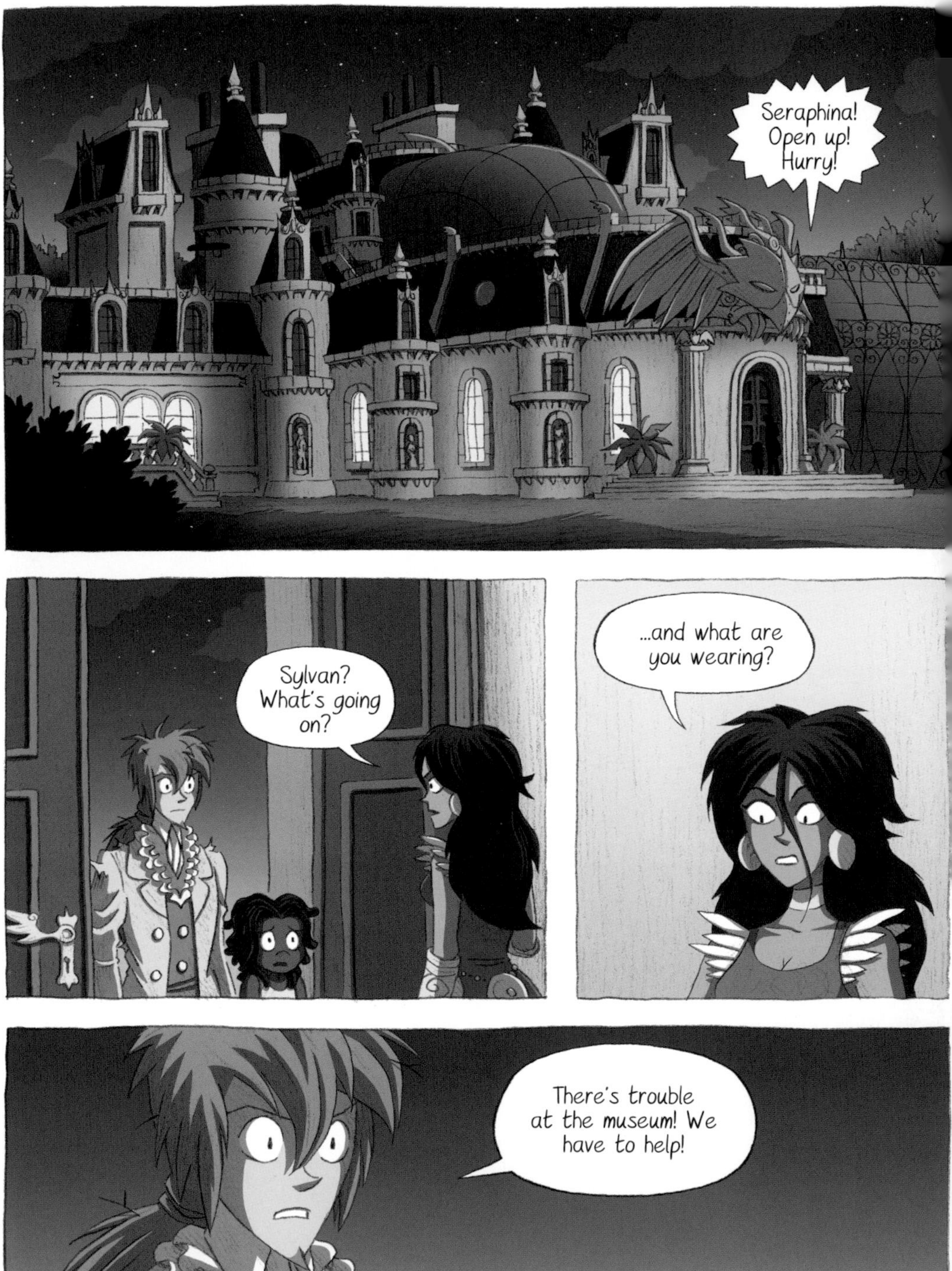
Seraphina! Open up! Hurry!
Sylvan? What's going on?
...and what are you wearing?
There's trouble at the museum! We have to help!

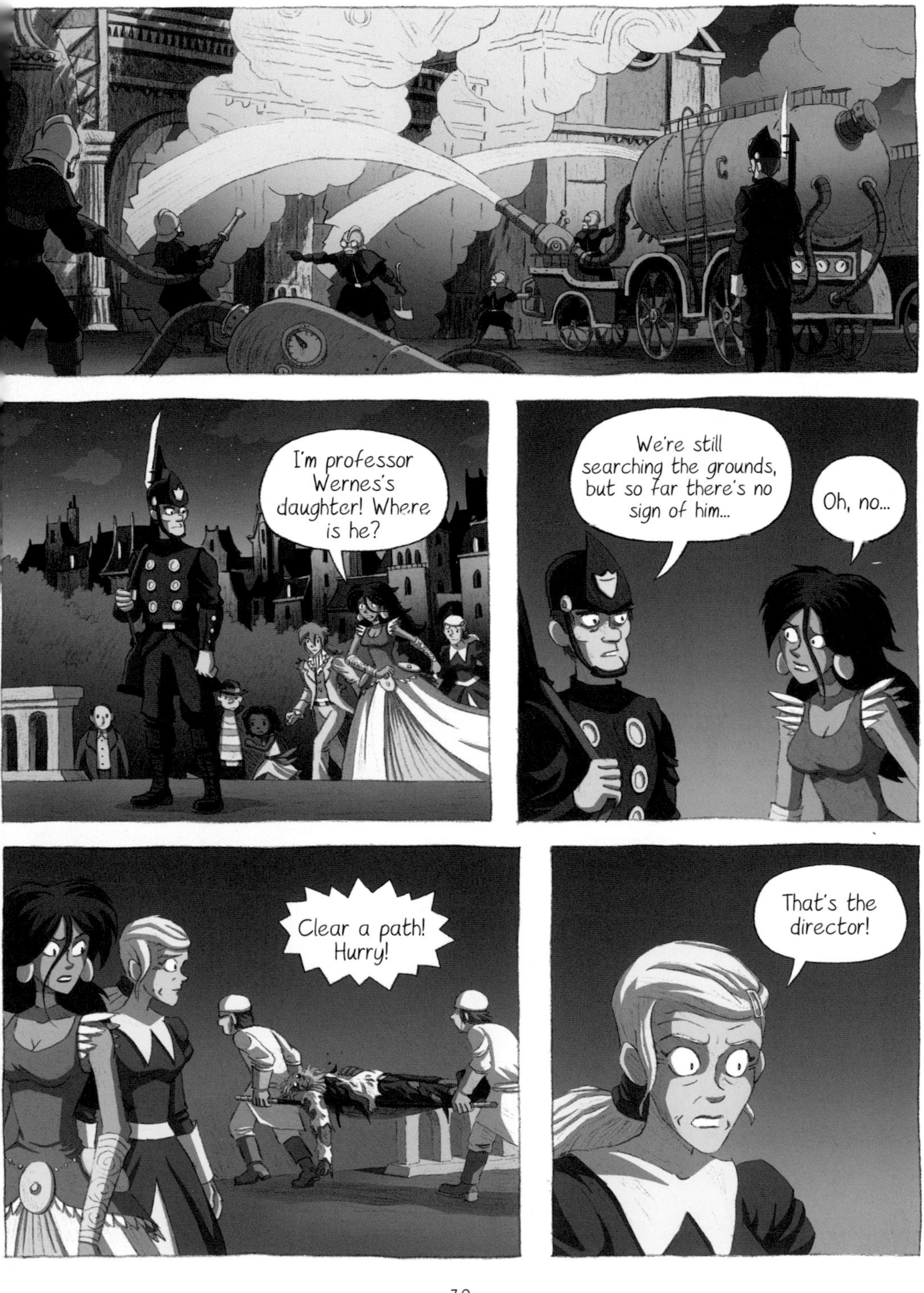
I'm professor Wernes's daughter! Where is he?
We're still searching the grounds, but so far there's no sign of him...
Oh, no...
Clear a path! Hurry!
That's the director!

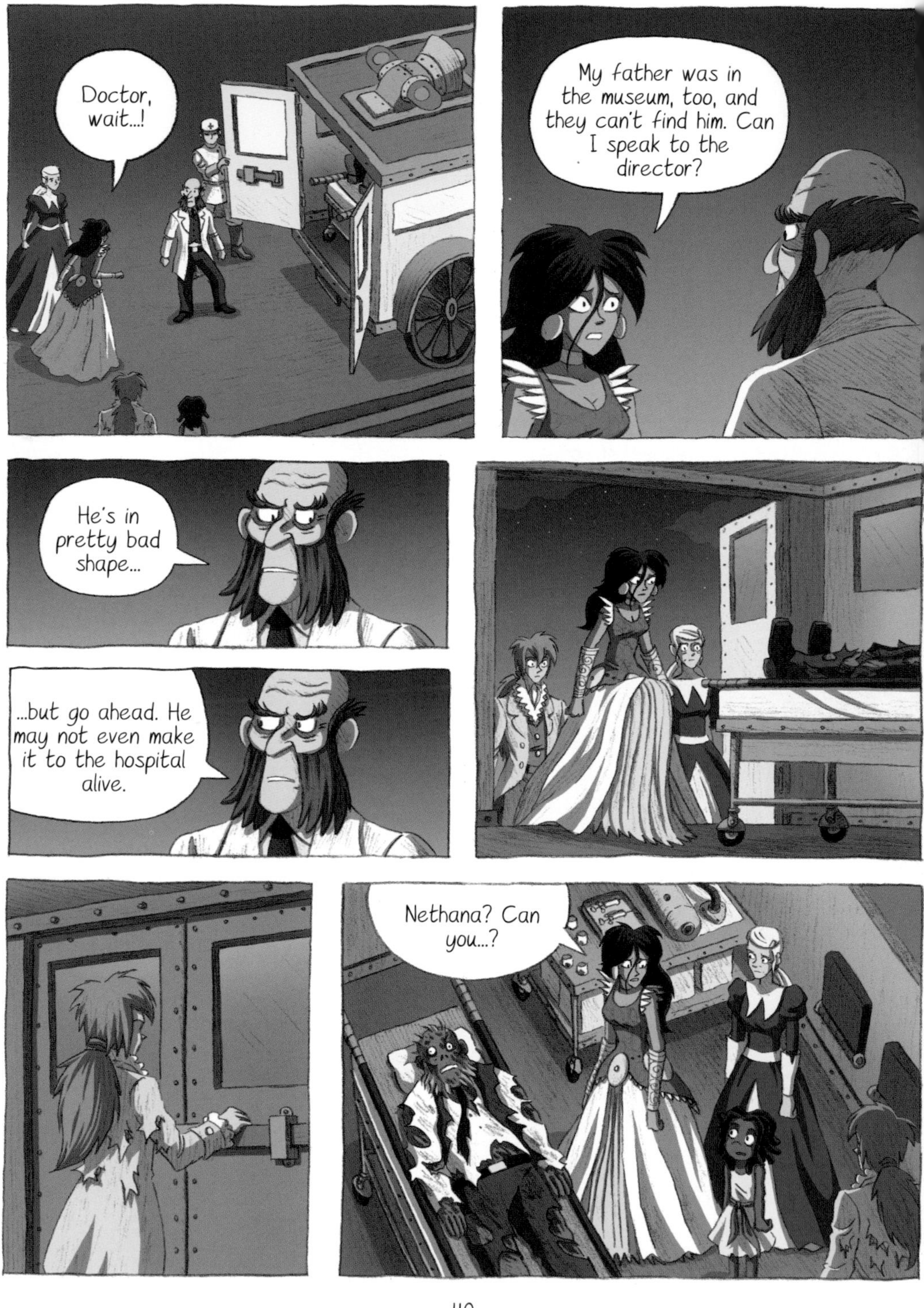
Doctor, wait...!
My father was in the museum, too, and they can't find him. Can I speak to the director?
He's in pretty bad shape...
...but go ahead. He may not even make it to the hospital alive.
Nethana? Can you...?

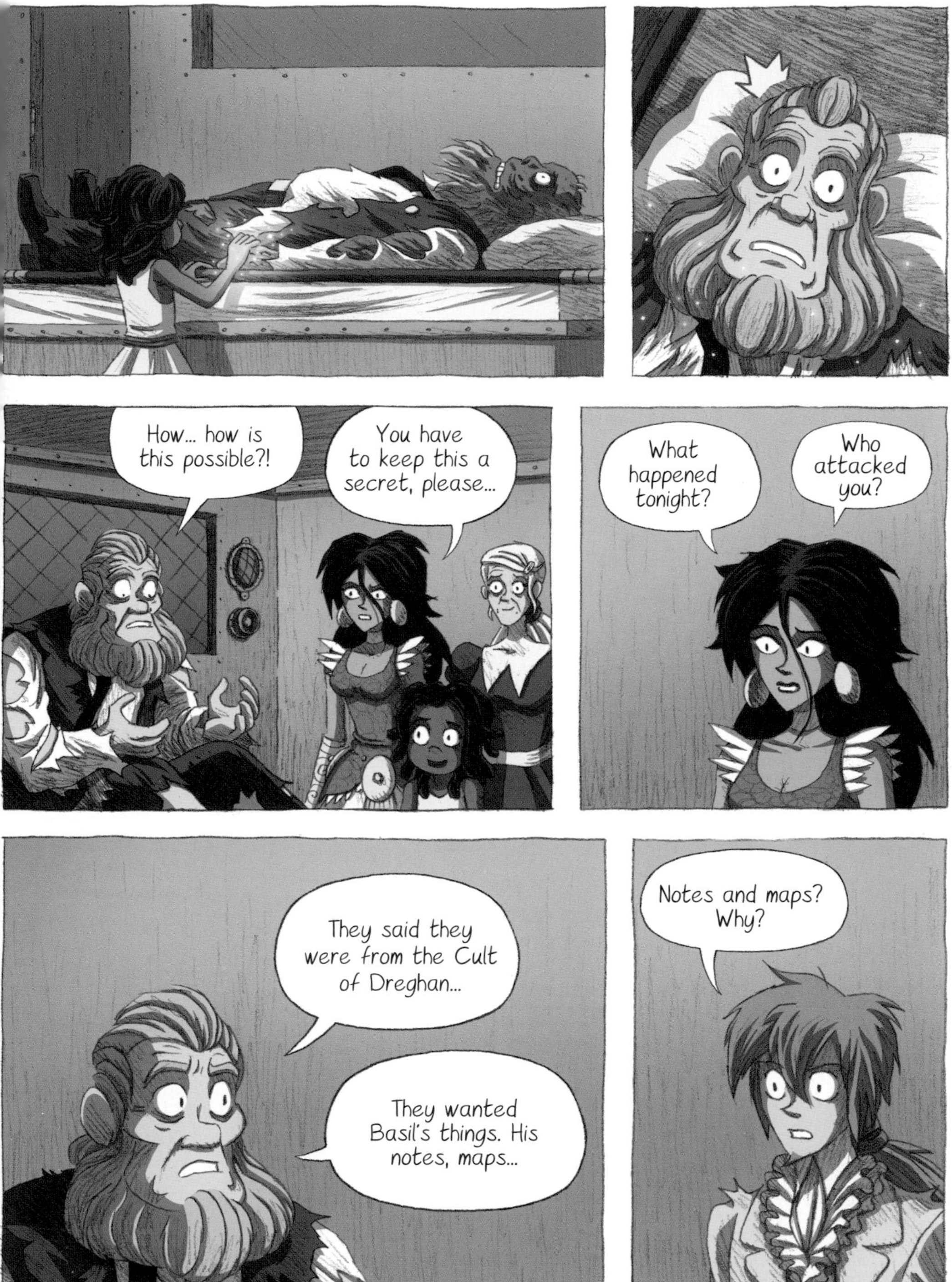
How... how is this possible?!
You have to keep this a secret, please...
What happened tonight?
Who attacked you?
They said they were from the Cult of Dreghan...
They wanted Basil's things. His notes, maps...
Notes and maps? Why?

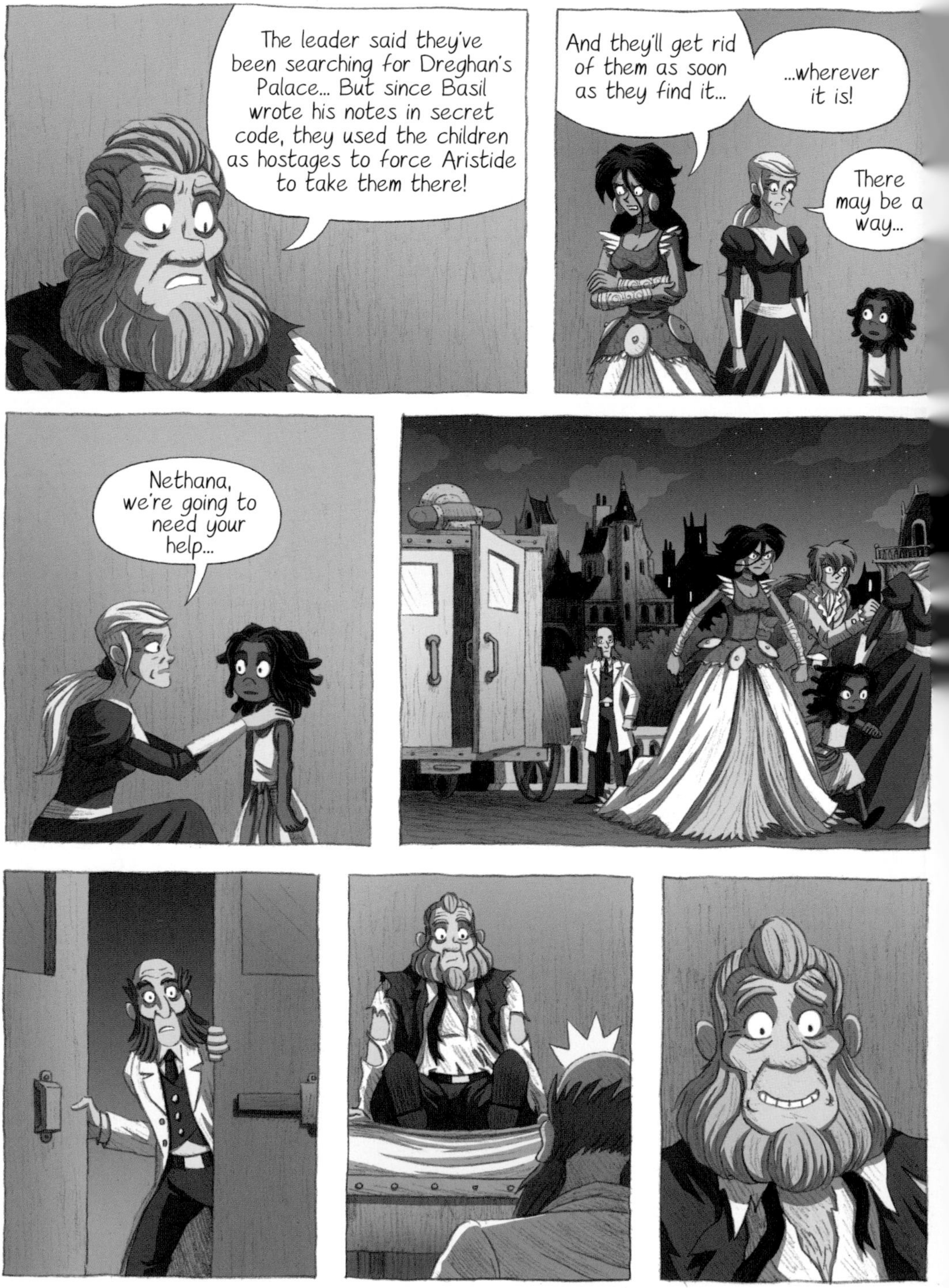
The leader said they've been searching for Dreghan's Palace... But since Basil wrote his notes in secret code, they used the children as hostages to force Aristide to take them there!
And they'll get rid of them as soon as they find it...
...wherever it is!
There may be a way...
Nethana, we're going to need your help...

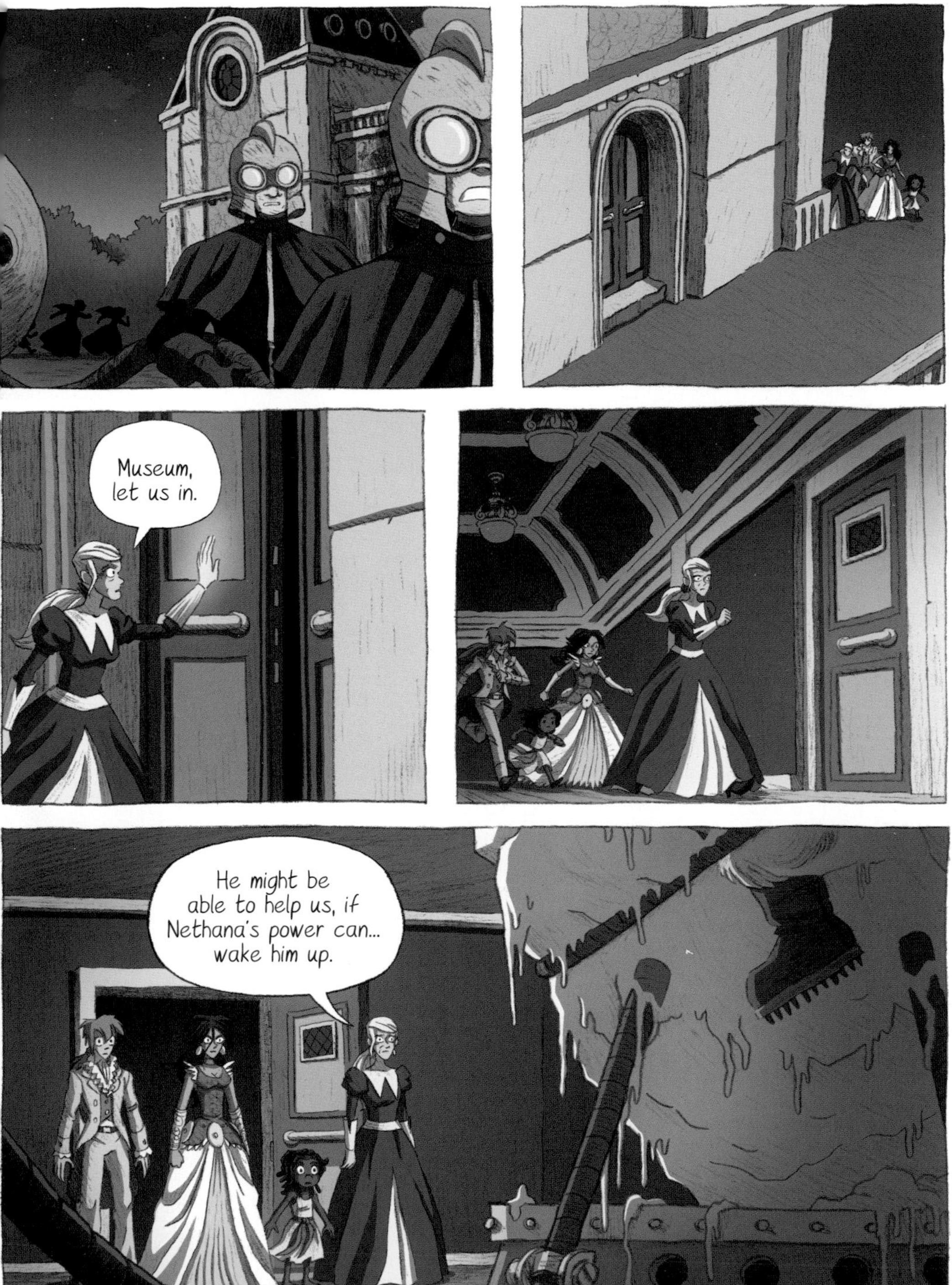
Museum, let us in.
He might be able to help us, if Nethana's power can... wake him up.

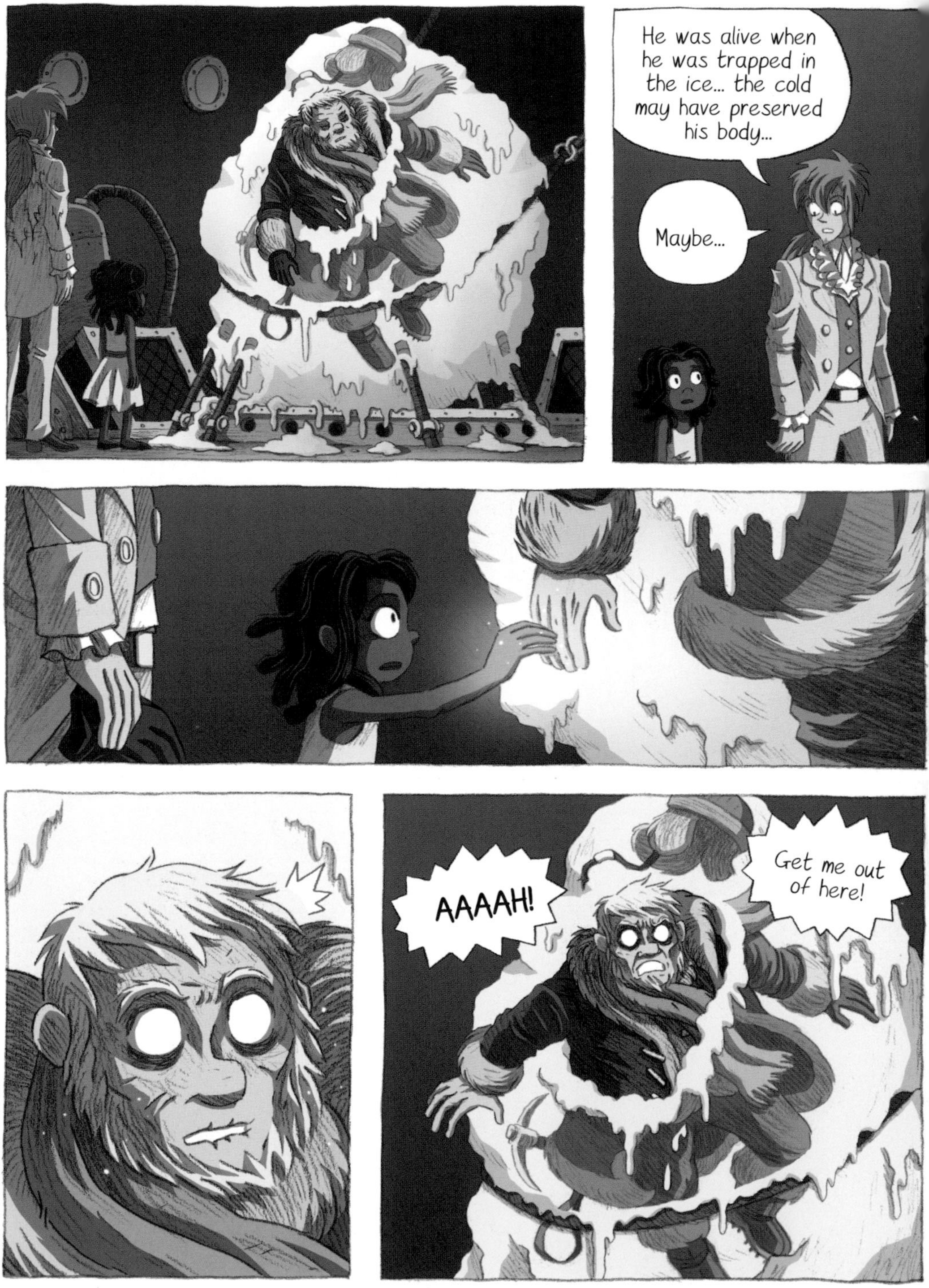
He was alive when he was trapped in the ice... the cold may have preserved his body...
Maybe...
AAAAH!
Get me out of here!

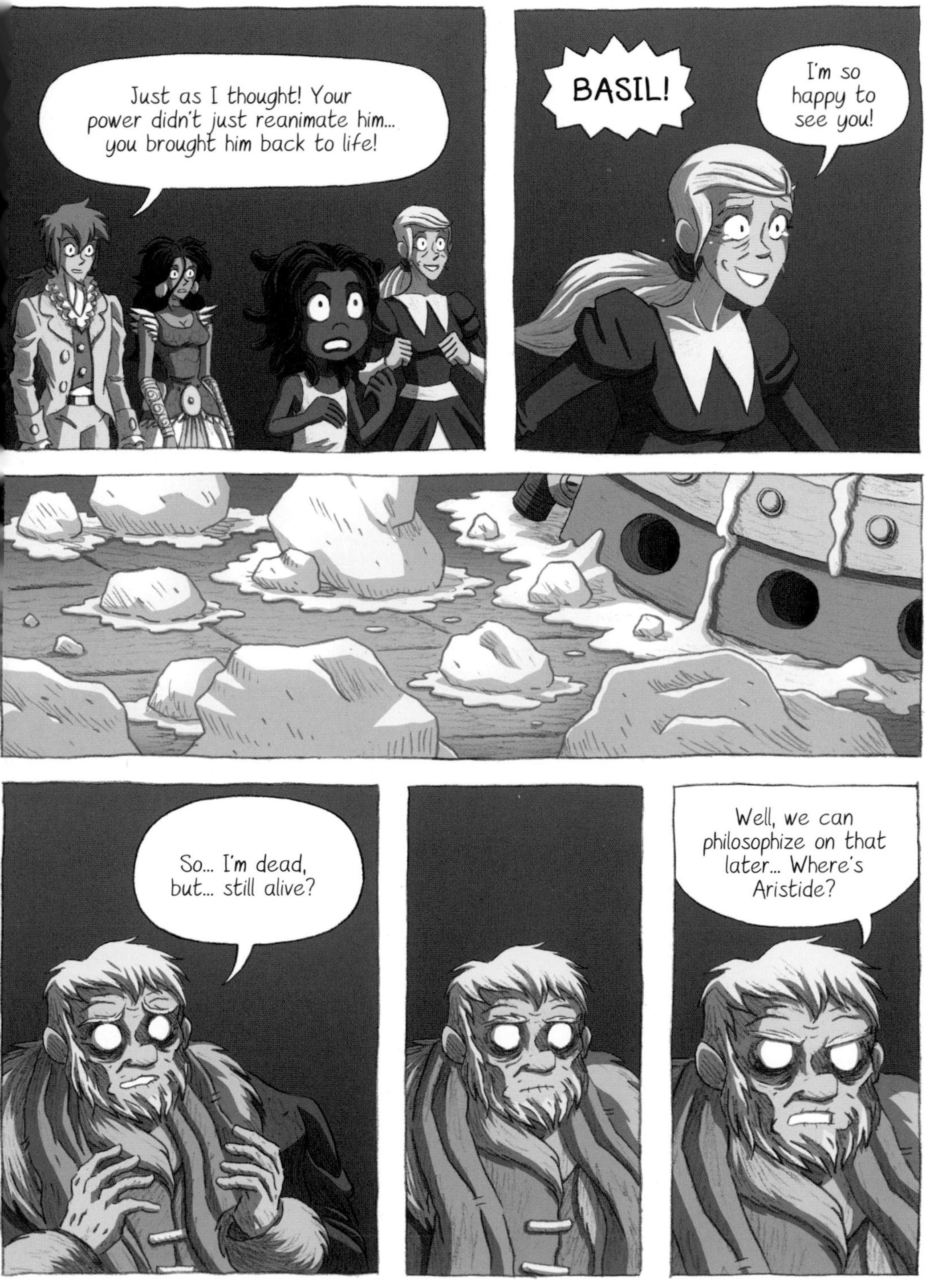
Just as I thought! Your power didn't just reanimate him... you brought him back to life!
BASIL!
I'm so happy to see you!
So... I'm dead, but... still alive?
Well, we can philosophize on that later... Where's Aristide?

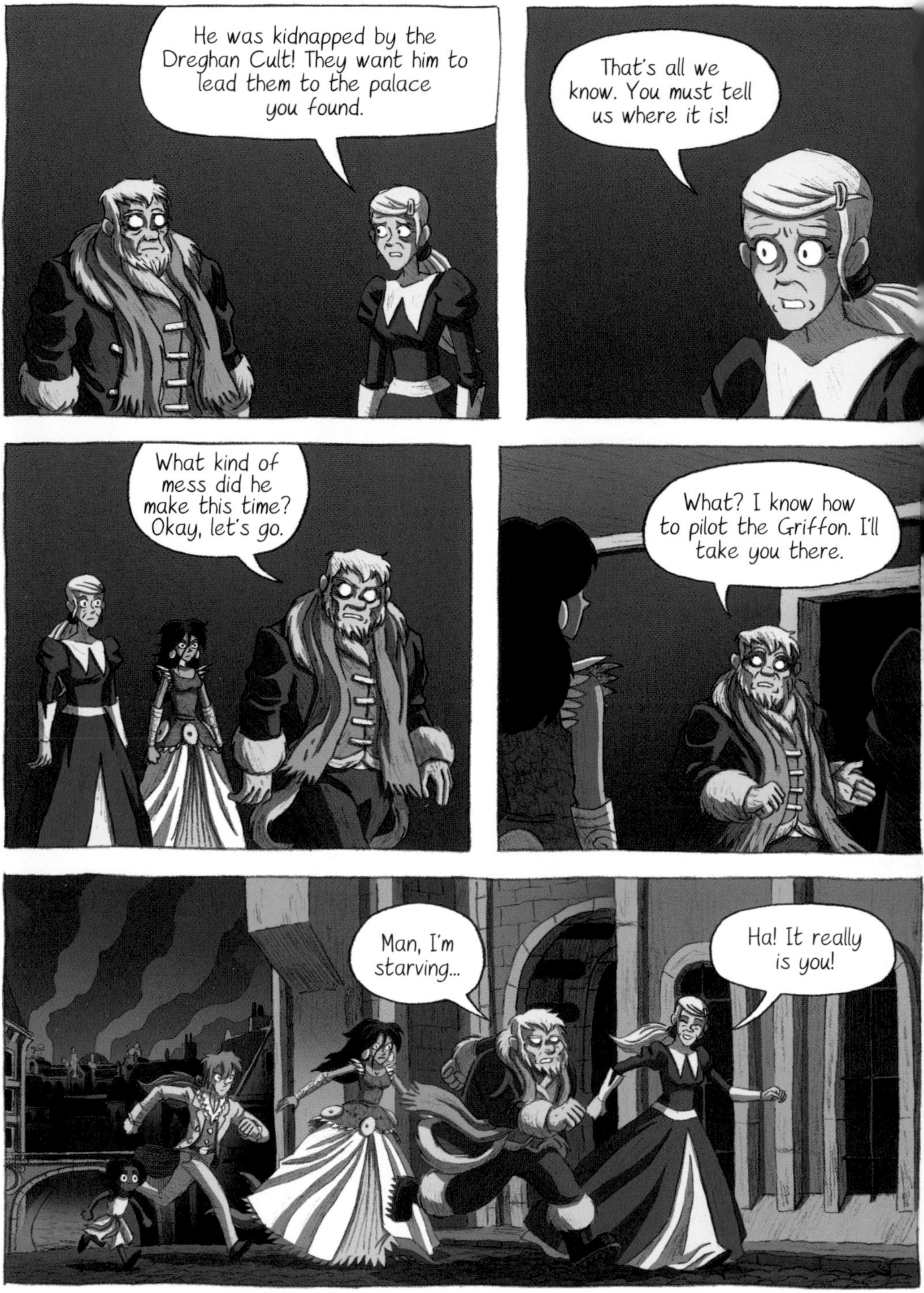
He was kidnapped by the Dreghan Cult! They want him to lead them to the palace you found.
That's all we know. You must tell us where it is!
What kind of mess did he make this time? Okay, let's go.
What? I know how to pilot the Griffon. I'll take you there.
Man, I'm starving...
Ha! It really is you!

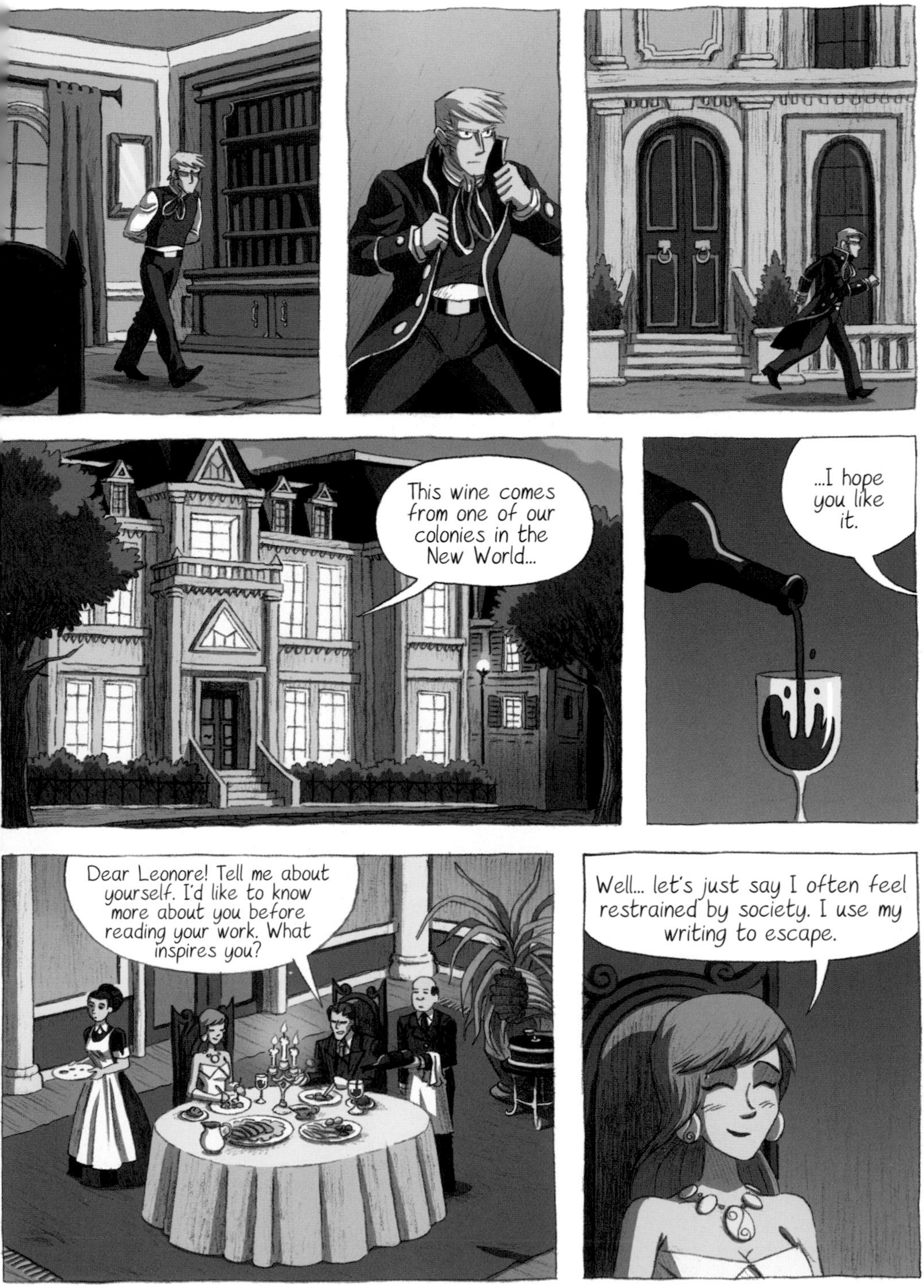
This wine comes from one of our colonies in the New World...
...I hope you like it.
Dear Leonore! Tell me about yourself. I'd like to know more about you before reading your work. What inspires you?
Well... let's just say I often feel restrained by society. I use my writing to escape.

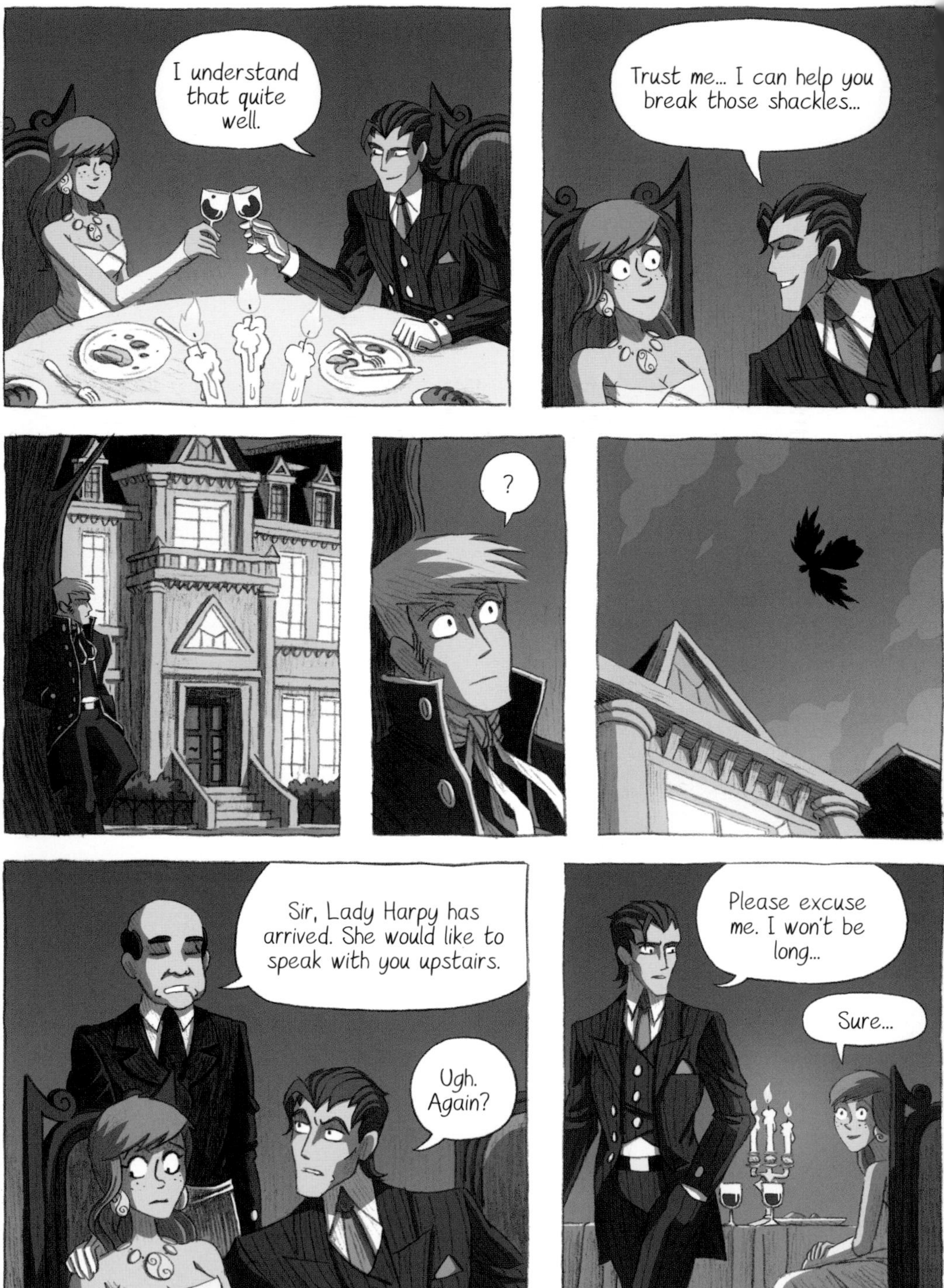

I understand that quite well.
Trust me... I can help you break those shackles...
?
Sir, Lady Harpy has arrived. She would like to speak with you upstairs.
Ugh. Again?
Please excuse me. I won't be long...
Sure...

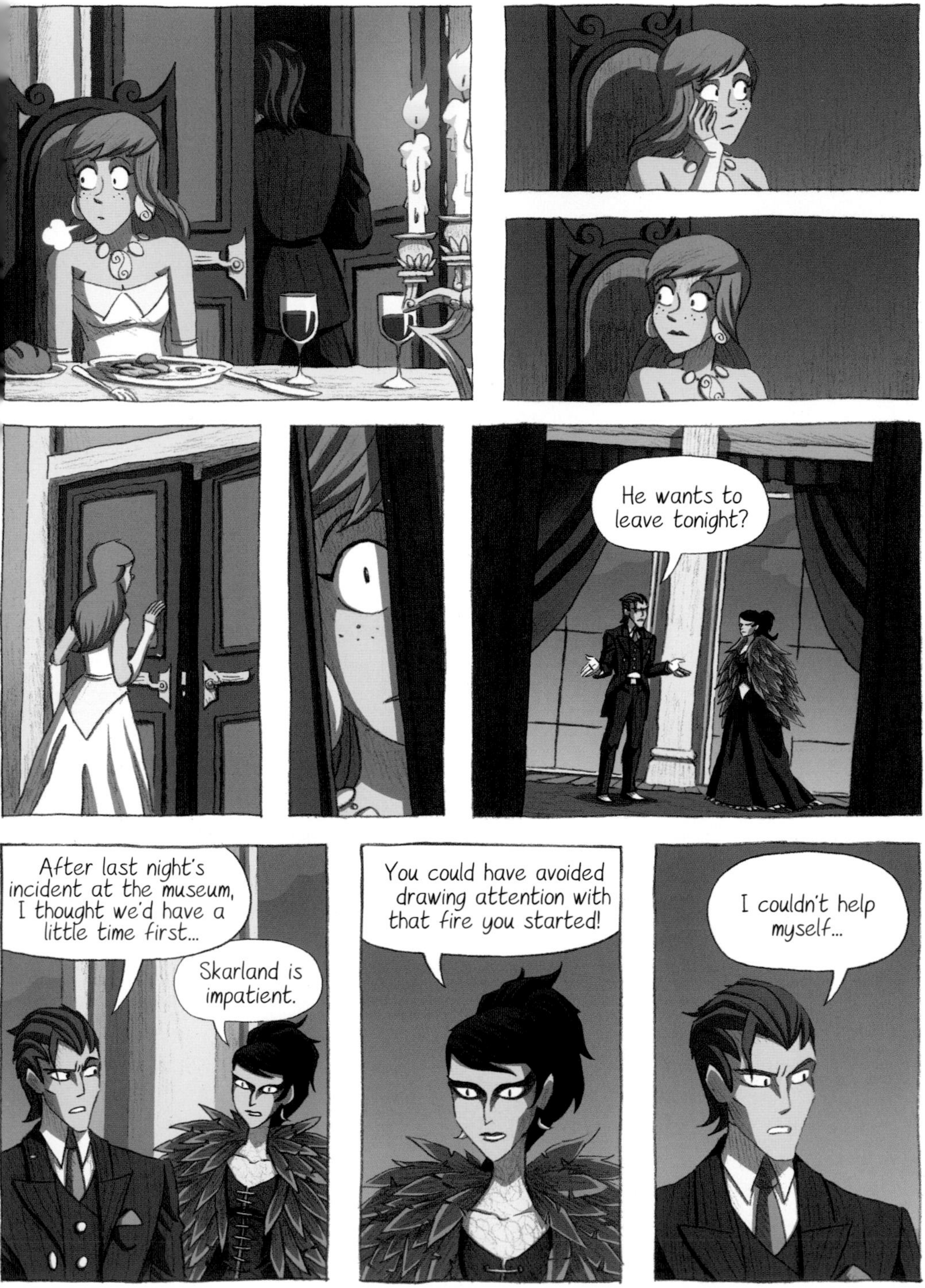
He wants to leave tonight?
After last night's incident at the museum, I thought we'd have a little time first...
Skarland is impatient.
You could have avoided drawing attention with that fire you started!
I couldn't help myself...

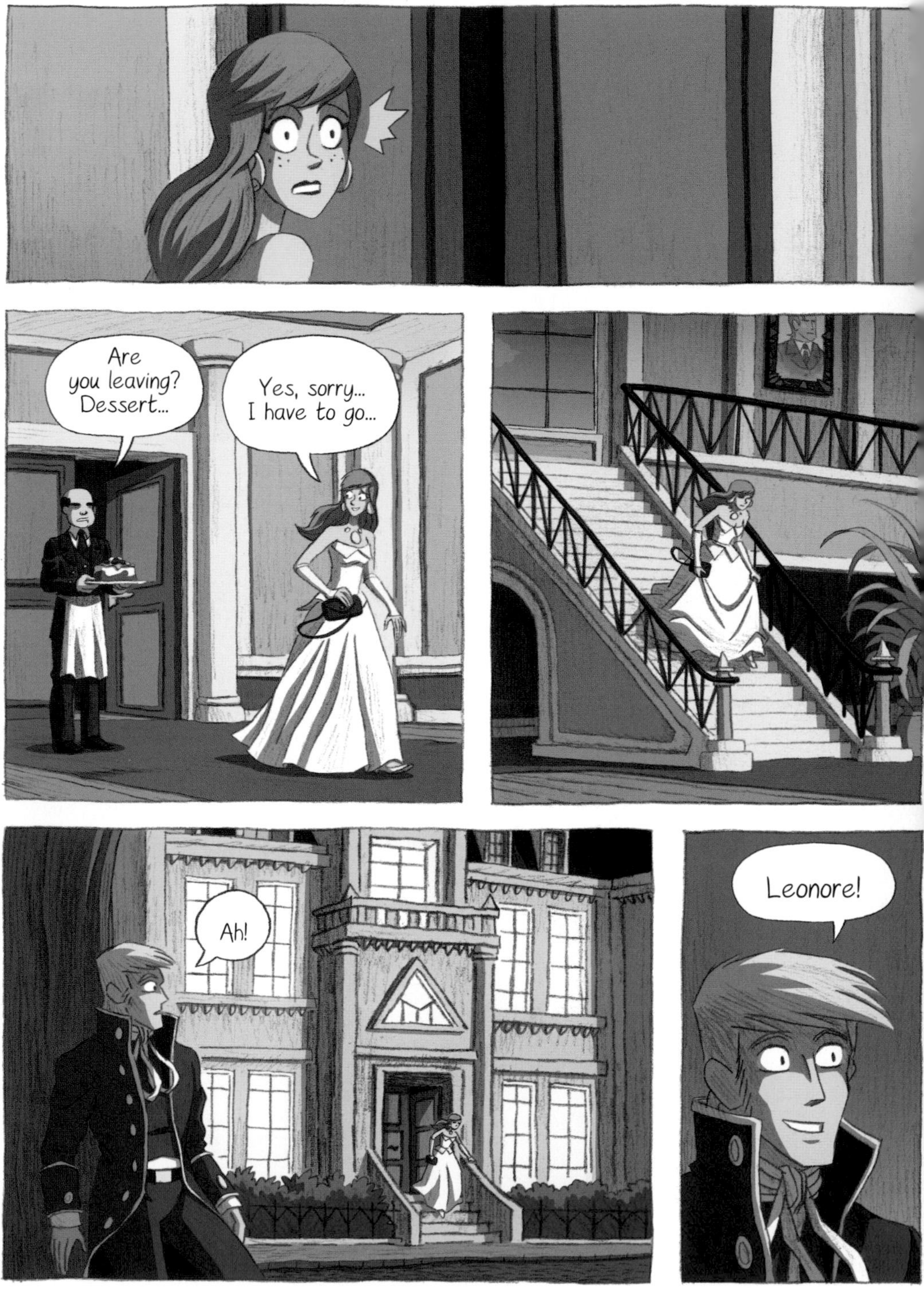
Are you leaving? Dessert...
Yes, sorry... I have to go...
Ah!
Leonore!

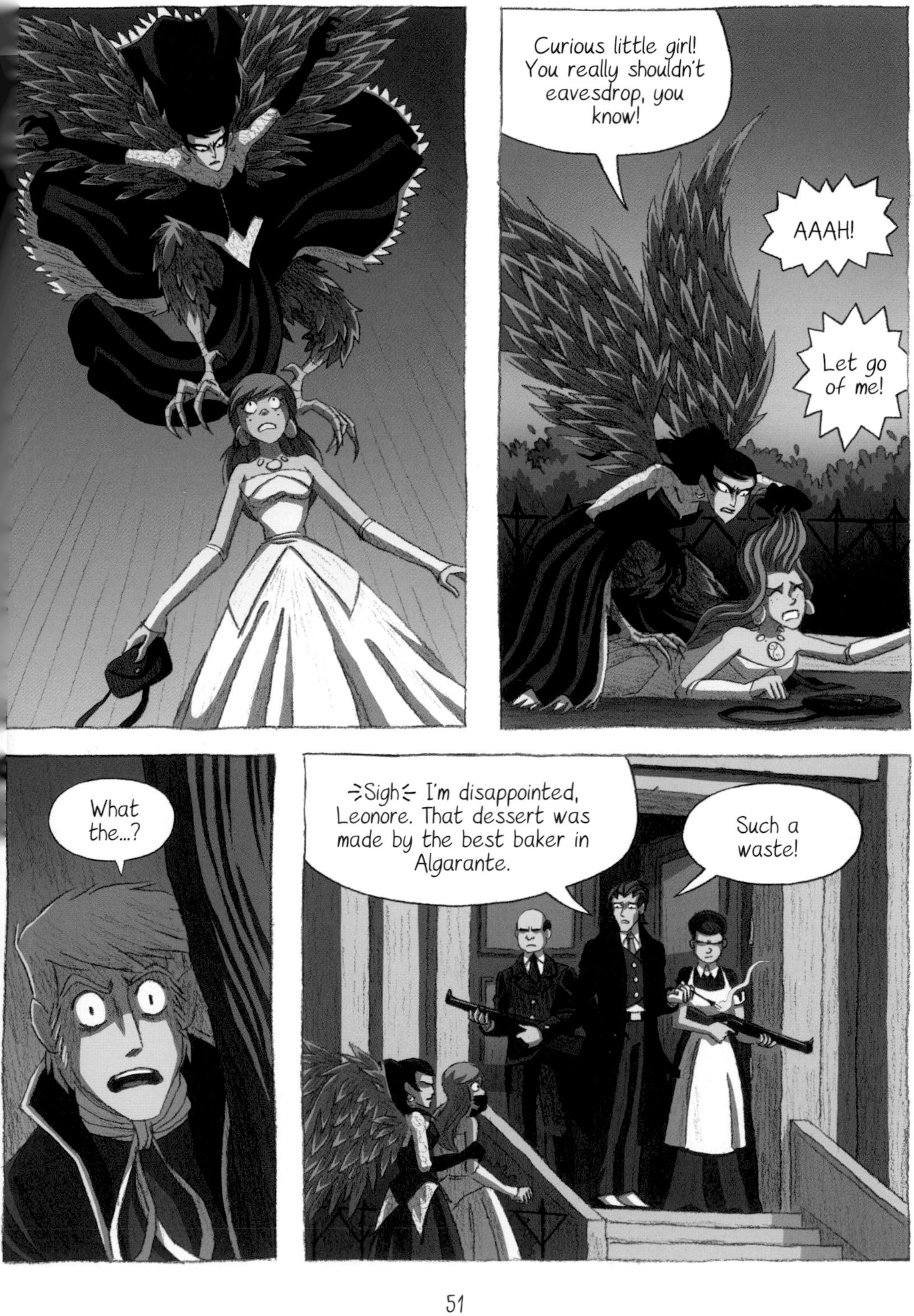
Curious little girl! You really shouldn't eavesdrop, you know!
AAAH!
Let go of me!
What the...?
⇒Sigh⇐ I'm disappointed, Leonore. That dessert was made by the best baker in Algarante.
Such a waste!

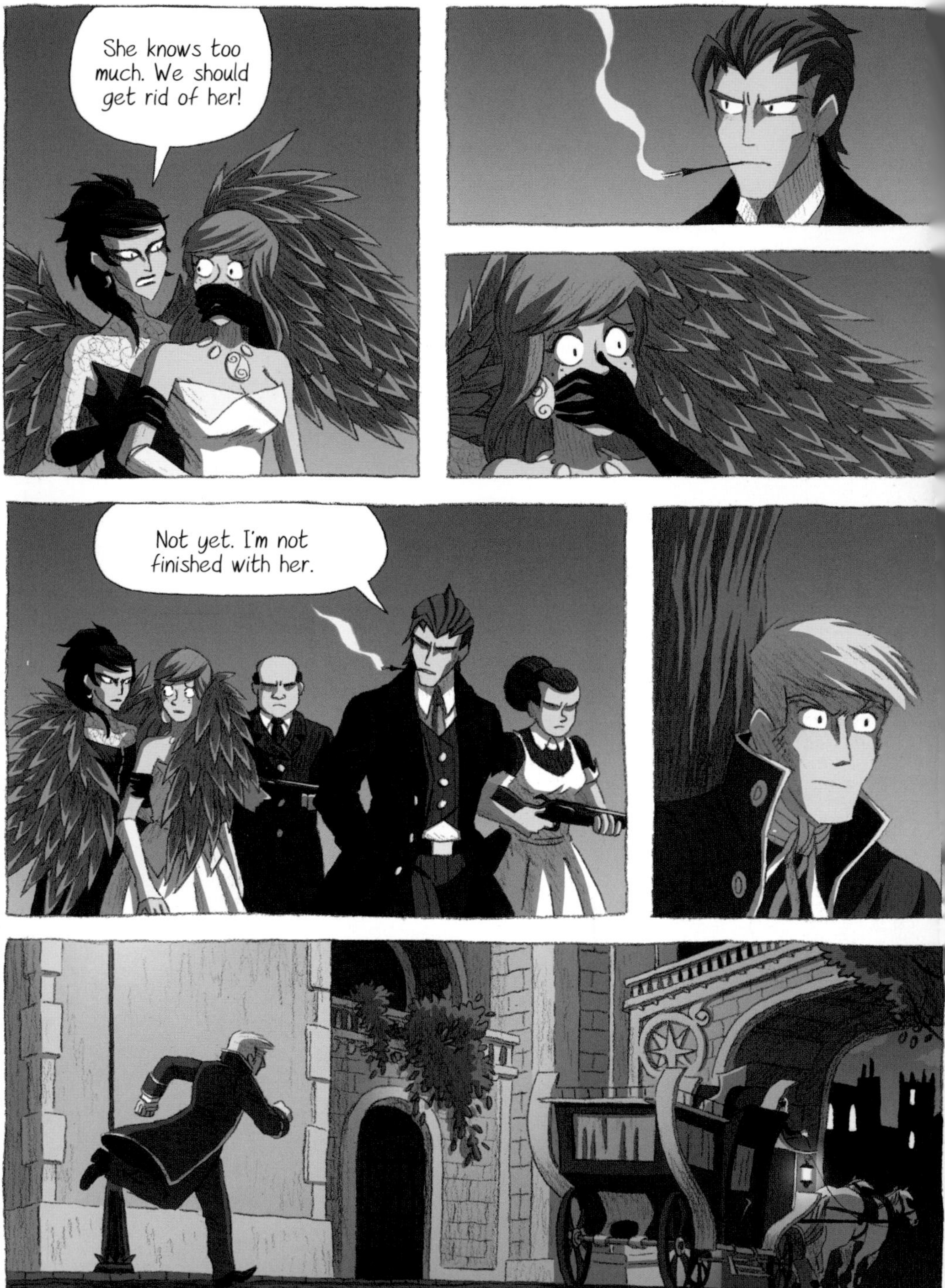
She knows too much. We should get rid of her!
Not yet. I'm not finished with her.

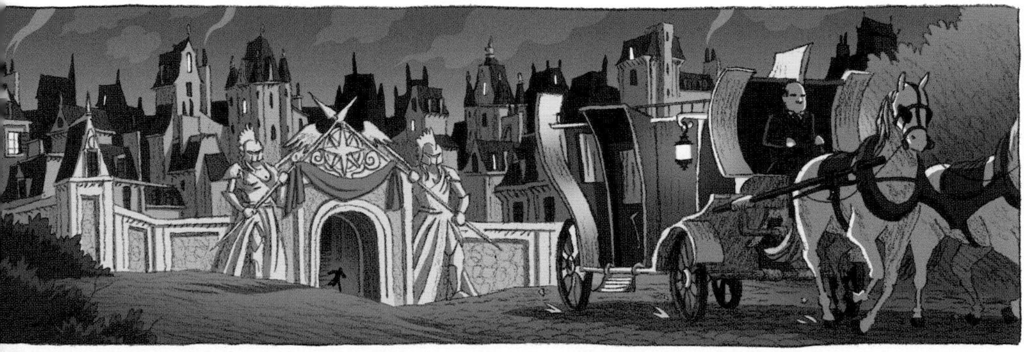

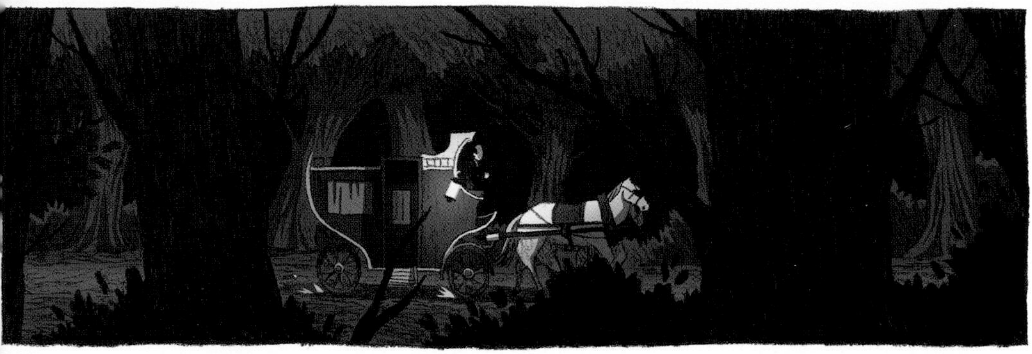

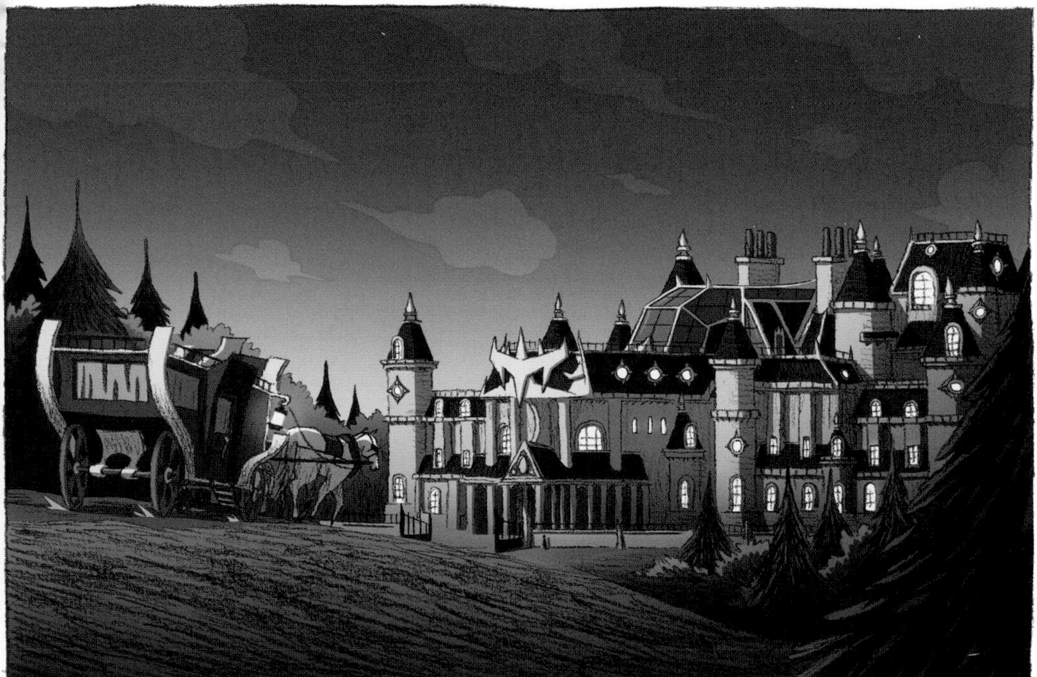

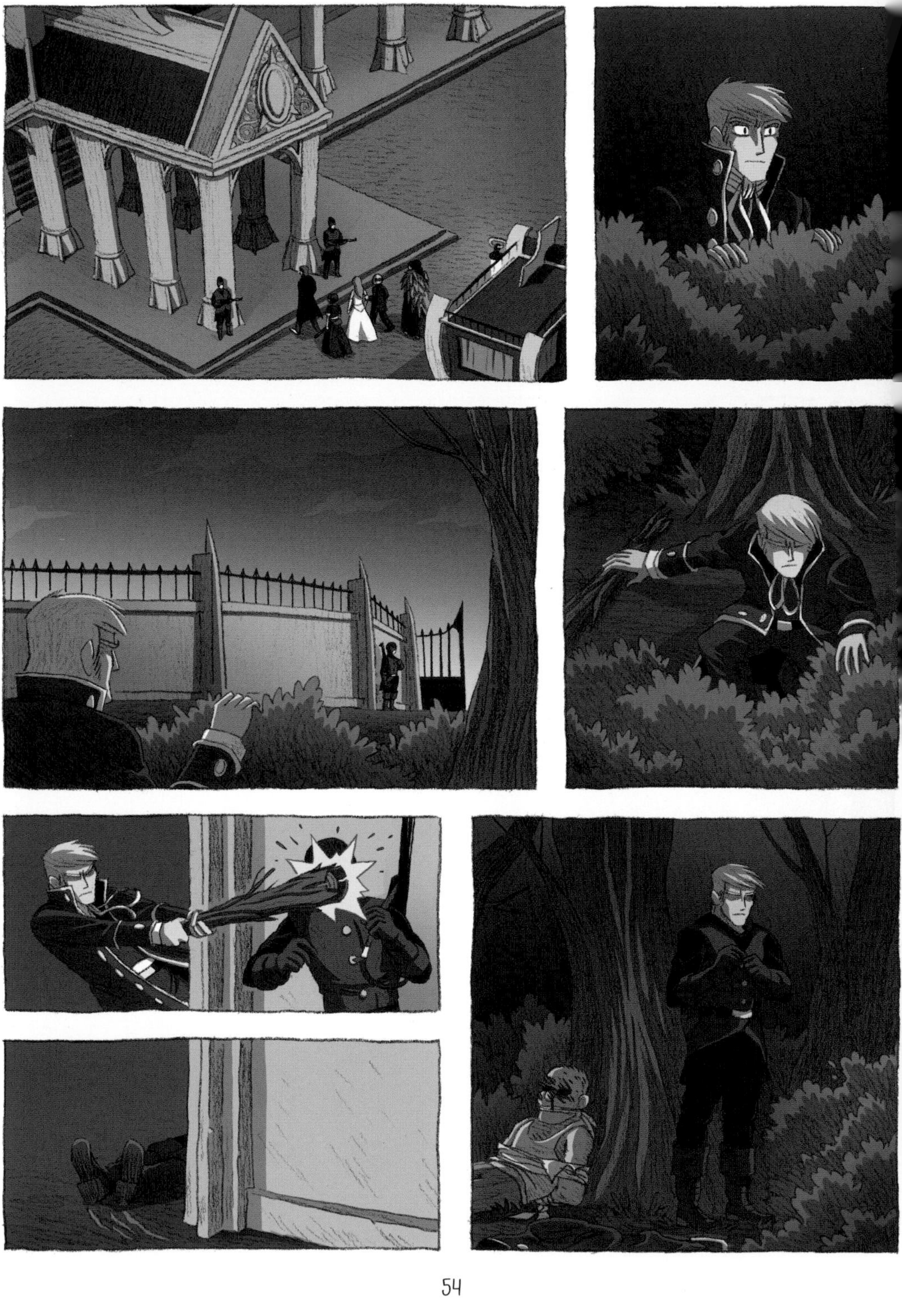

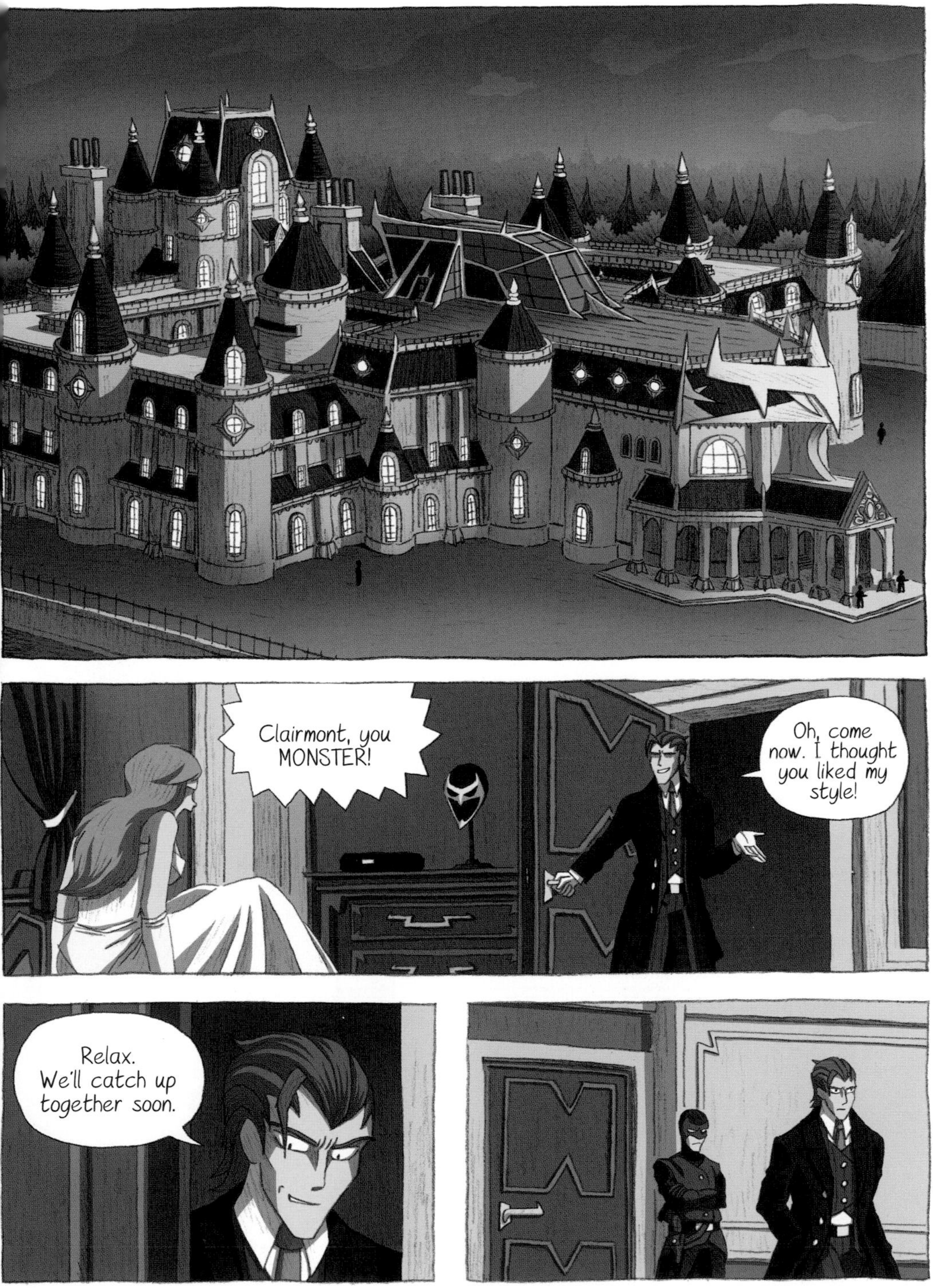
Clairmont, you MONSTER!
Oh, come now. I thought you liked my style!
Relax. We'll catch up together soon.

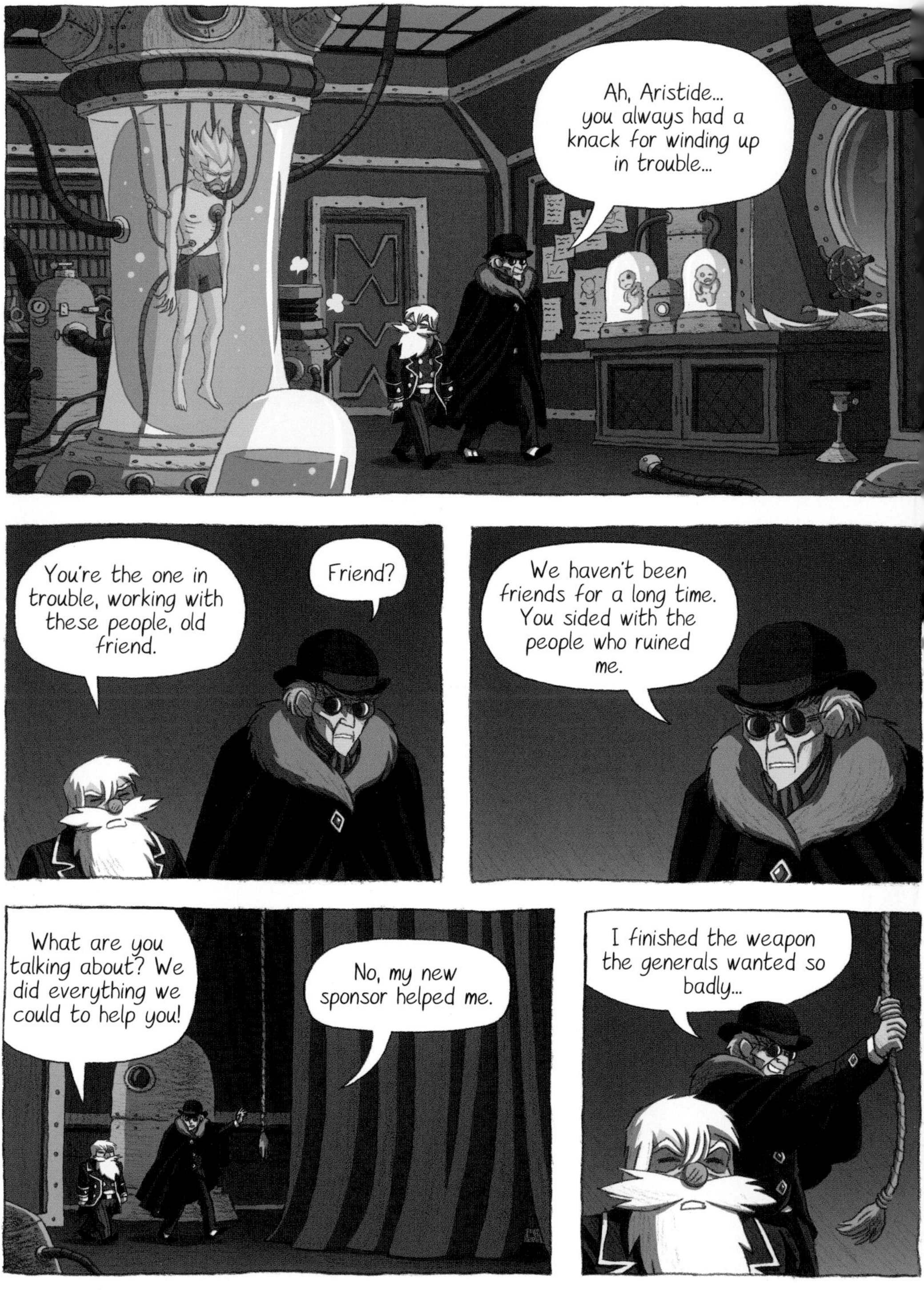
Ah, Aristide... you always had a knack for winding up in trouble...
You're the one in trouble, working with these people, old friend.
Friend?
We haven't been friends for a long time. You sided with the people who ruined me.
What are you talking about? We did everything we could to help you!
No, my new sponsor helped me.
I finished the weapon the generals wanted so badly...

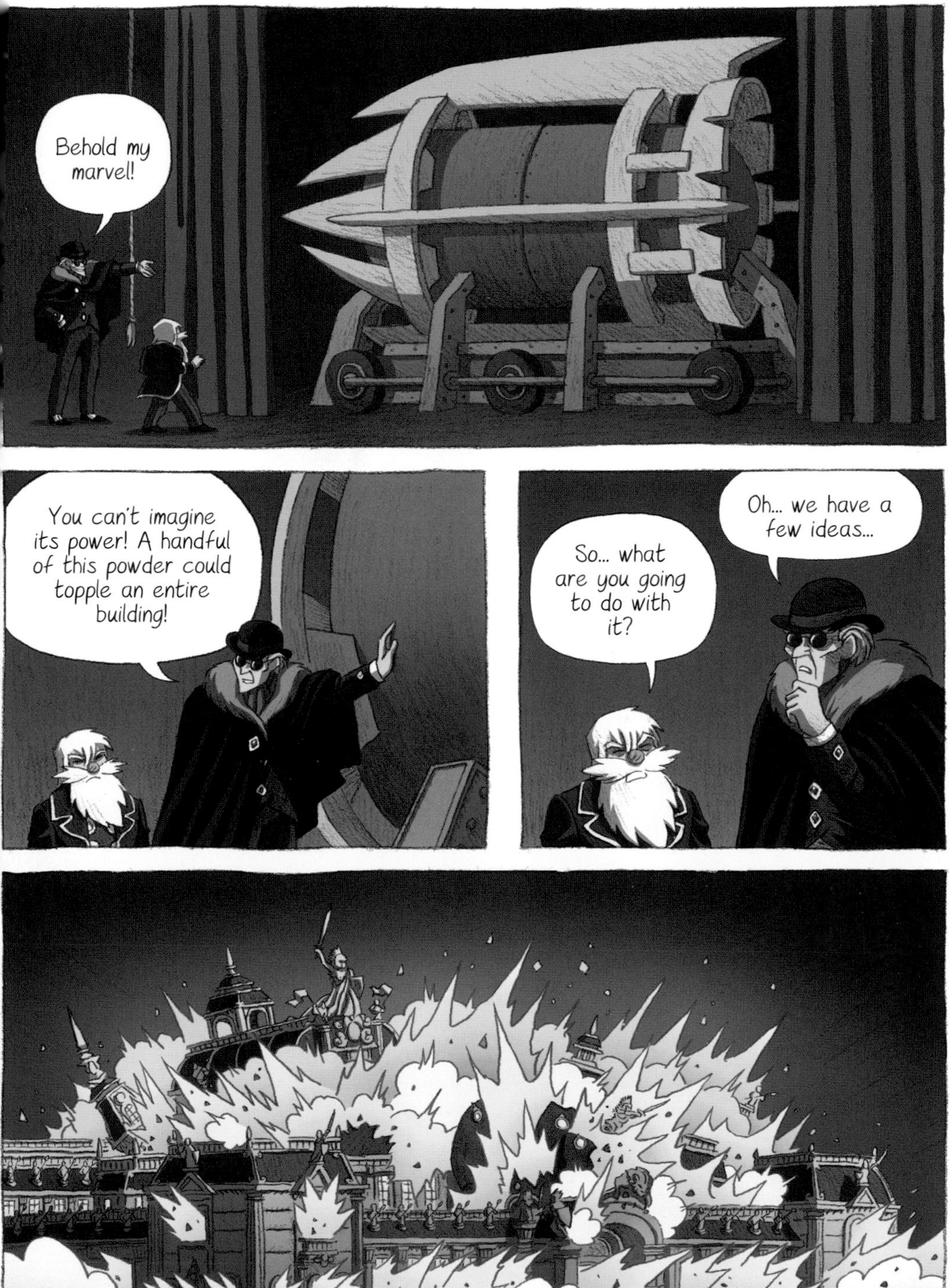

Behold my marvel!
You can't imagine its power! A handful of this powder could topple an entire building!
So... what are you going to do with it?
Oh... we have a few ideas...

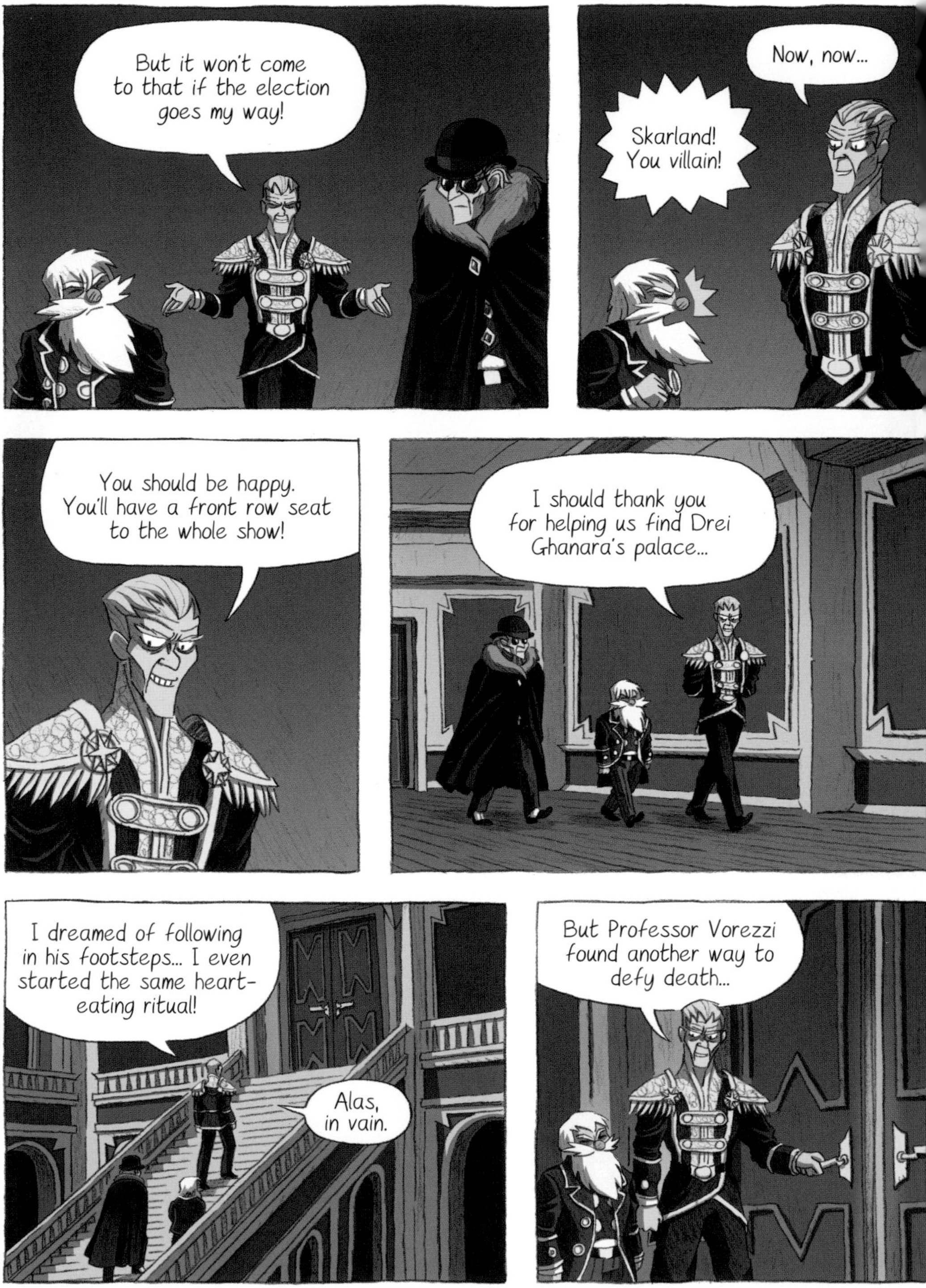

But it won't come to that if the election goes my way!
Skarland! You villain!
Now, now...
You should be happy. You'll have a front row seat to the whole show!
I should thank you for helping us find Drei Ghanara's palace...
I dreamed of following in his footsteps... I even started the same heart-eating ritual!
Alas, in vain.
But Professor Vorezzi found another way to defy death...

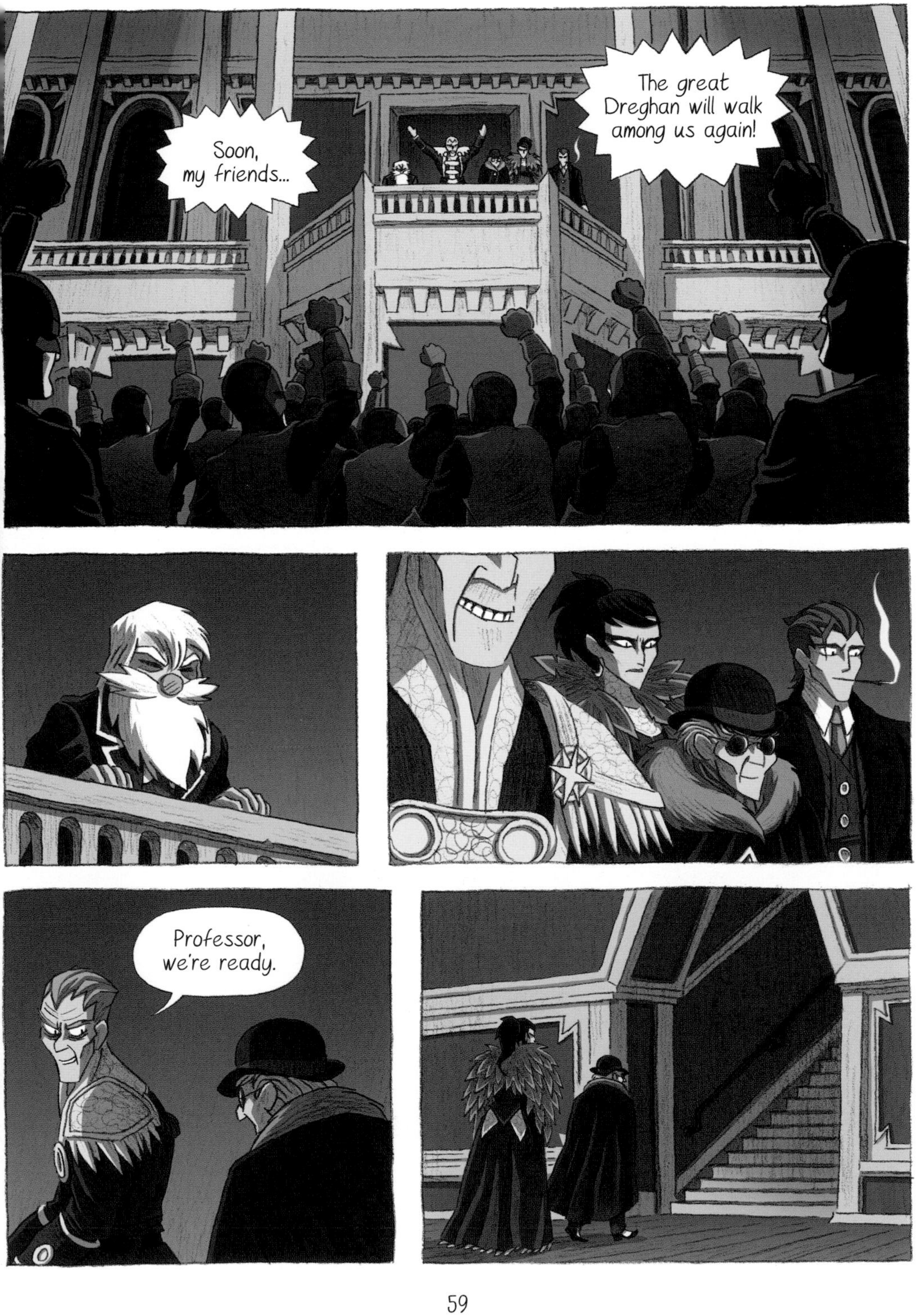
Soon, my friends...
The great Dreghan will walk among us again!
Professor, we're ready.

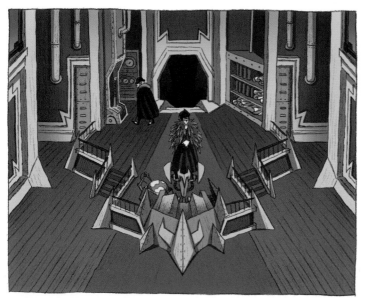

CLANK!

KLRKLRKLRKLRKLRRL LKL

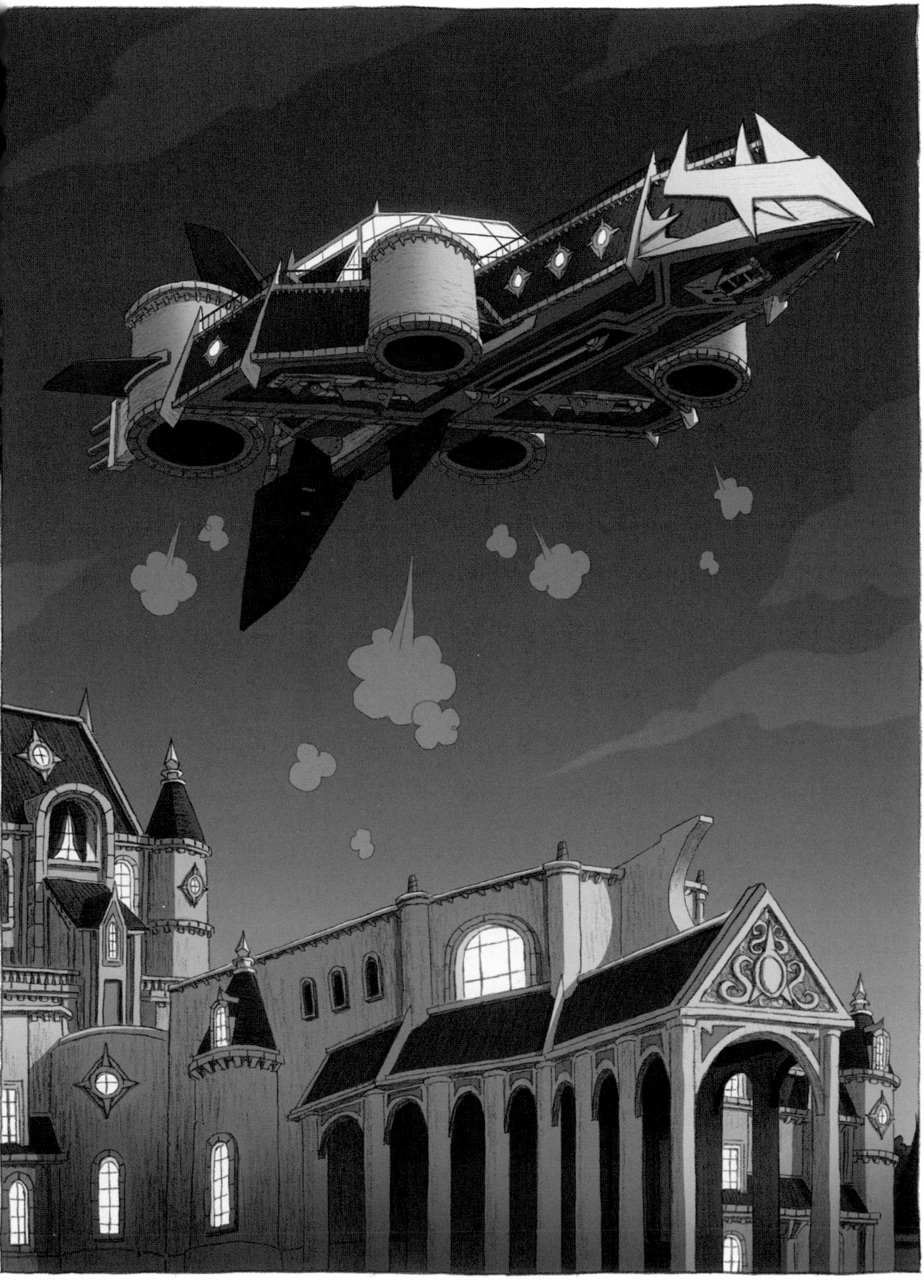

The Dreghan Cult was founded several decades ago. They worshiped the wicked spirit they hoped would "bite" them, and took to torturing and murdering people to feed it...

Its members came from all levels of society, from nobles and aristocrats...

...to artisans and simple folk.

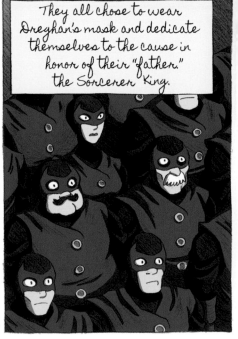

They all chose to wear Dreghan's mask and dedicate themselves to the cause in honor of their "father," the Sorcerer King.

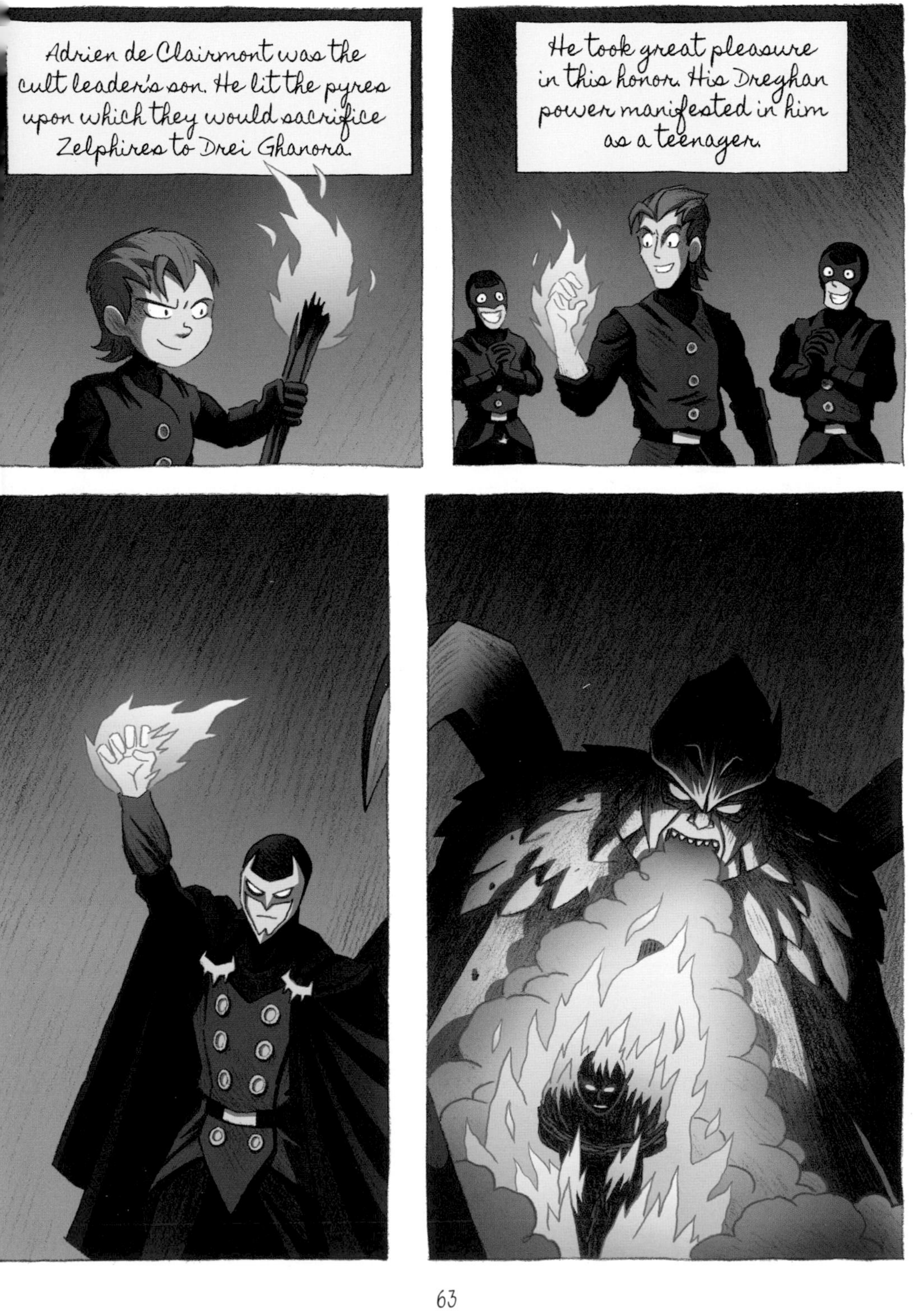
Adrien de Clairmont was the cult leader's son. He lit the pyres upon which they would sacrifice Zelphires to Drei Ghanora.
He took great pleasure in this honor. His Dreghan power manifested in him as a teenager.

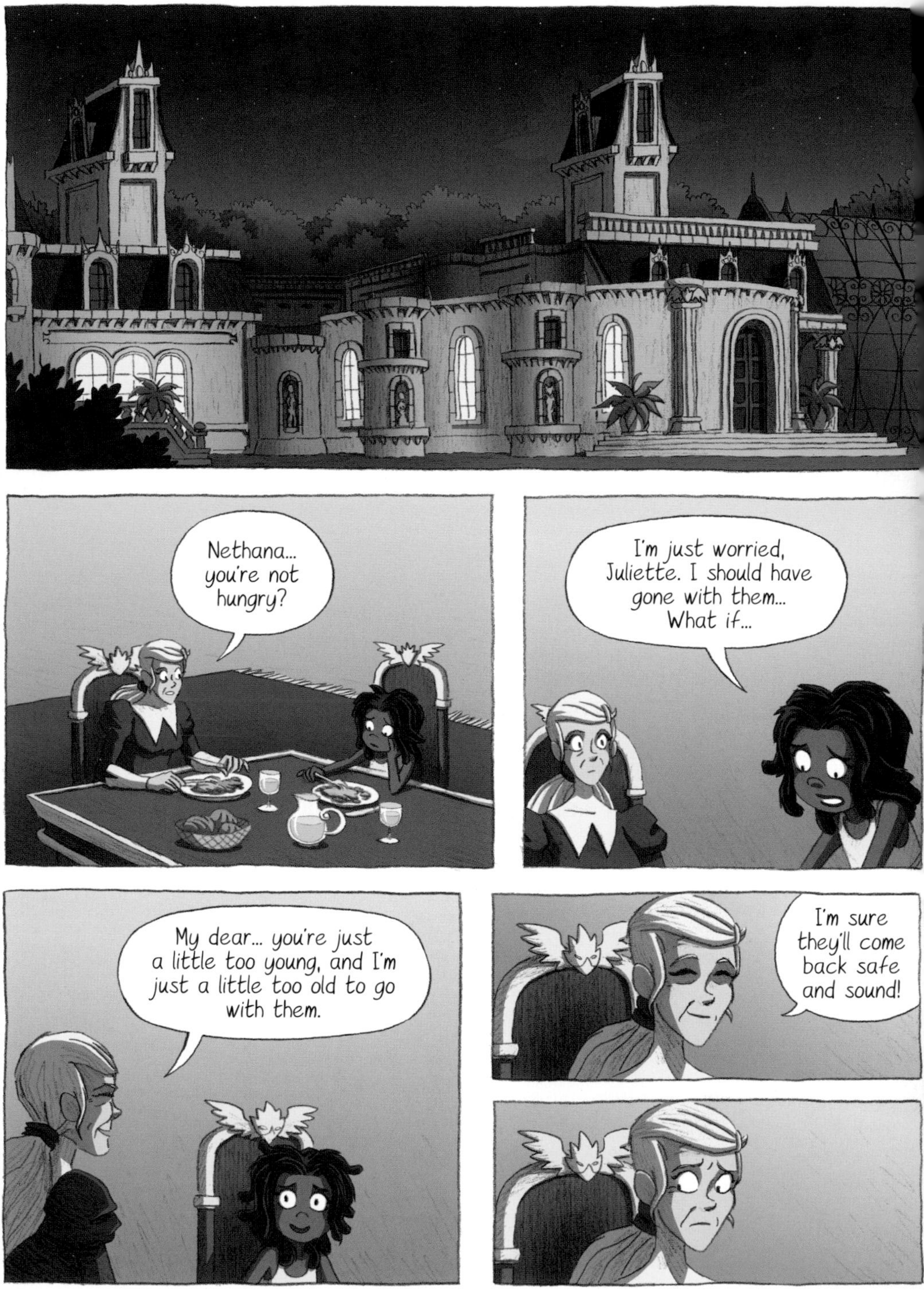
Nethana... you're not hungry?
I'm just worried, Juliette. I should have gone with them... What if...
My dear... you're just a little too young, and I'm just a little too old to go with them.
I'm sure they'll come back safe and sound!

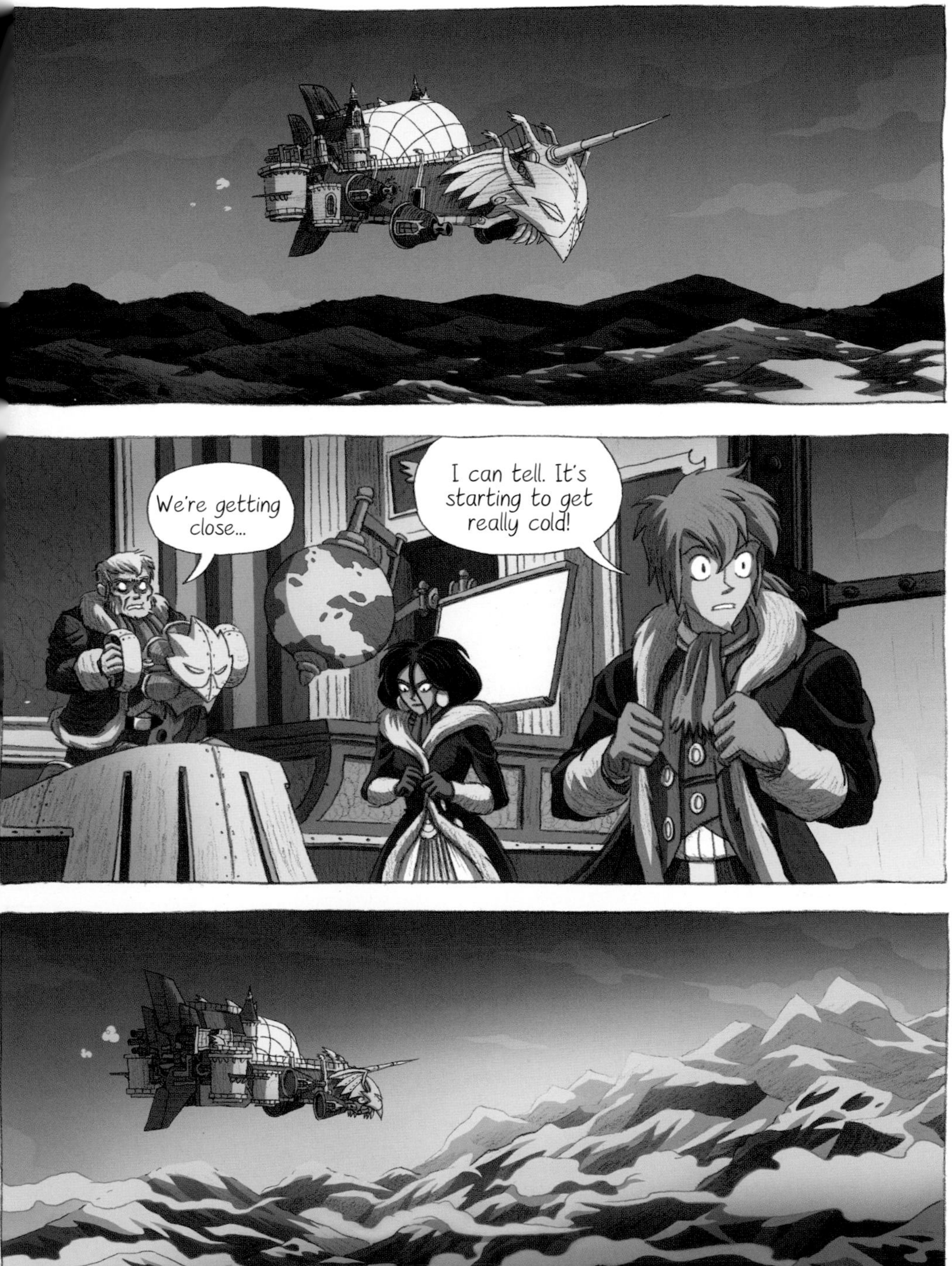
We're getting close...
I can tell. It's starting to get really cold!

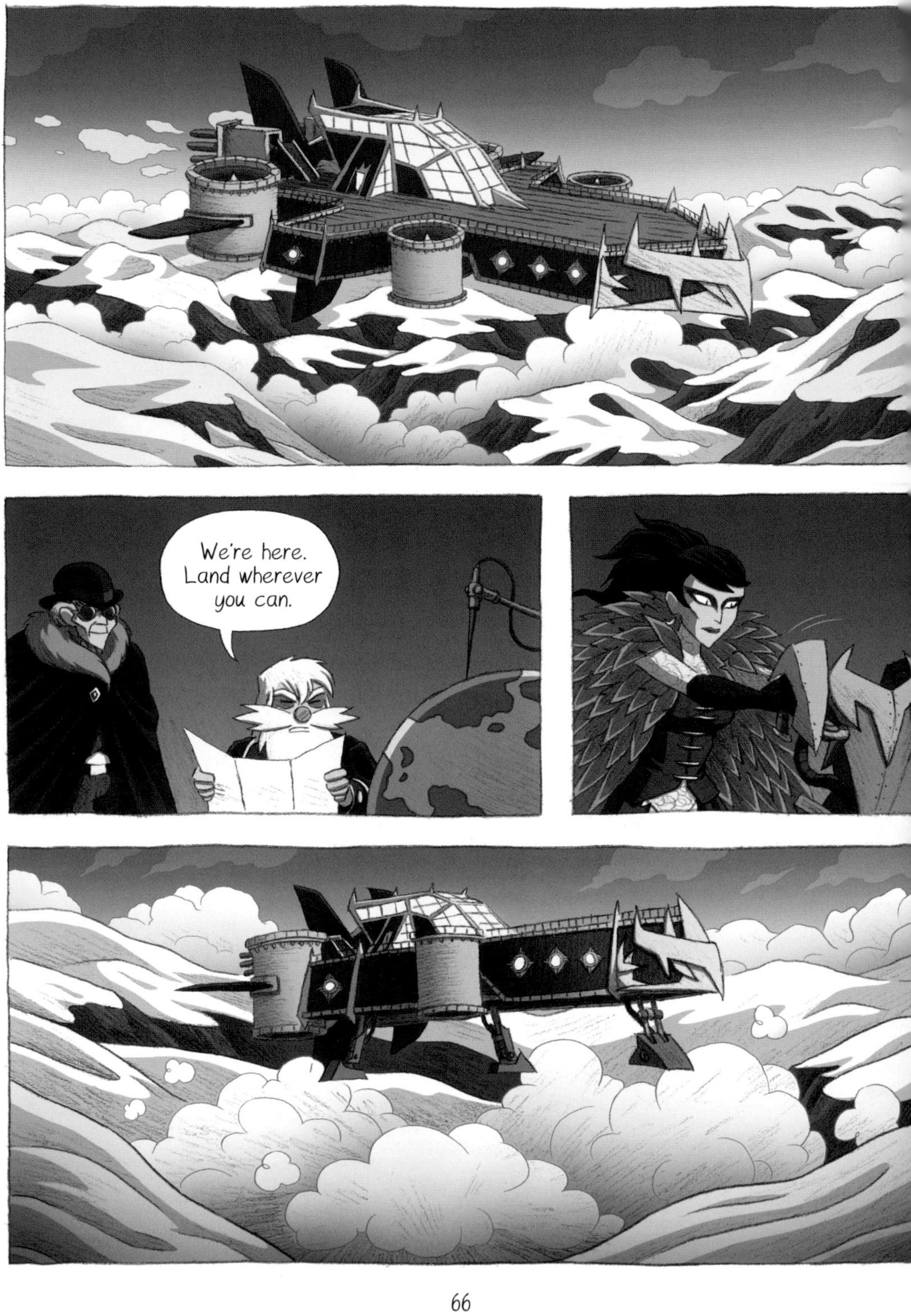
We're here. Land wherever you can.

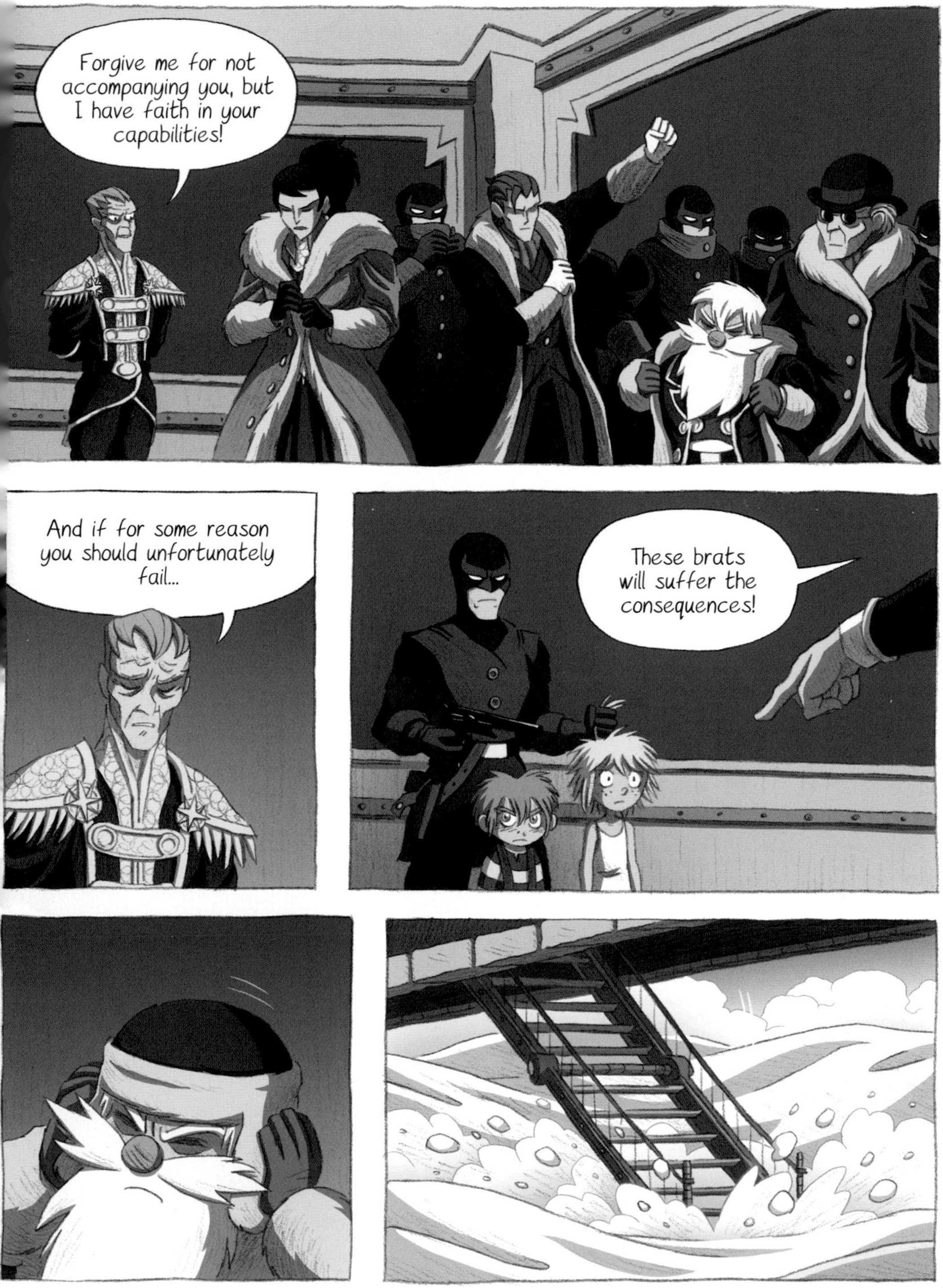
Forgive me for not accompanying you, but I have faith in your capabilities!
And if for some reason you should unfortunately fail...
These brats will suffer the consequences!

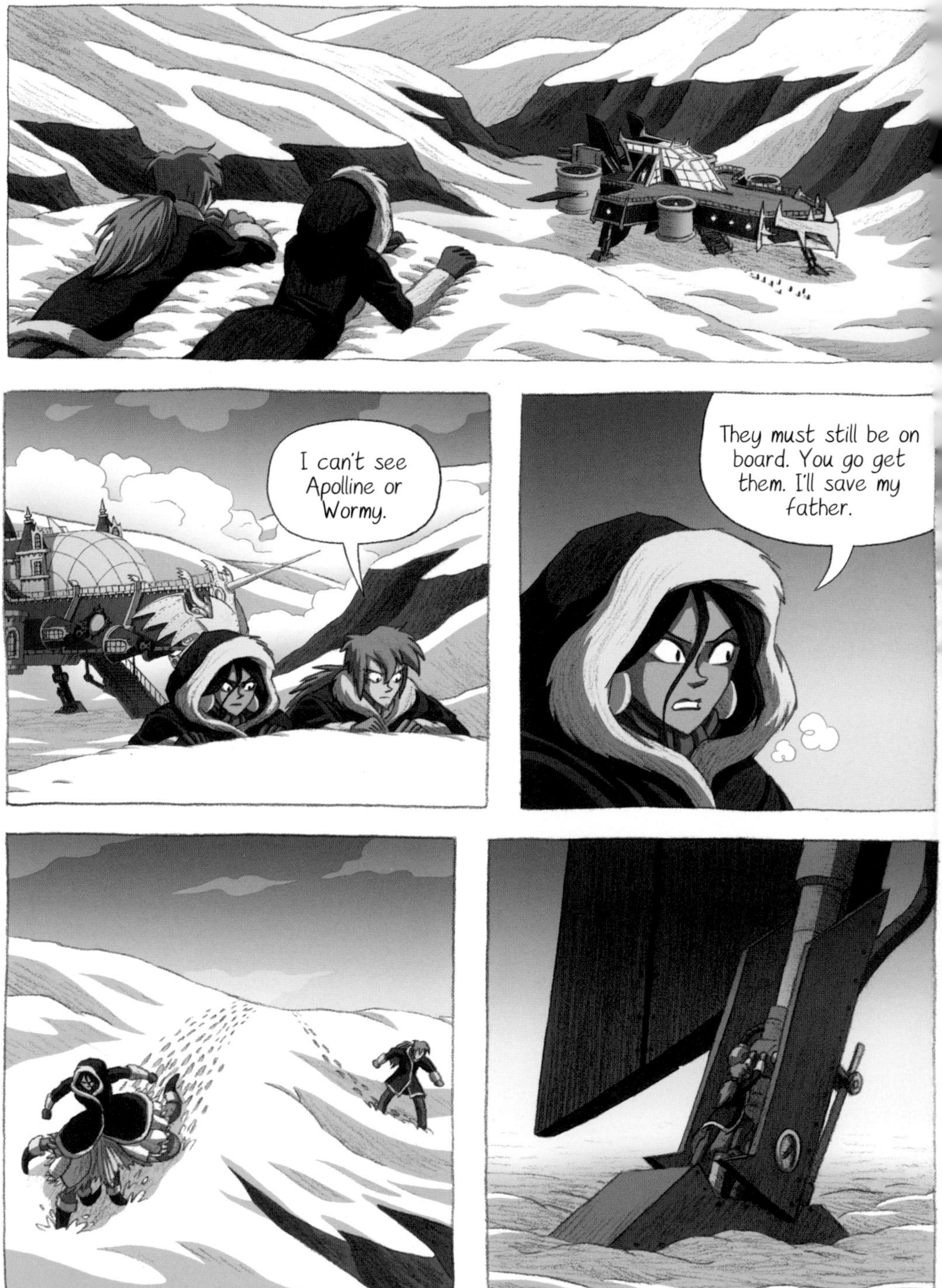
I can't see Apolline or Wormy.
They must still be on board. You go get them. I'll save my father.

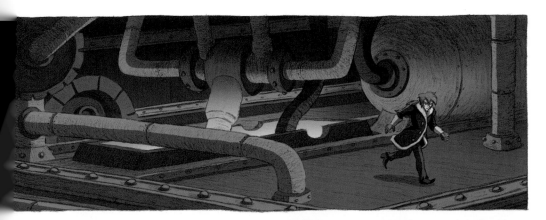

Not much further... we should almost...

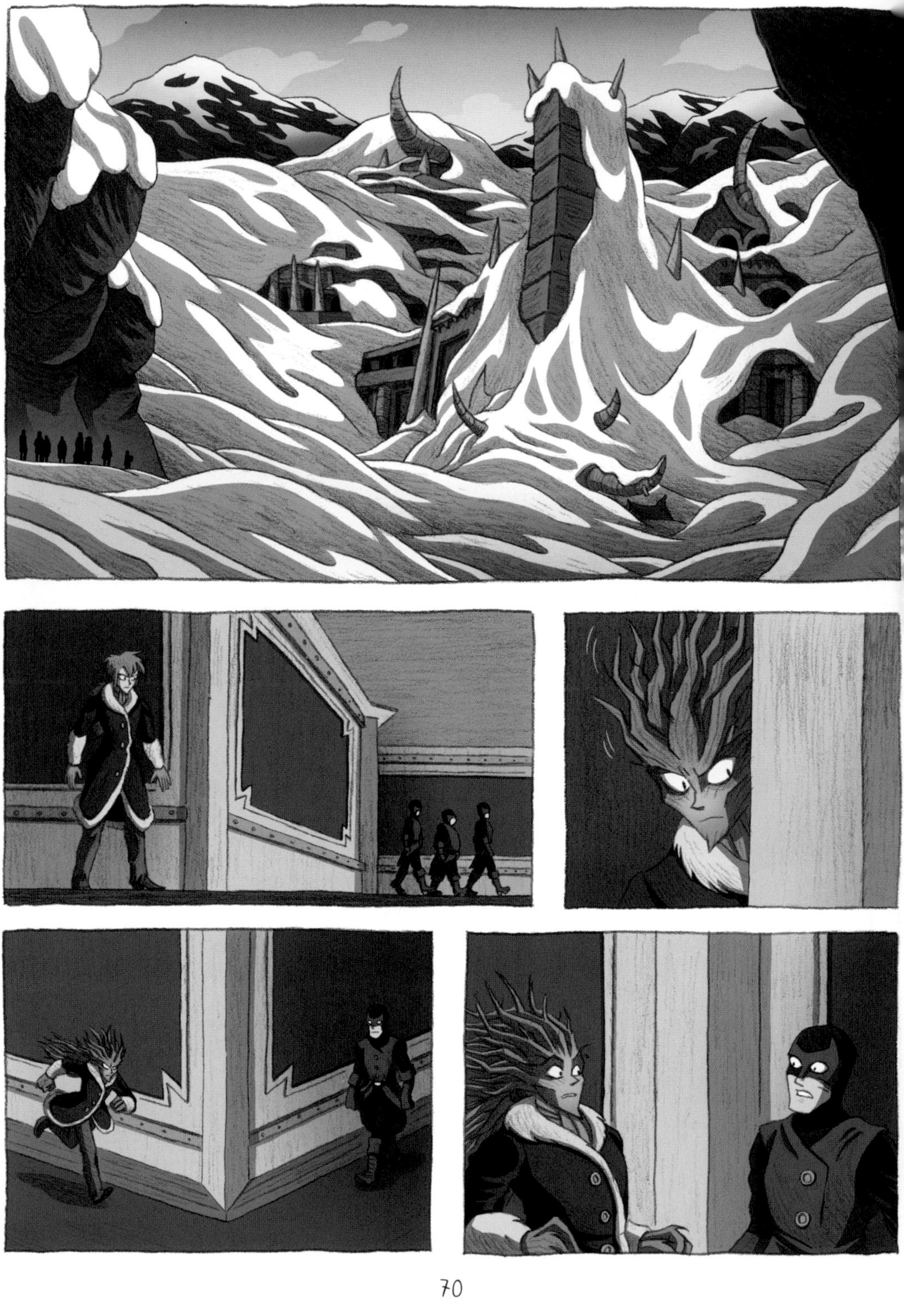

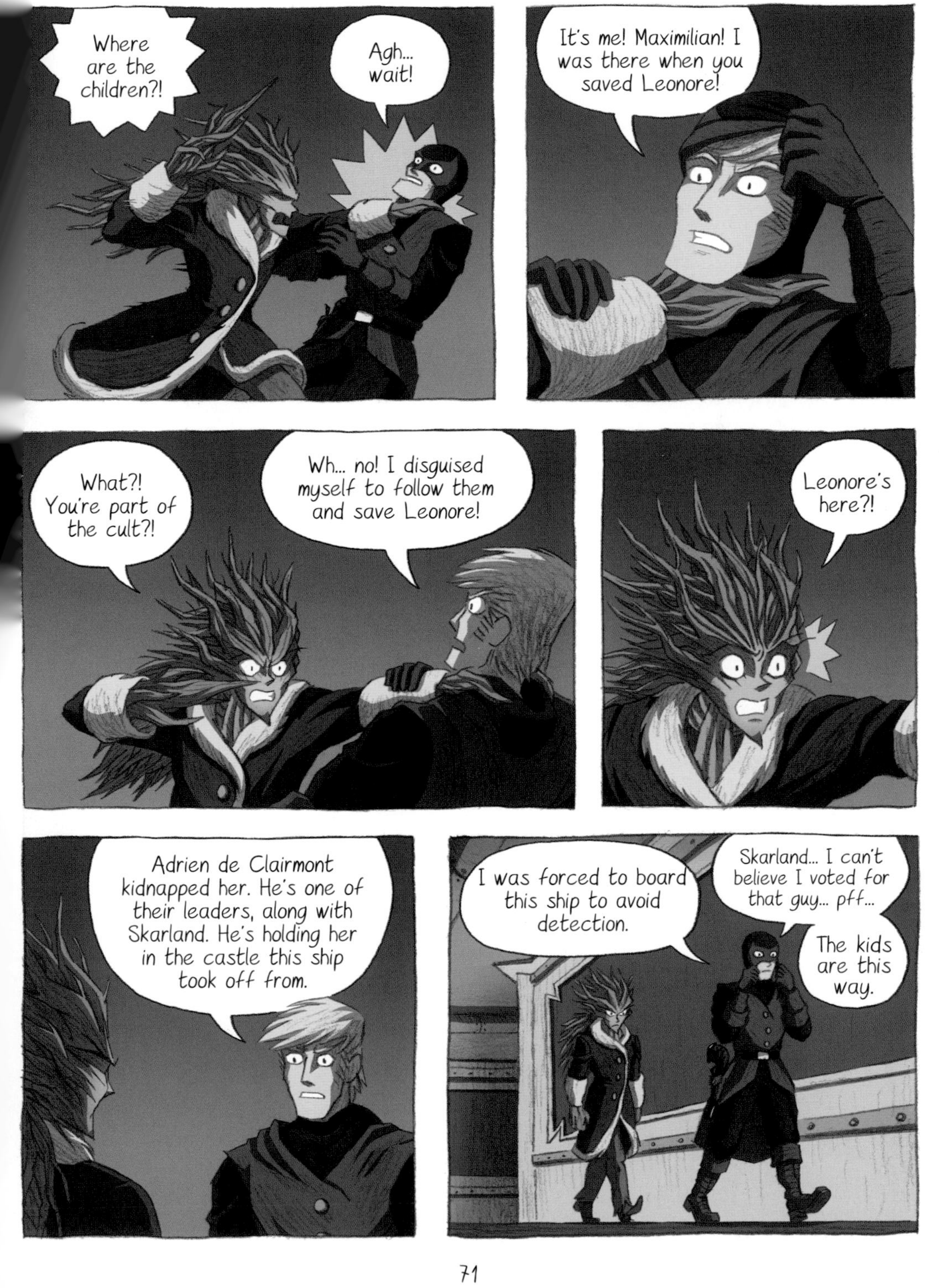
Where are the children?!
Agh... wait!
It's me! Maximilian! I was there when you saved Leonore!
What?! You're part of the cult?!
Wh... no! I disguised myself to follow them and save Leonore!
Leonore's here?!
Adrien de Clairmont kidnapped her. He's one of their leaders, along with Skarland. He's holding her in the castle this ship took off from.
I was forced to board this ship to avoid detection.
Skarland... I can't believe I voted for that guy... pff...
The kids are this way.

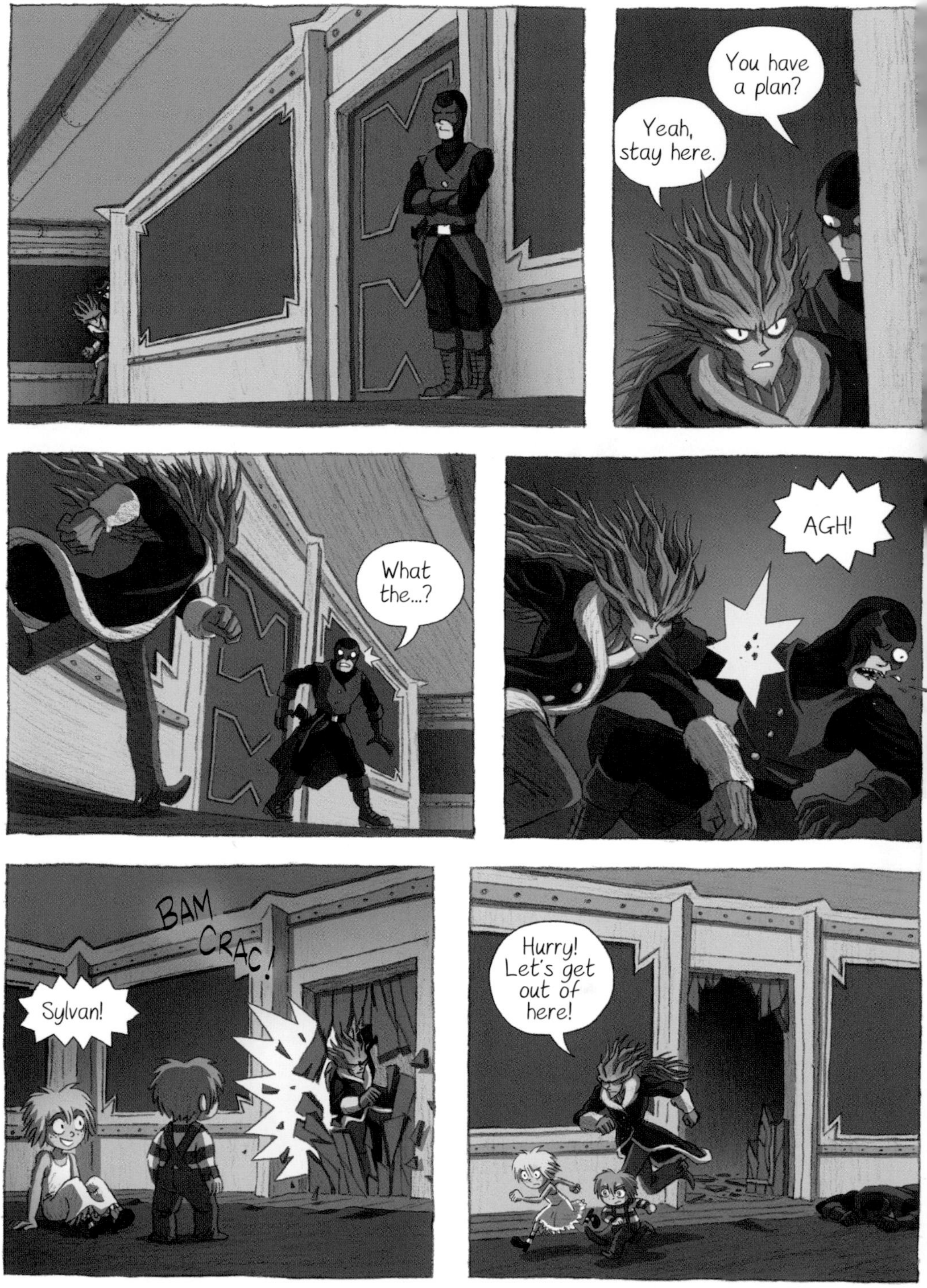

You have a plan?
Yeah, stay here.
What the...?
AGH!
BAM
CRAC!
Sylvan!
Hurry! Let's get out of here!

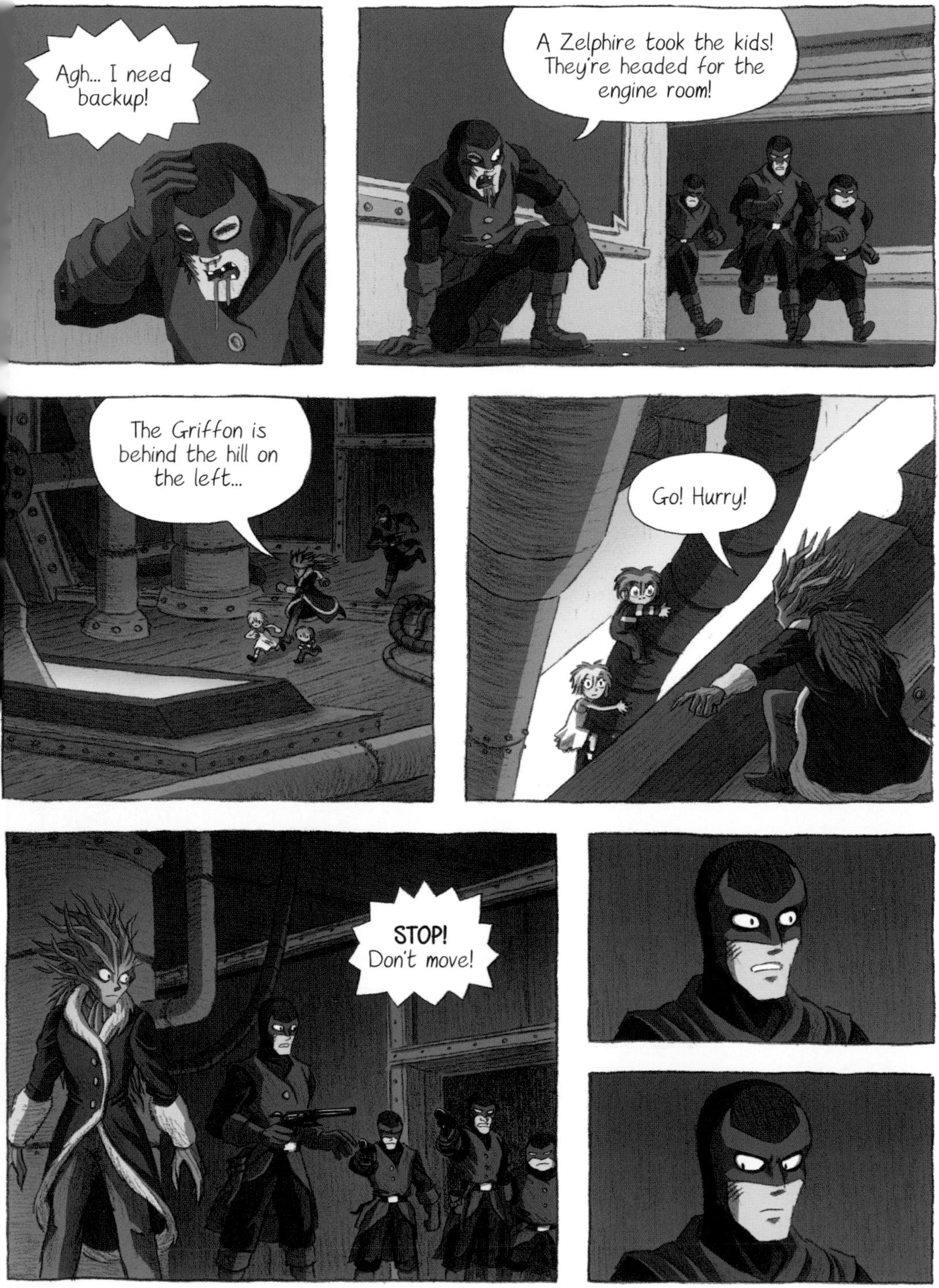
Agh... I need backup!
A Zelphire took the kids! They're headed for the engine room!
The Griffon is behind the hill on the left...
Go! Hurry!
STOP! Don't move!

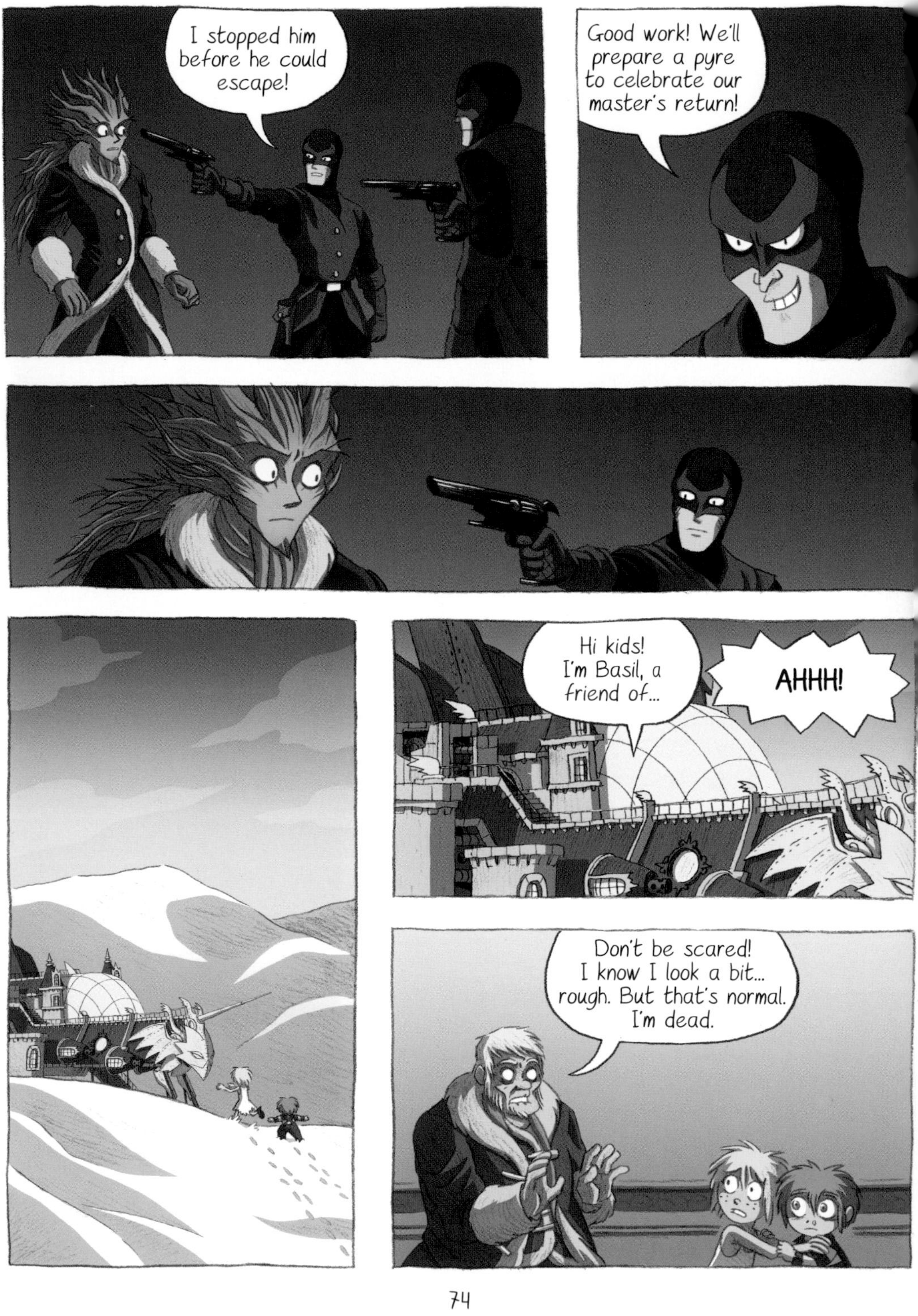

I stopped him before he could escape!
Good work! We'll prepare a pyre to celebrate our master's return!
Hi kids! I'm Basil, a friend of...
AHHH!
Don't be scared! I know I look a bit... rough. But that's normal. I'm dead.

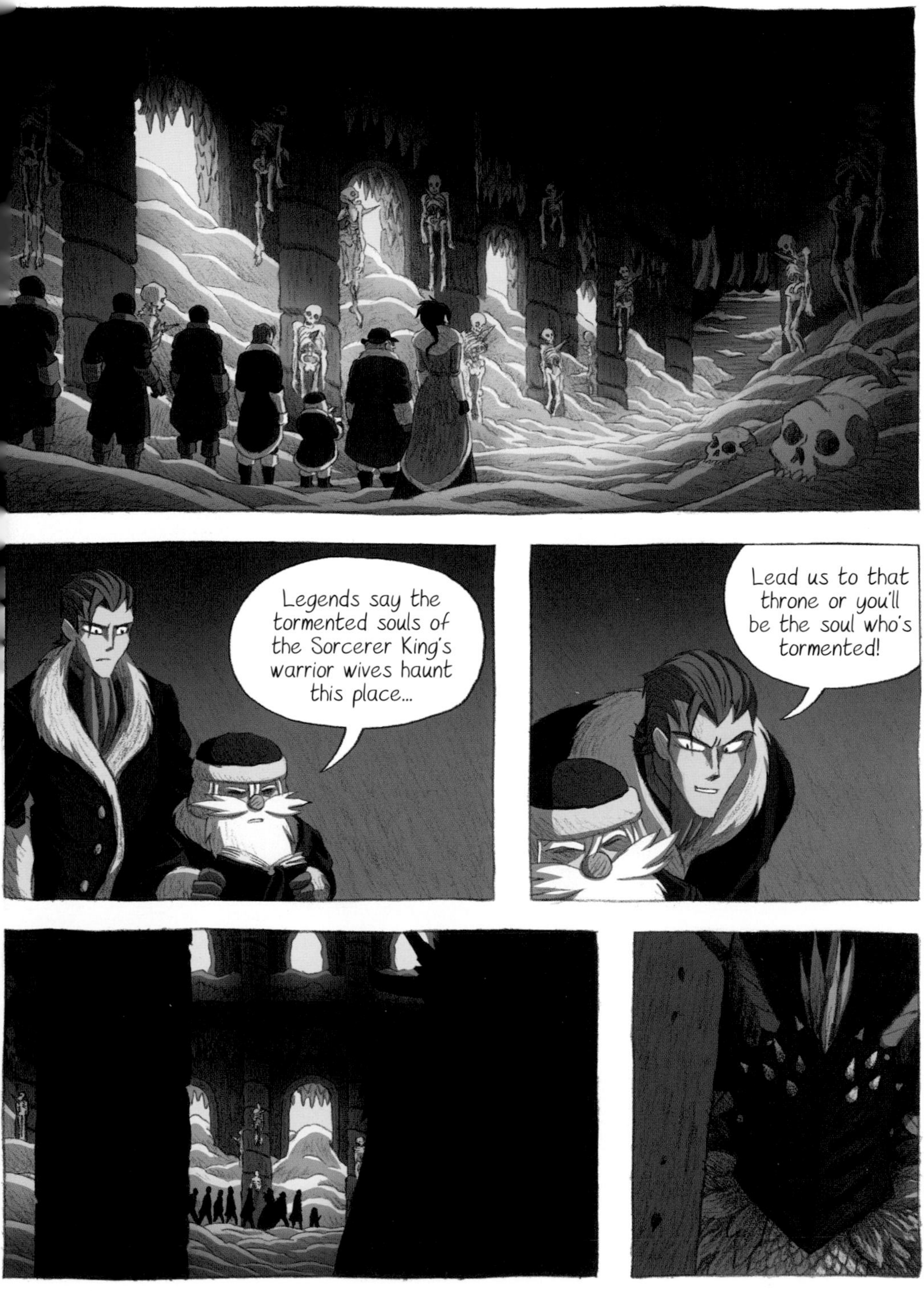
Legends say the tormented souls of the Sorcerer King's warrior wives haunt this place...
Lead us to that throne or you'll be the soul who's tormented!

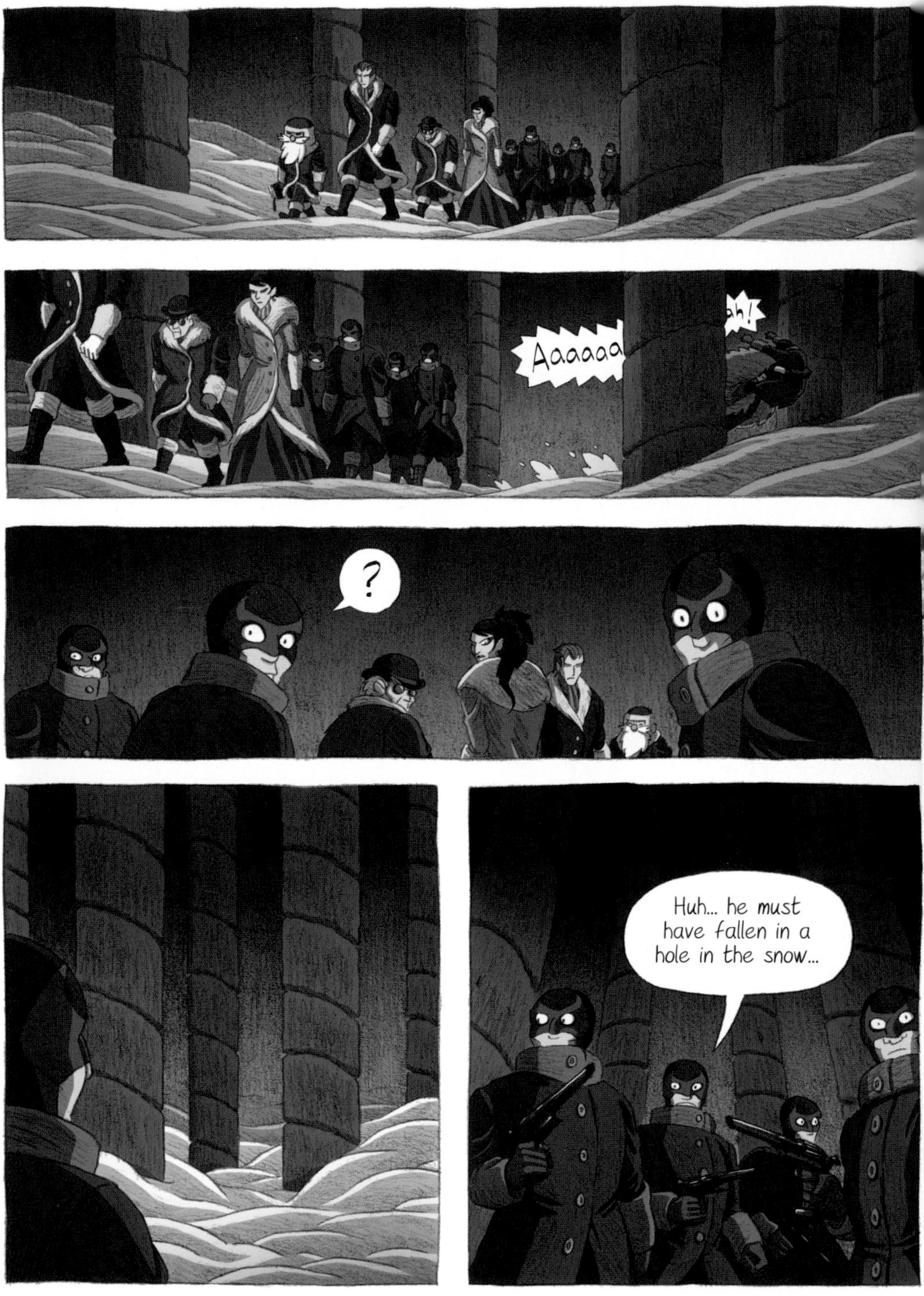
Aaaaa
ah!
?
Huh... he must have fallen in a hole in the snow...

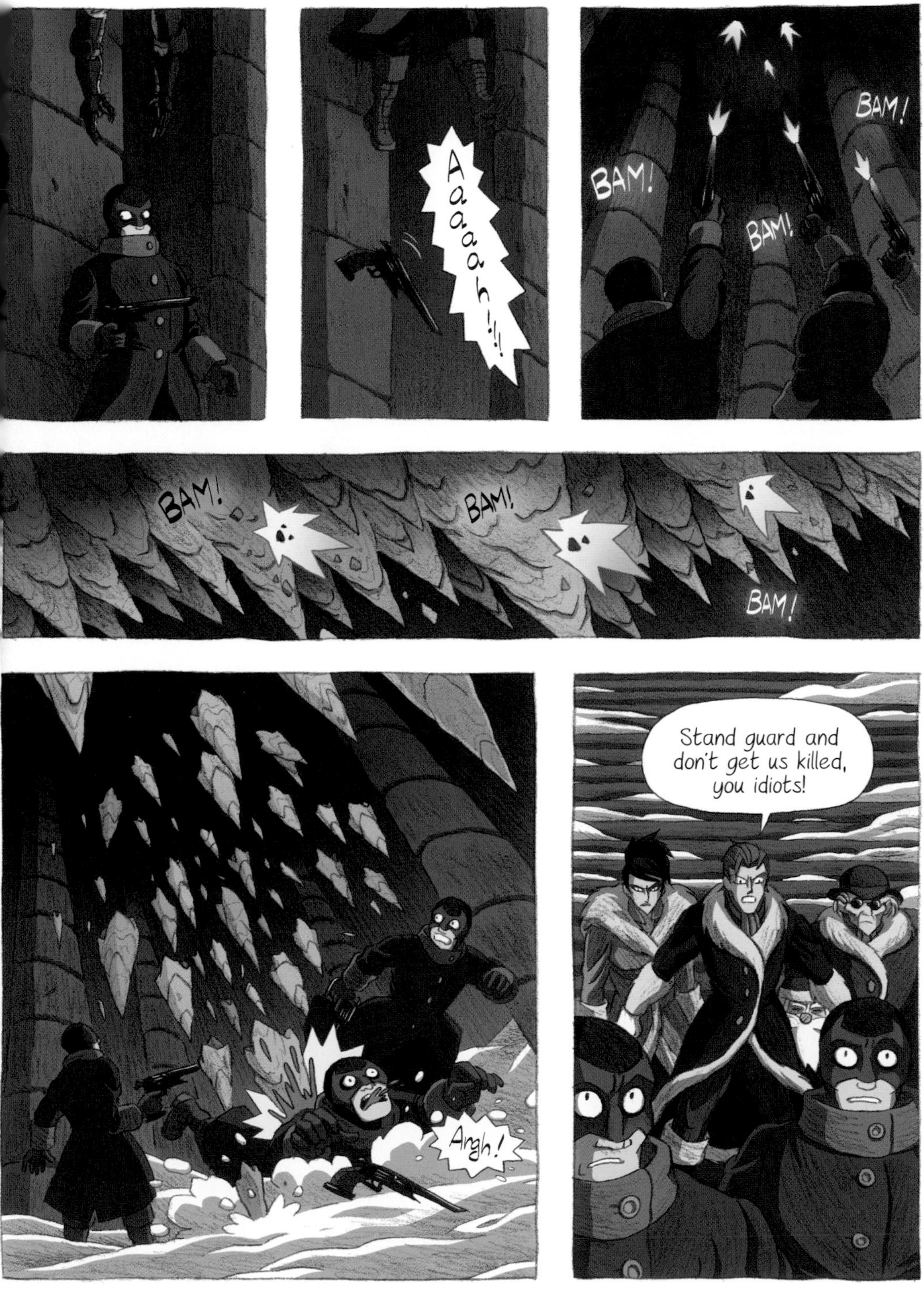
Aaaaah!!!
BAM!
BAM!
BAM!
BAM!
BAM!
BAM!
Argh!
Stand guard and don't get us killed, you idiots!

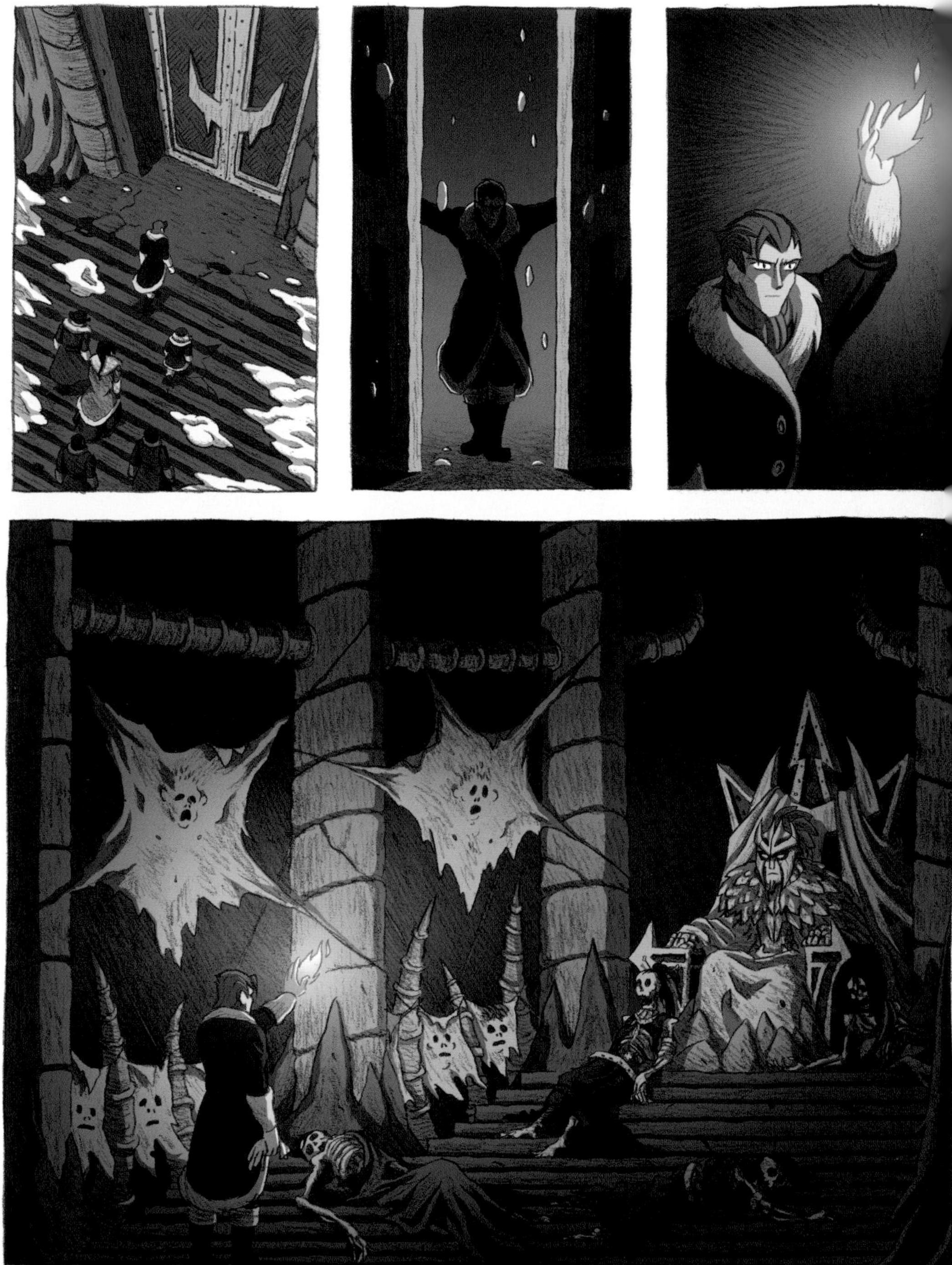

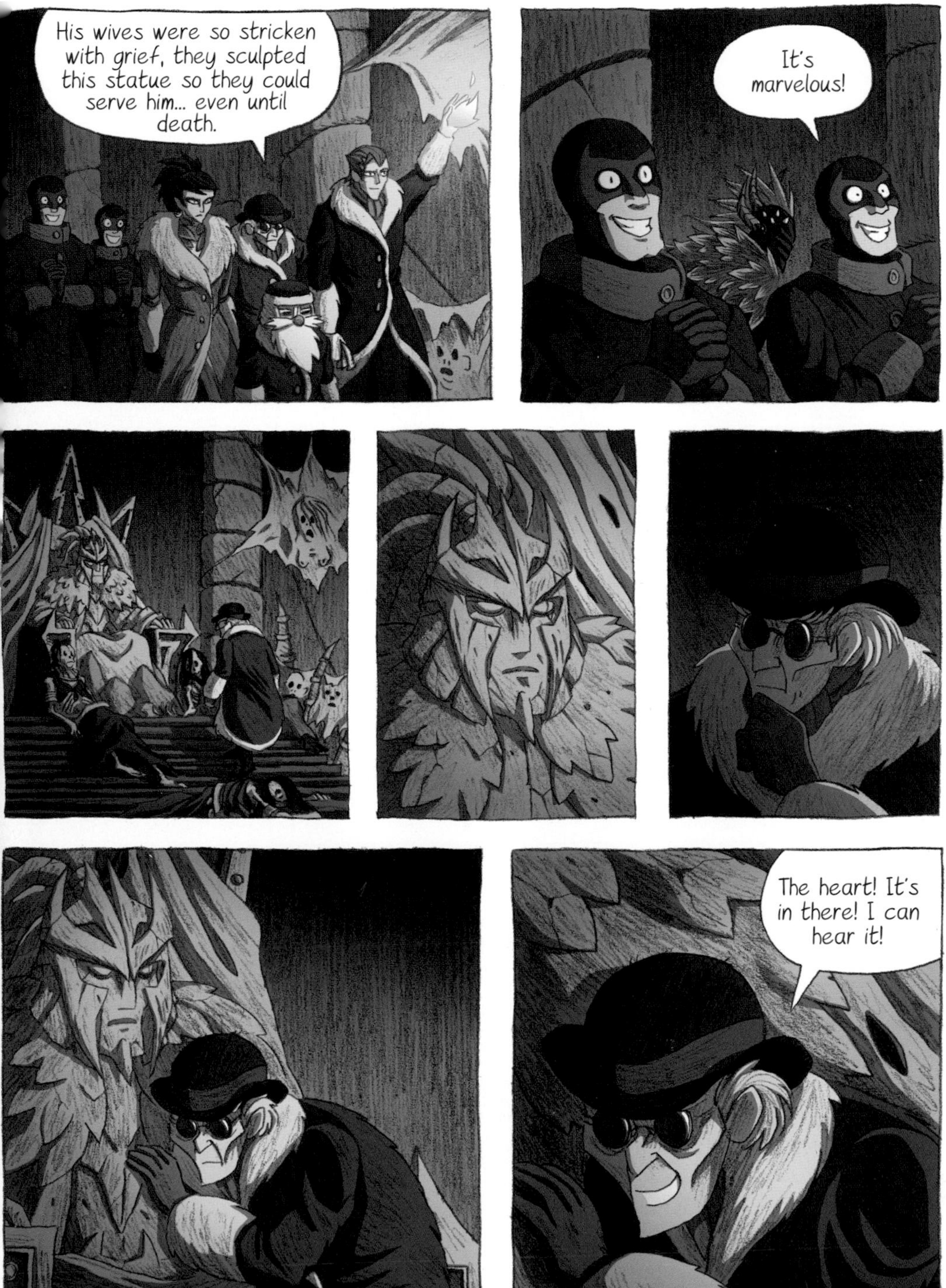
His wives were so stricken with grief, they sculpted this statue so they could serve him... even until death.
It's marvelous!
The heart! It's in there! I can hear it!

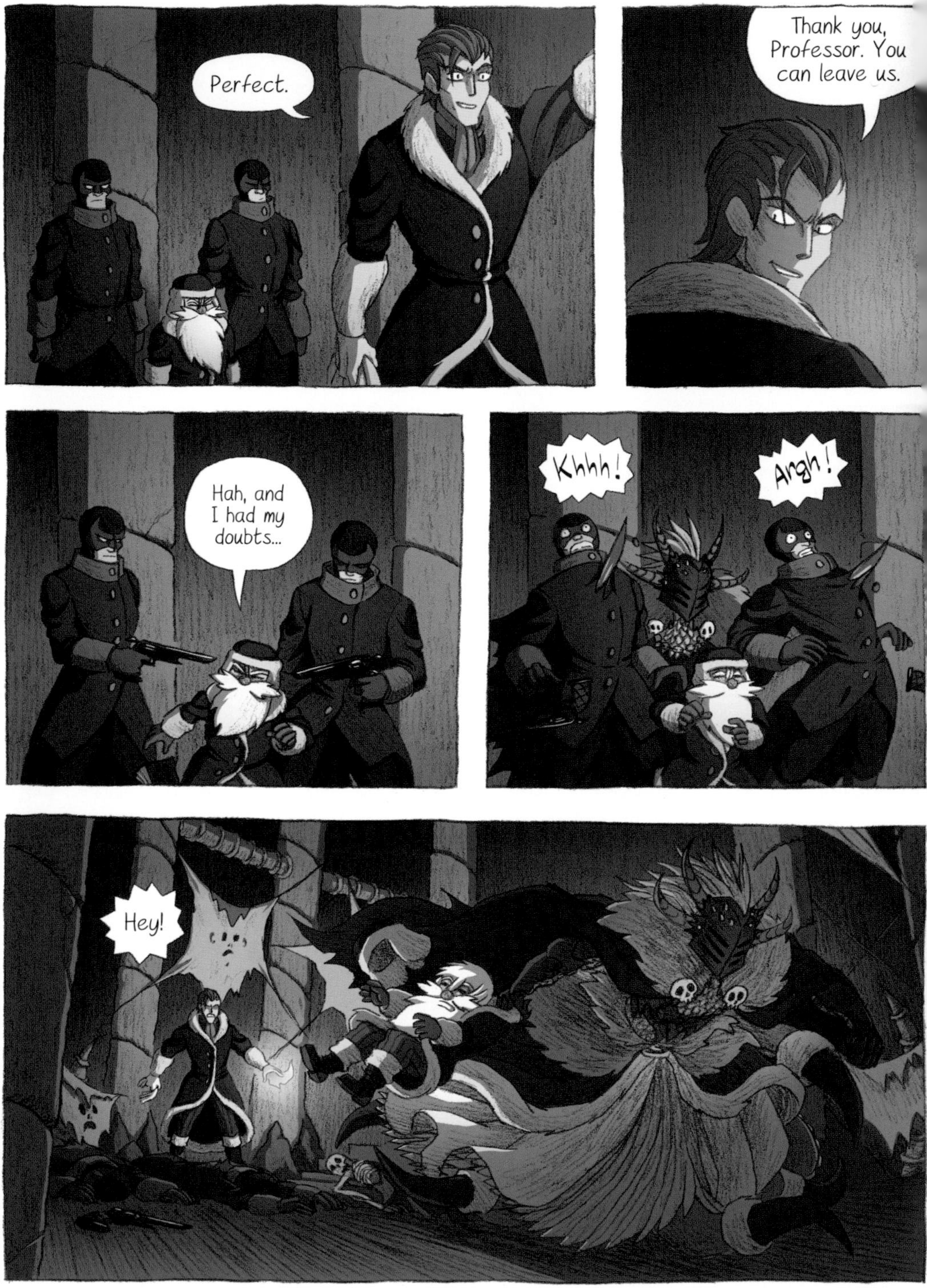
Perfect.
Thank you, Professor. You can leave us.
Hah, and I had my doubts...
Khhh!
Argh!
Hey!

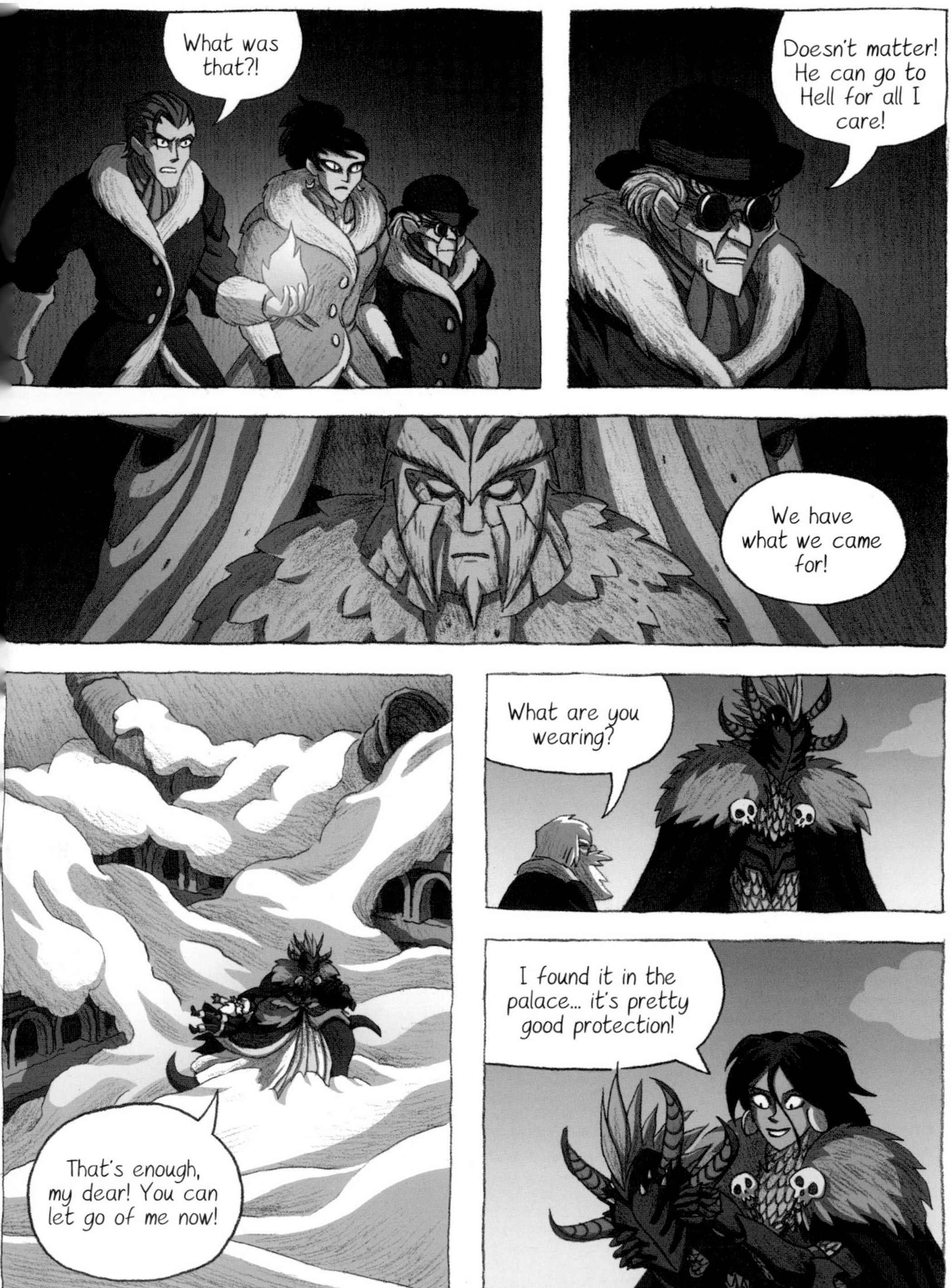
What was that?!
Doesn't matter! He can go to Hell for all I care!
We have what we came for!
That's enough, my dear! You can let go of me now!
What are you wearing?
I found it in the palace... it's pretty good protection!

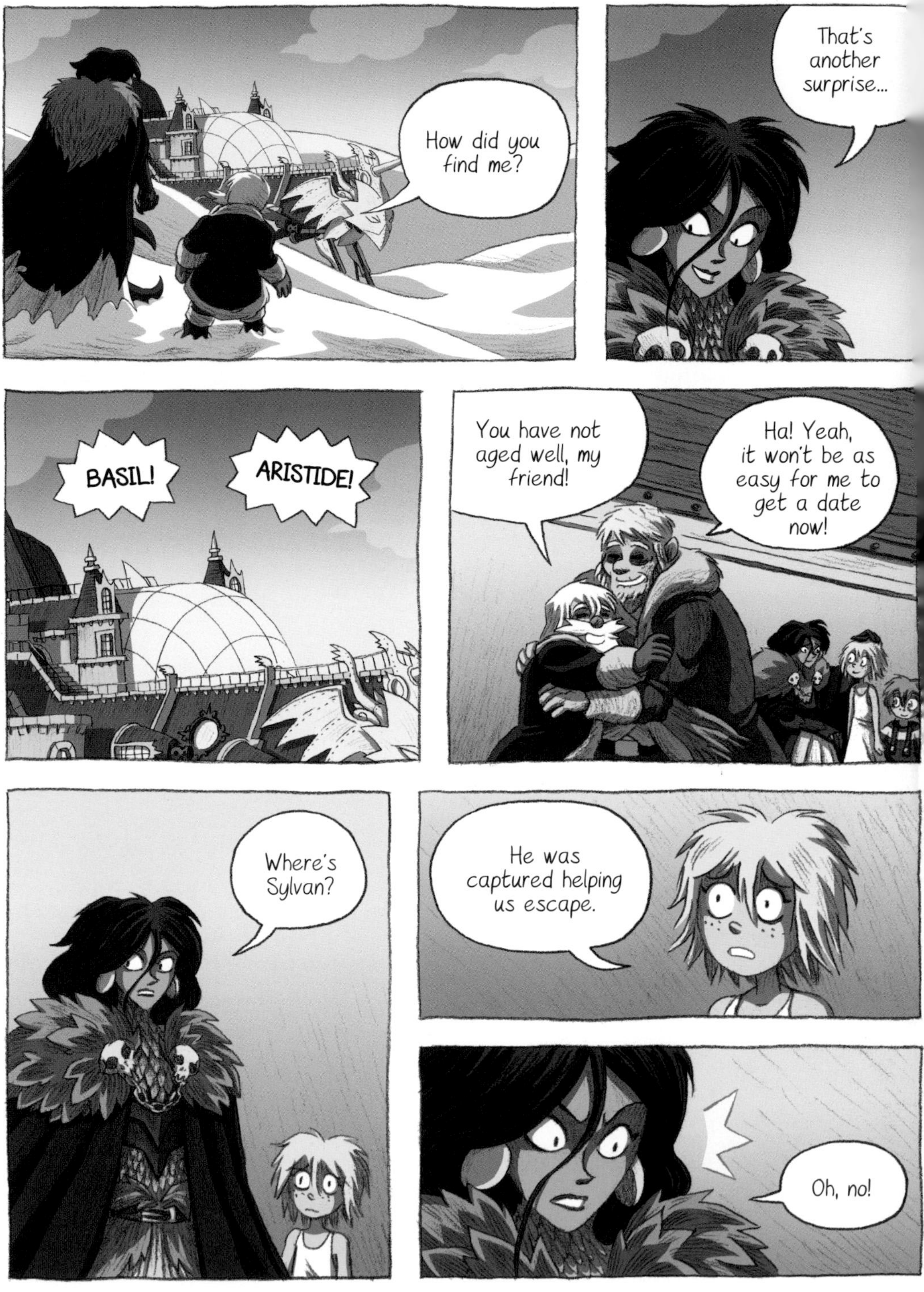
How did you find me?
That's another surprise...
BASIL!
ARISTIDE!
You have not aged well, my friend!
Ha! Yeah, it won't be as easy for me to get a date now!
Where's Sylvan?
He was captured helping us escape.
Oh, no!

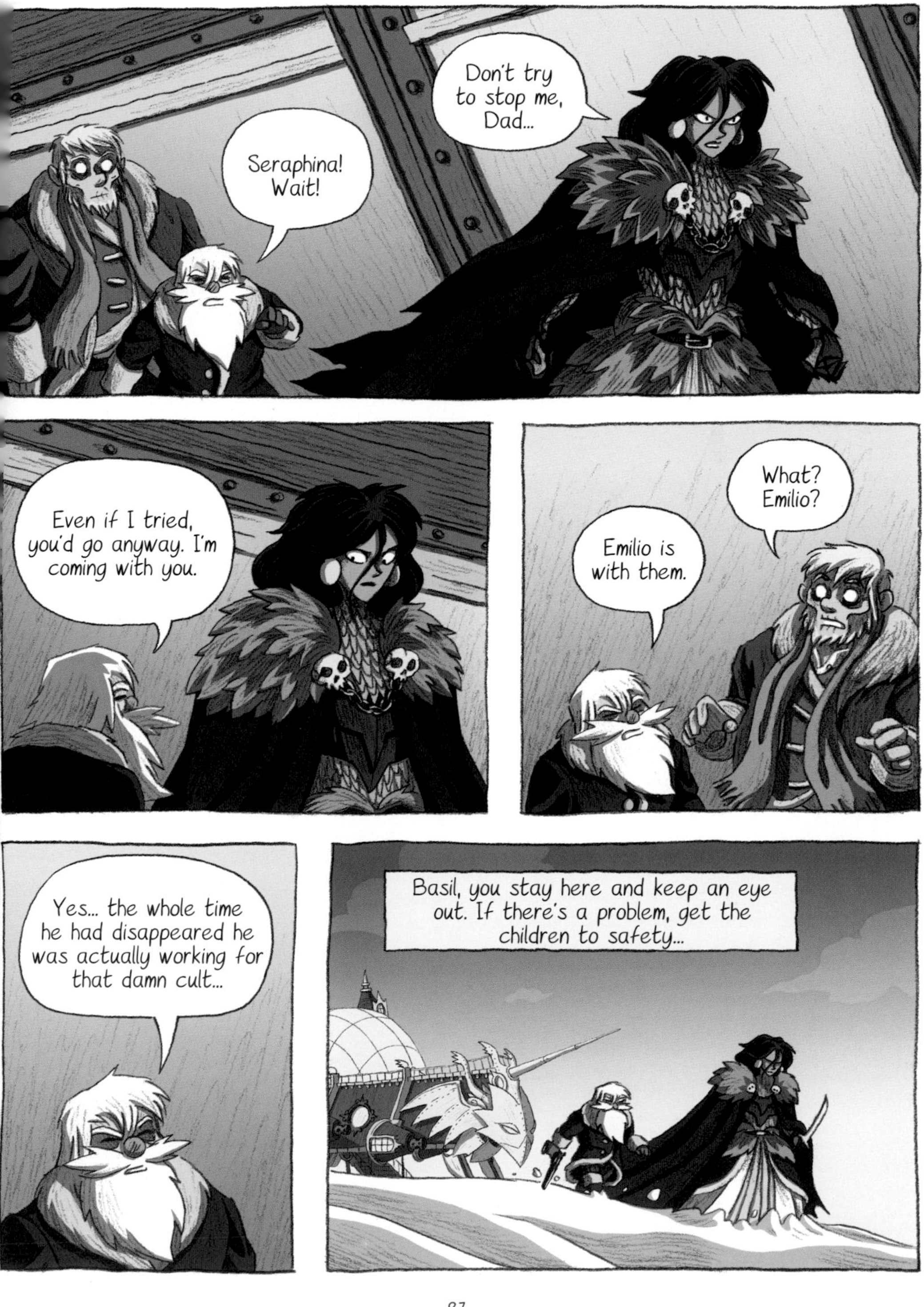
Seraphina! Wait!
Don't try to stop me, Dad...
Even if I tried, you'd go anyway. I'm coming with you.
Emilio is with them.
What? Emilio?
Yes... the whole time he had disappeared he was actually working for that damn cult...
Basil, you stay here and keep an eye out. If there's a problem, get the children to safety...

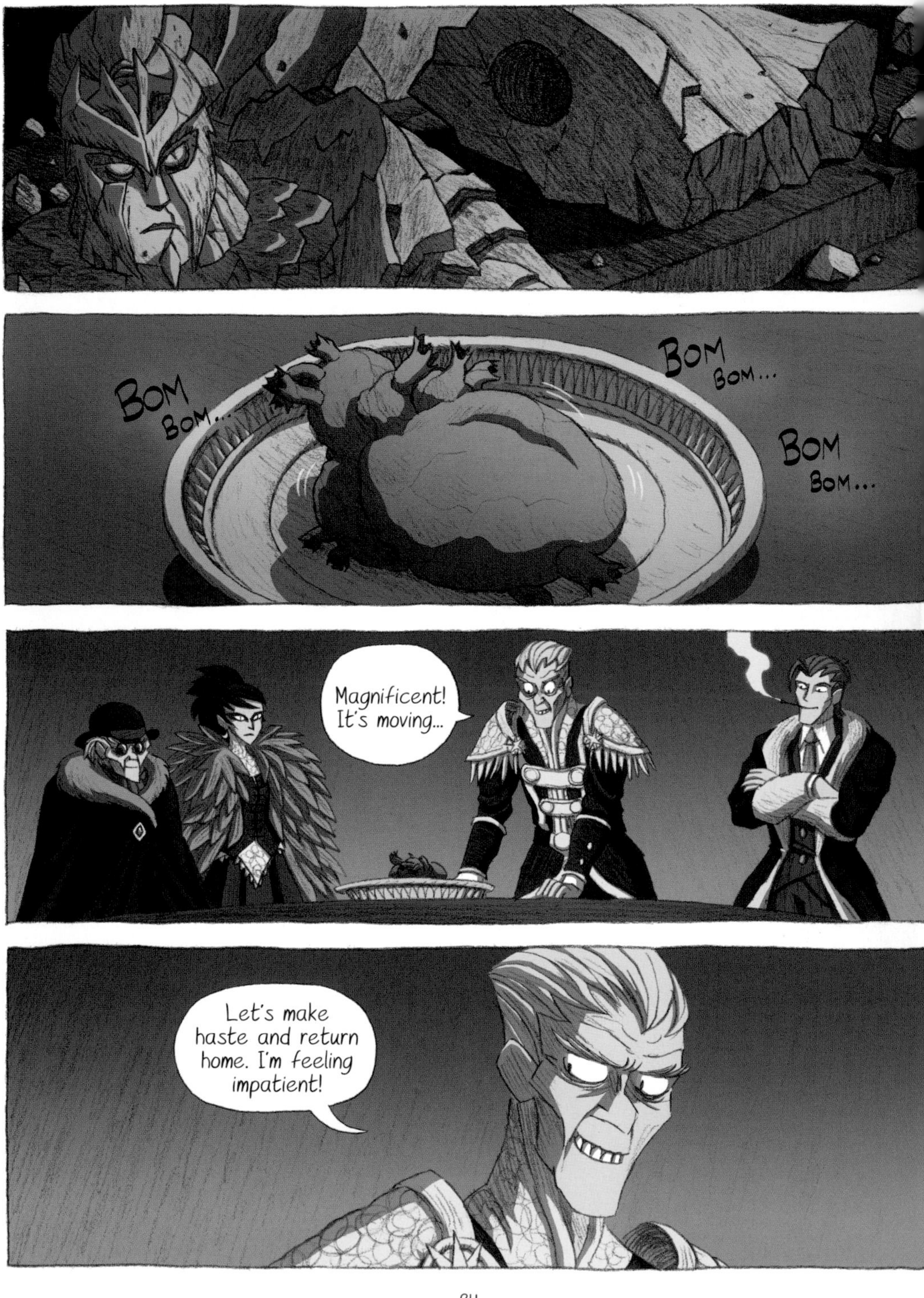
BOM
BOM...
BOM
BOM...
BOM
BOM...
Magnificent! It's moving...
Let's make haste and return home. I'm feeling impatient!

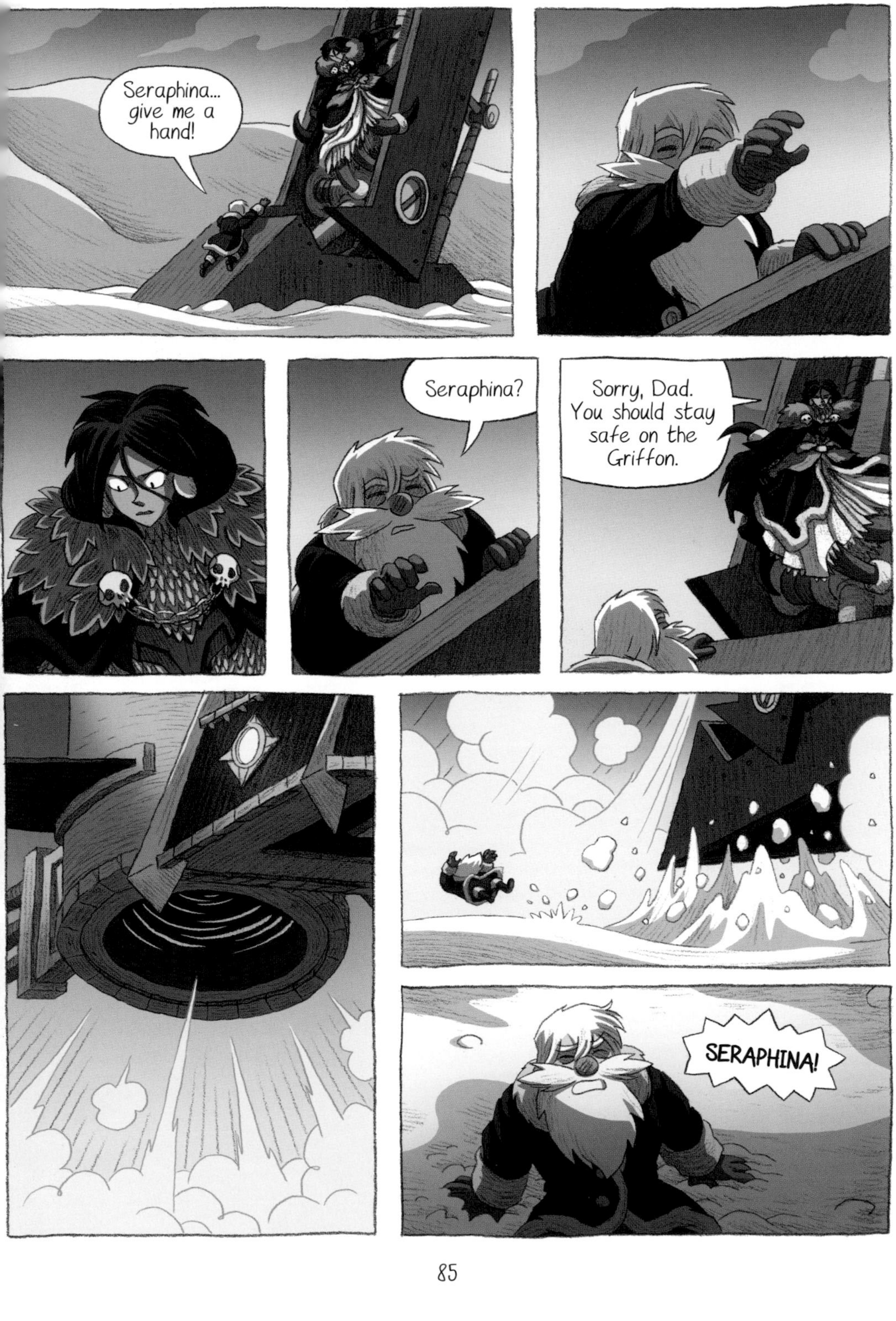
Seraphina... give me a hand!
Seraphina?
Sorry, Dad. You should stay safe on the Griffon.
SERAPHINA!

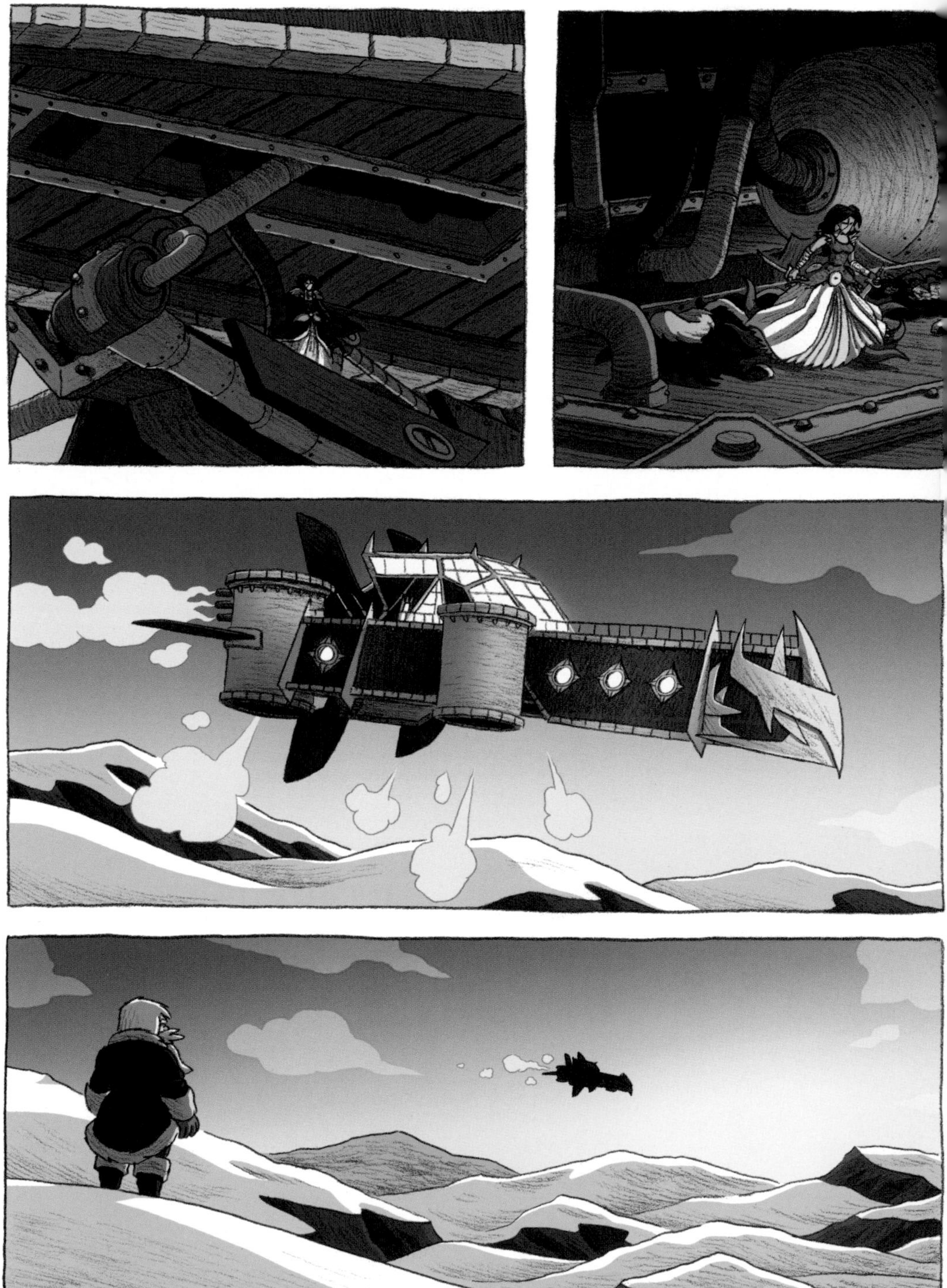

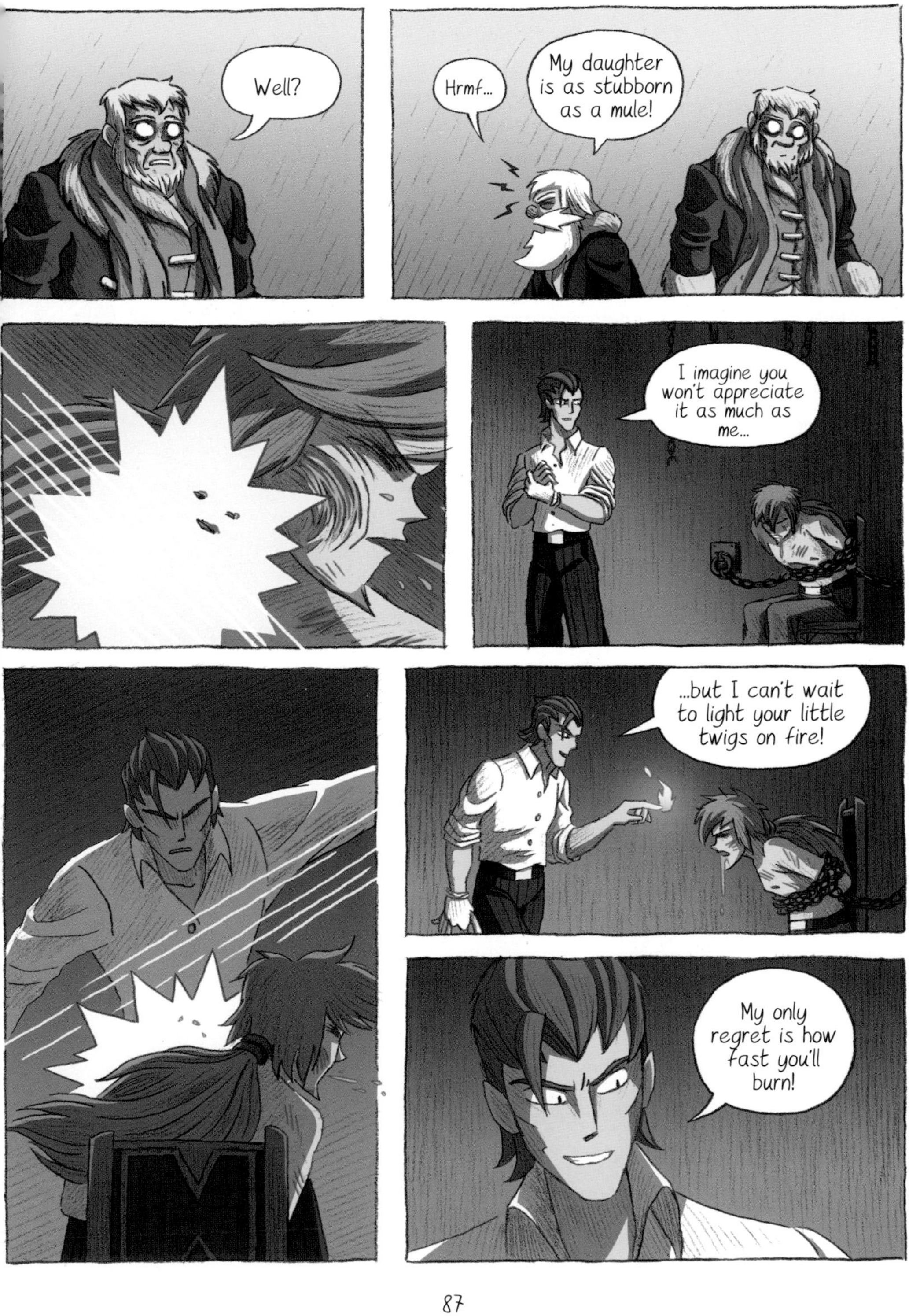
Well?
Hrmf...
My daughter is as stubborn as a mule!
I imagine you won't appreciate it as much as me...
...but I can't wait to light your little twigs on fire!
My only regret is how fast you'll burn!

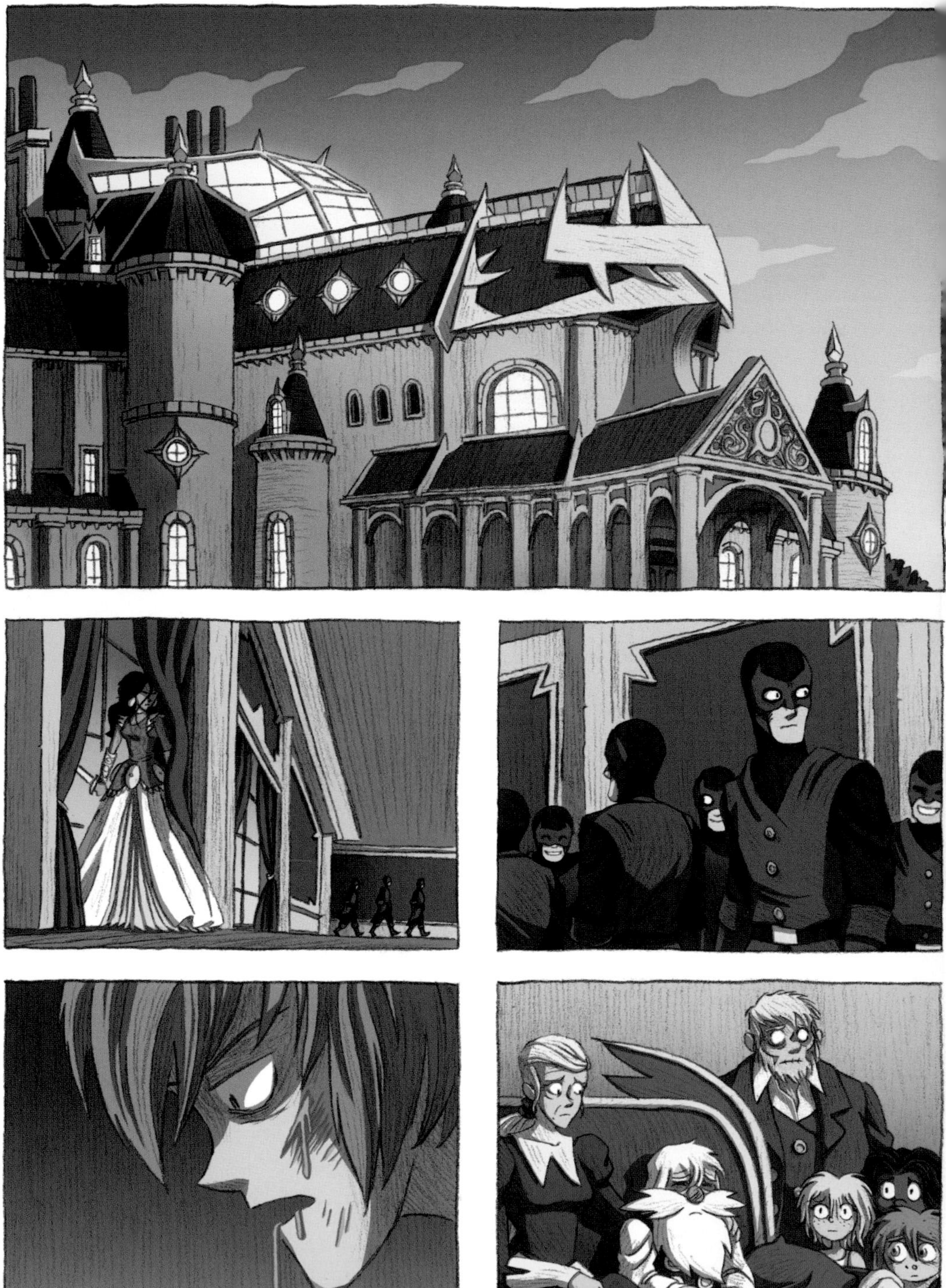

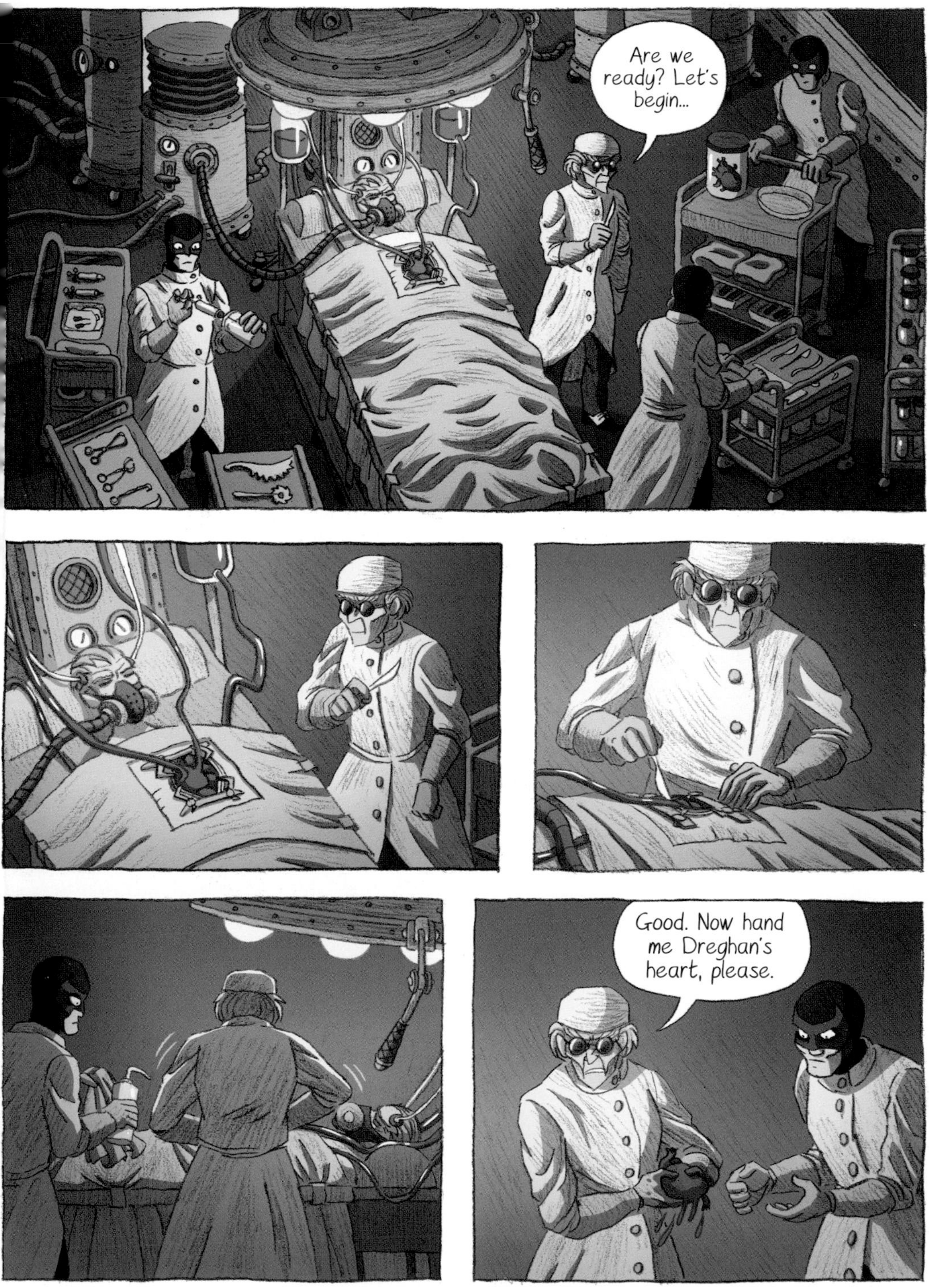
Are we ready? Let's begin...
Good. Now hand me Dreghan's heart, please.

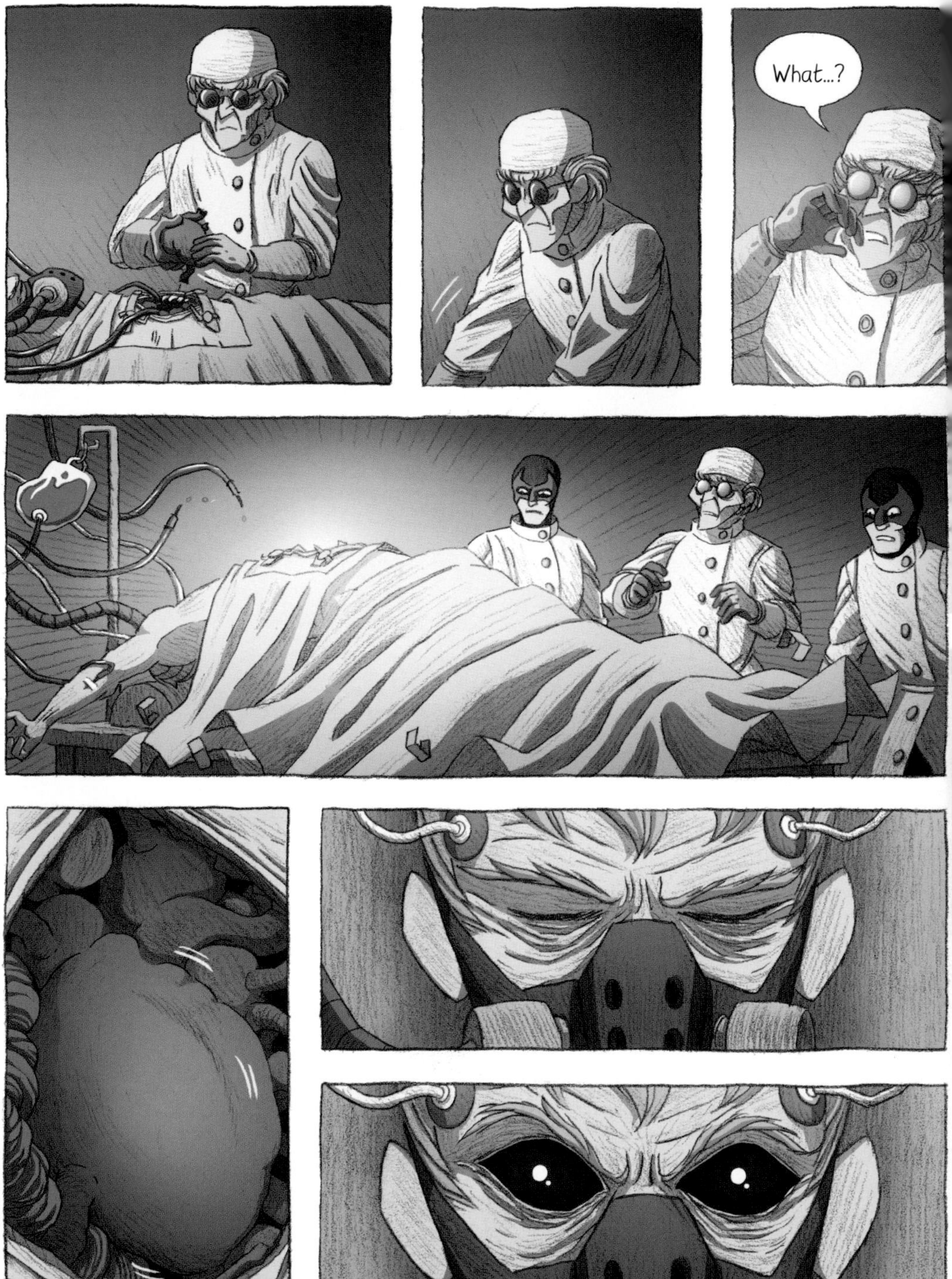
What...?

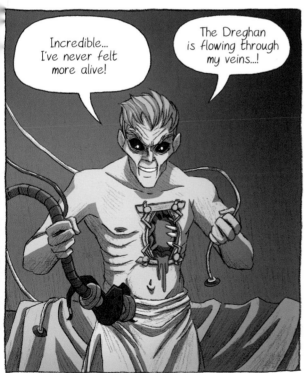

Incredible... I've never felt more alive!

The Dreghan is flowing through my veins...!

Gather everyone in the main hall... and don't forget the Zelphire!

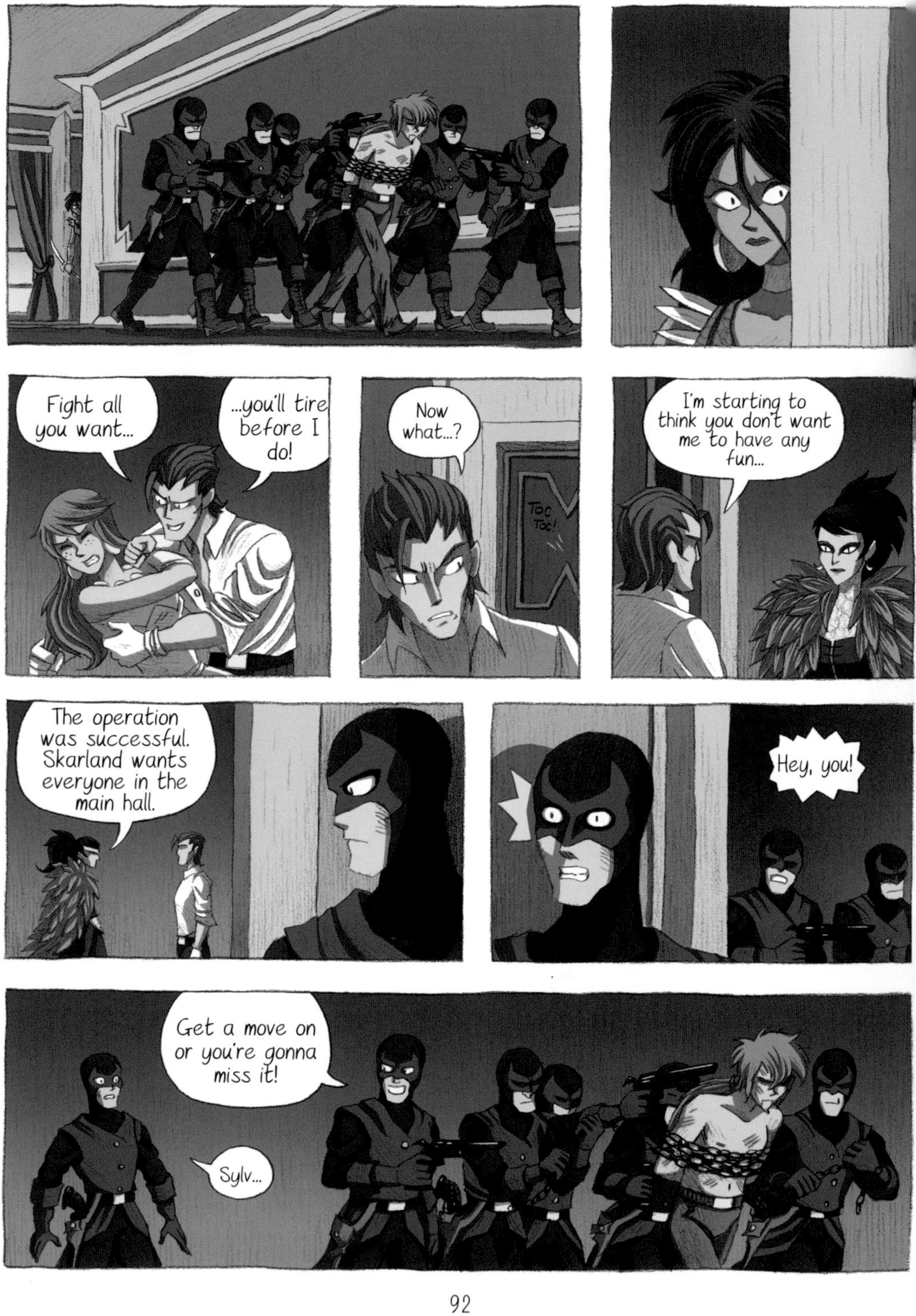
Fight all you want...
...you'll tire before I do!
Now what...?
Toc Toc!
I'm starting to think you don't want me to have any fun...
The operation was successful. Skarland wants everyone in the main hall.
Hey, you!
Get a move on or you're gonna miss it!
Sylv...

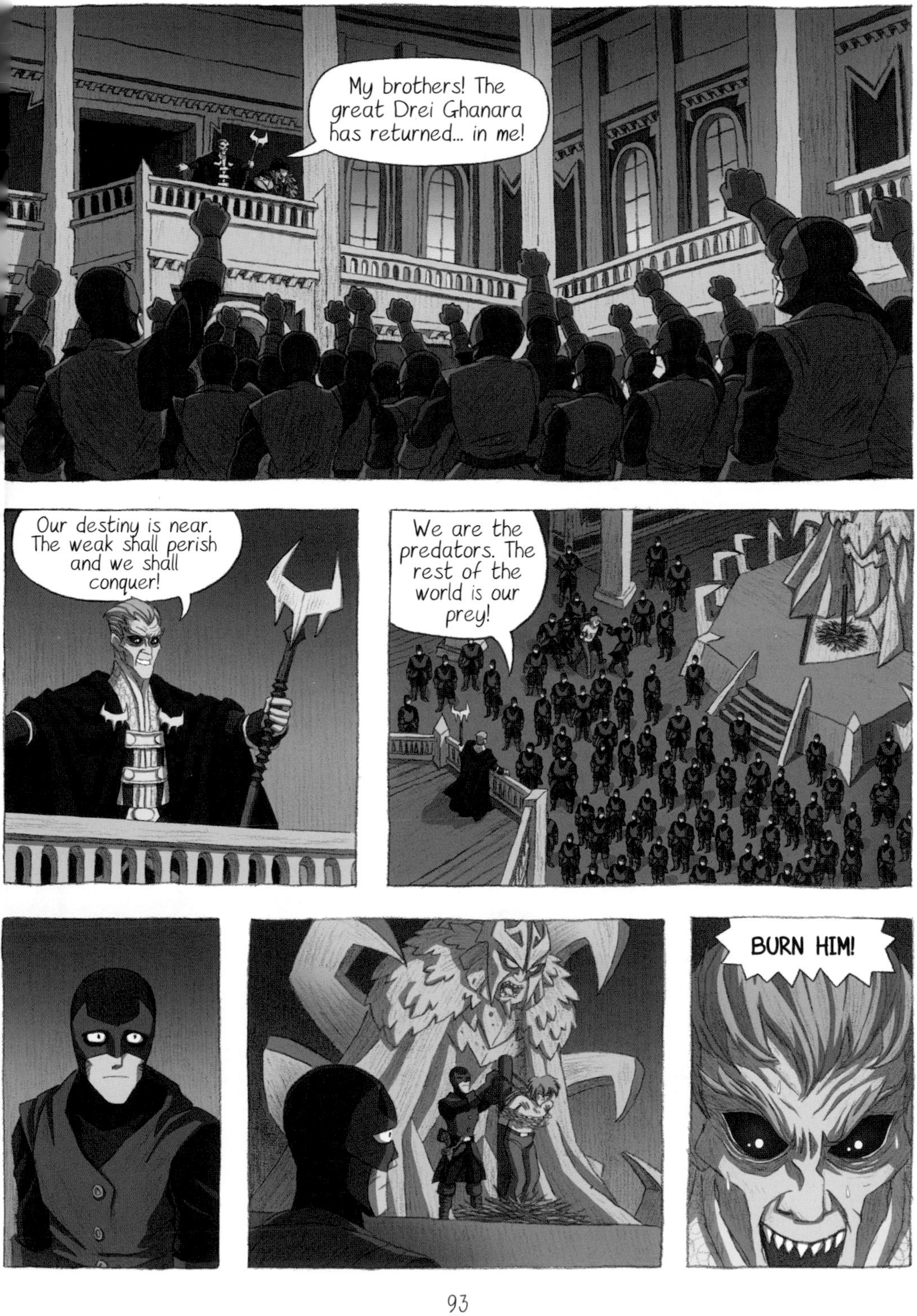
My brothers! The great Drei Ghanara has returned... in me!
Our destiny is near. The weak shall perish and we shall conquer!
We are the predators. The rest of the world is our prey!
BURN HIM!

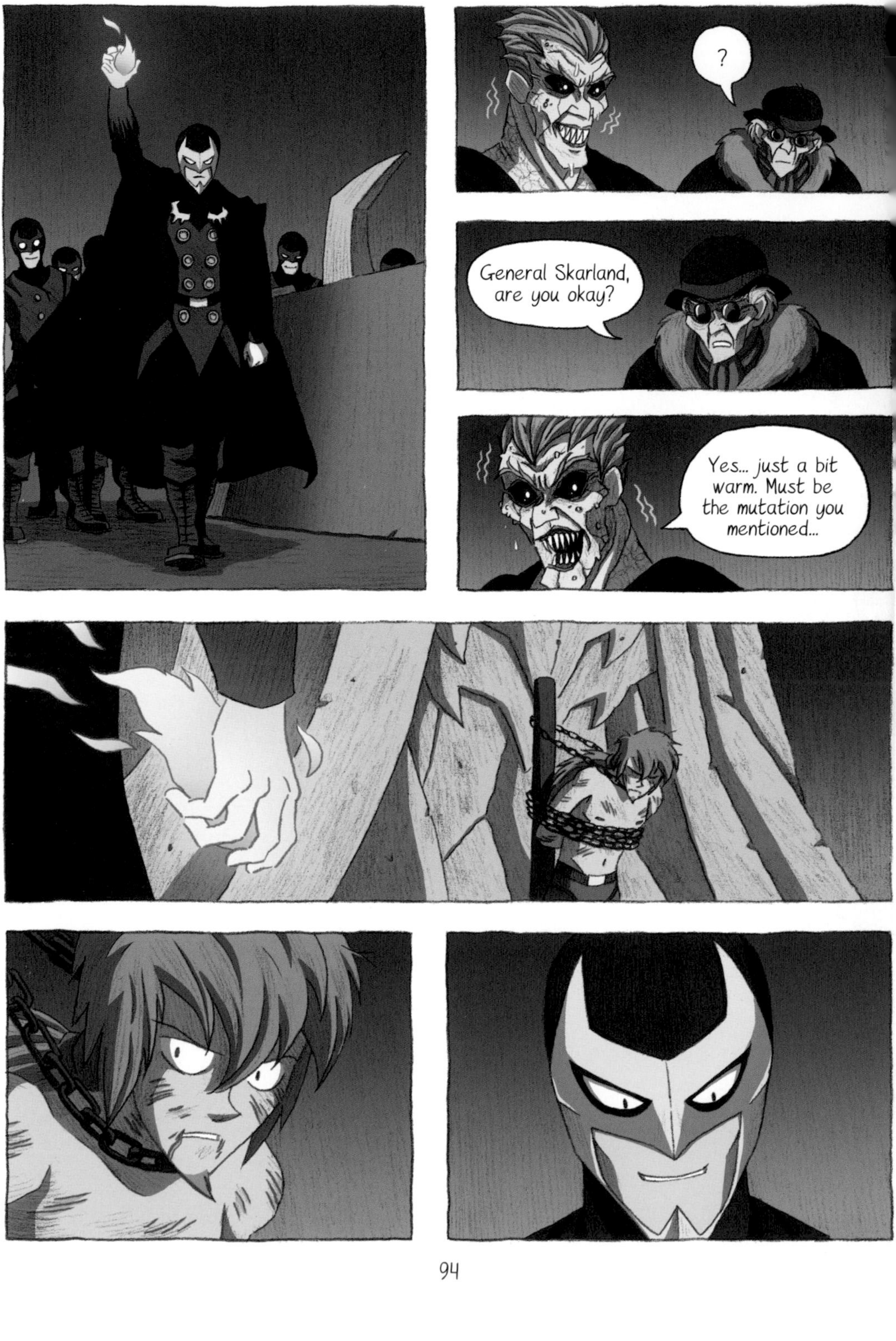
?
General Skarland, are you okay?
Yes... just a bit warm. Must be the mutation you mentioned...

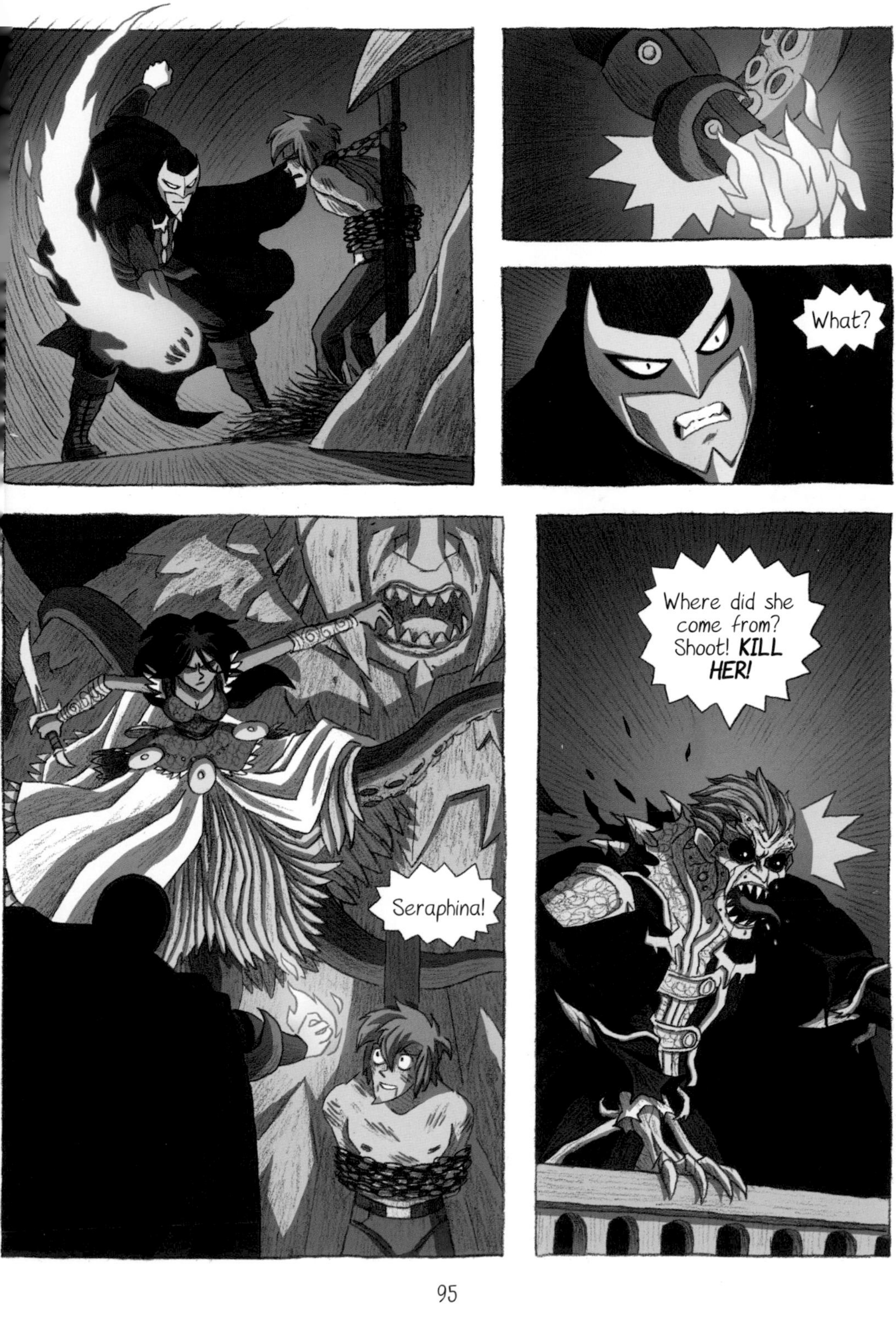
What?
Seraphina!
Where did she come from? Shoot! **KILL HER!**

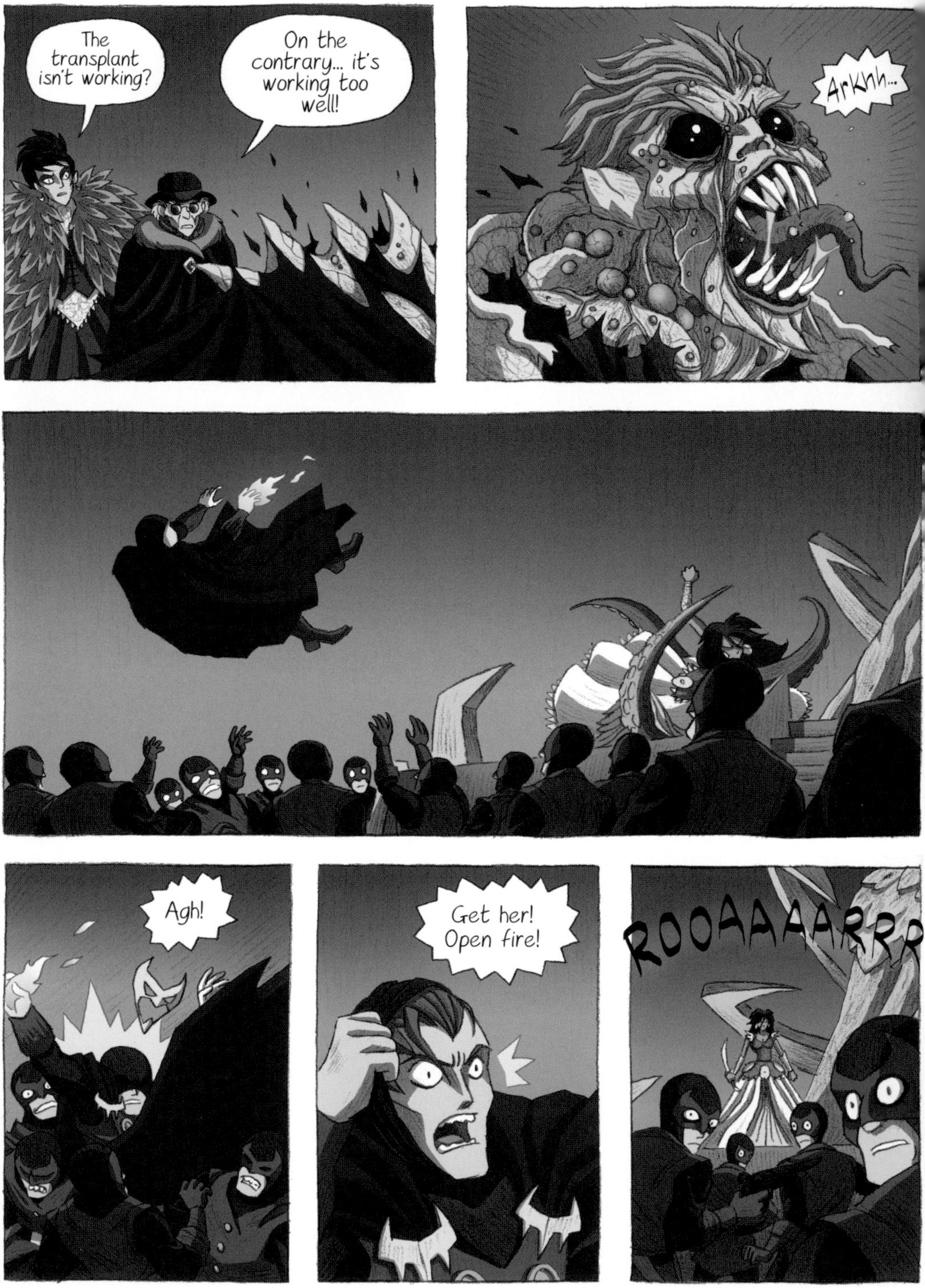
The transplant isn't working?
On the contrary... it's working too well!
Arkhh...
Agh!
Get her! Open fire!
ROOAAAARRR

RAAAAARGGGHHARGH!!

Whoa...

Aaaaahh!

Aaaa... aaaaahh!!!

97

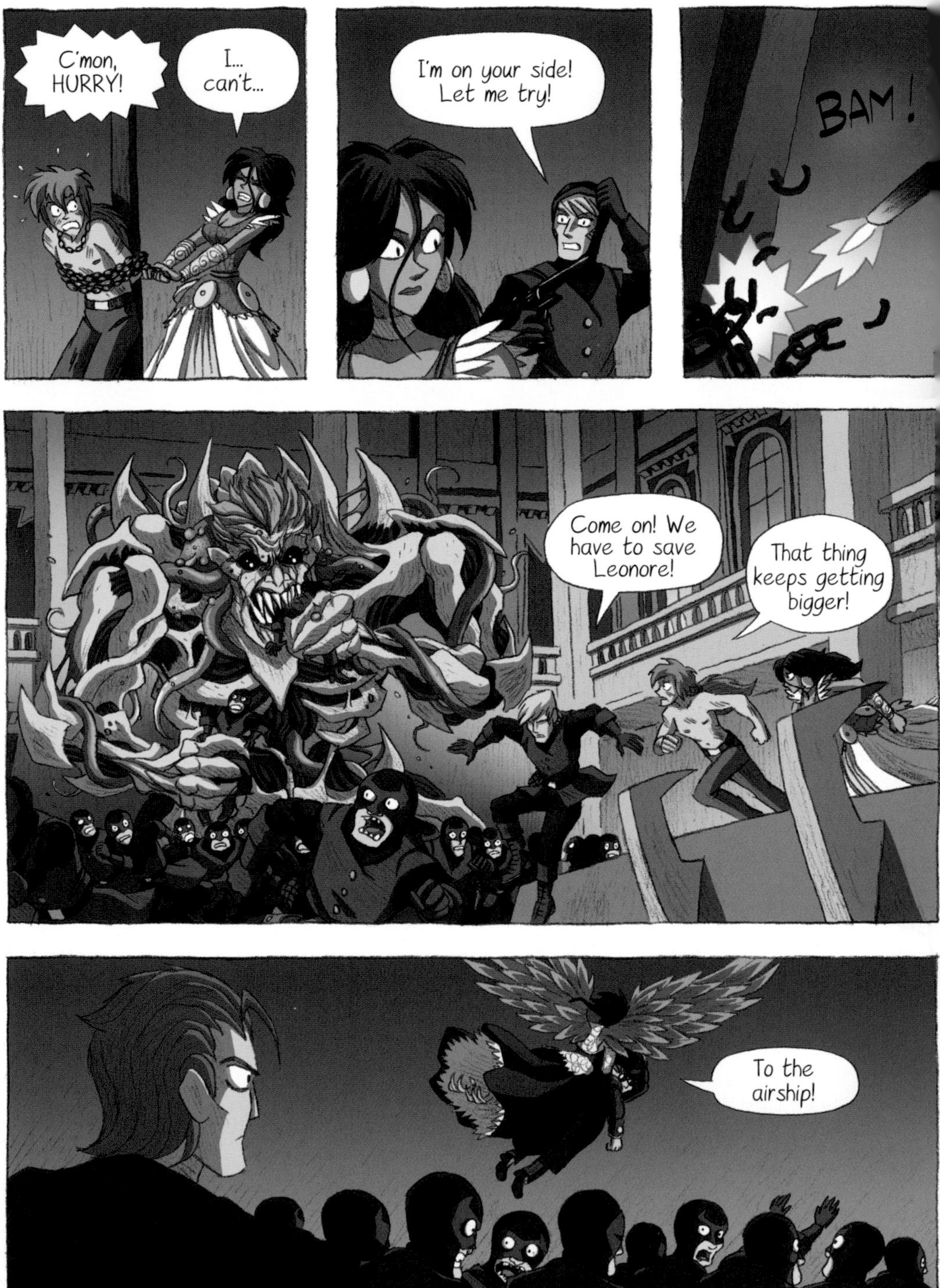
C'mon, HURRY!
I... can't...
I'm on your side! Let me try!
BAM!
Come on! We have to save Leonore!
That thing keeps getting bigger!
To the airship!

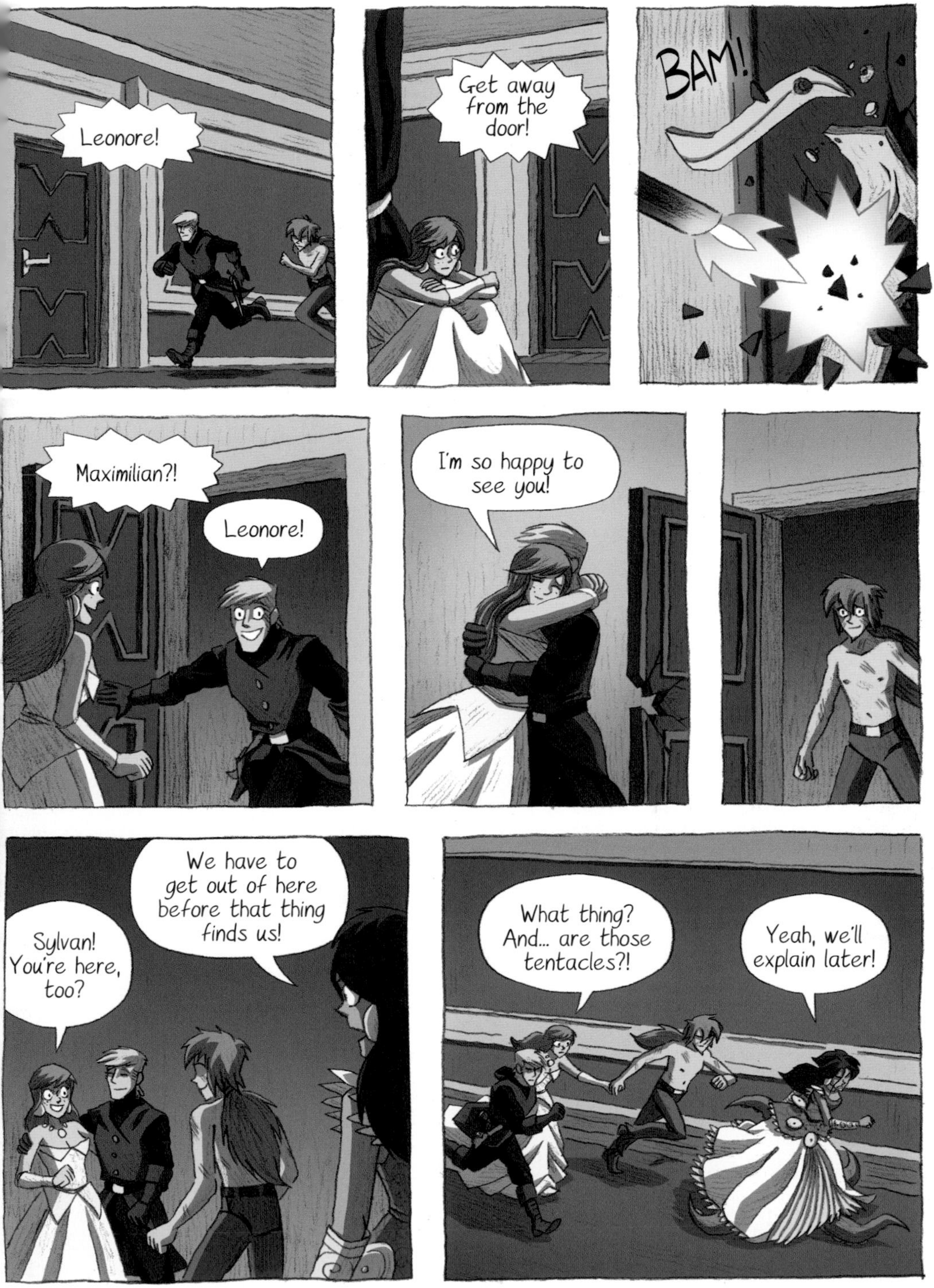
Leonore!
Get away from the door!
BAM!
Maximilian?!
Leonore!
I'm so happy to see you!
Sylvan! You're here, too?
We have to get out of here before that thing finds us!
What thing? And... are those tentacles?!
Yeah, we'll explain later!

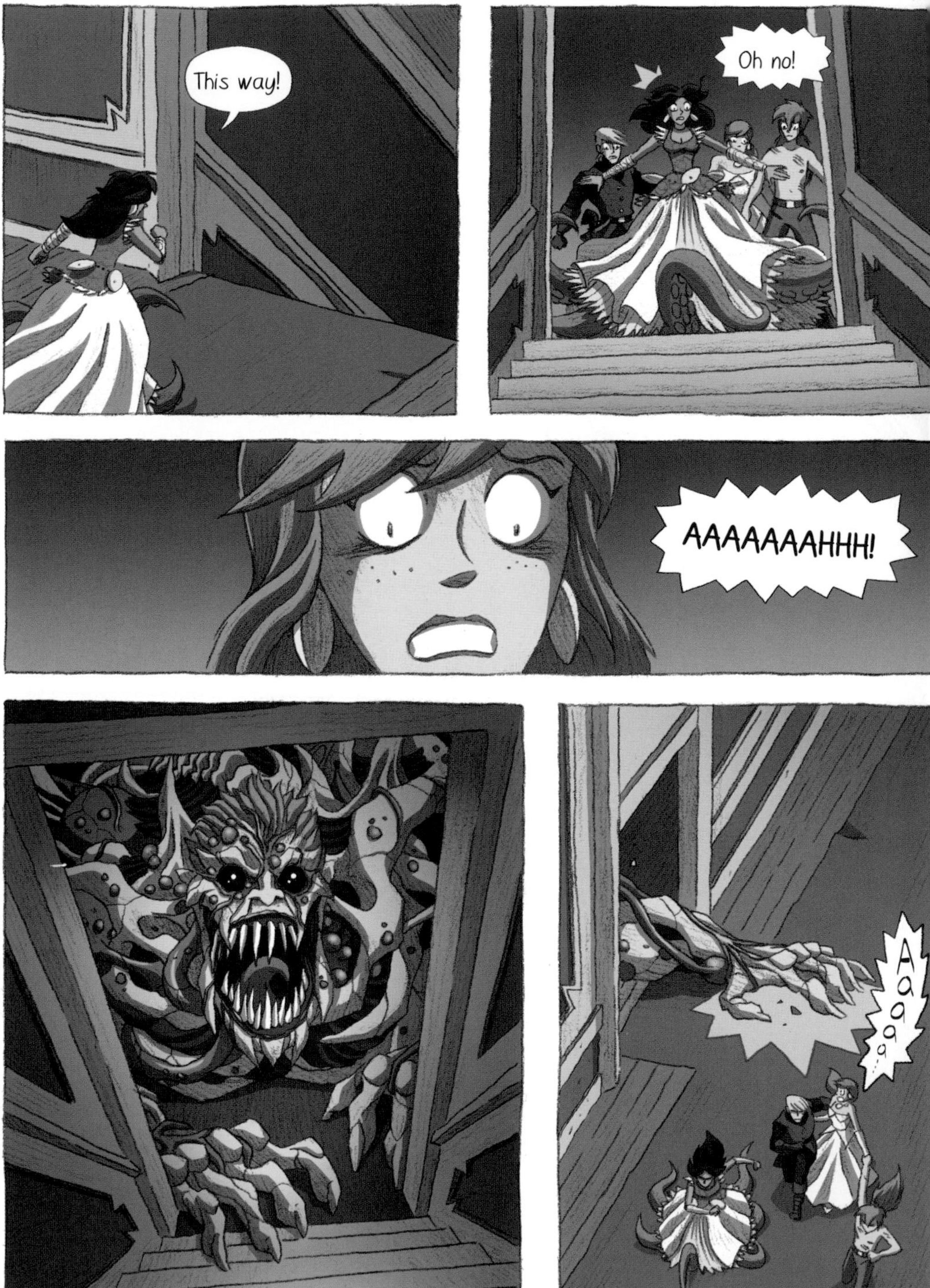
This way!
Oh no!
AAAAAAAHHH!
Aaggg...

KRRRRRRR...

Well, what a surprise! Our friends have come to join us!

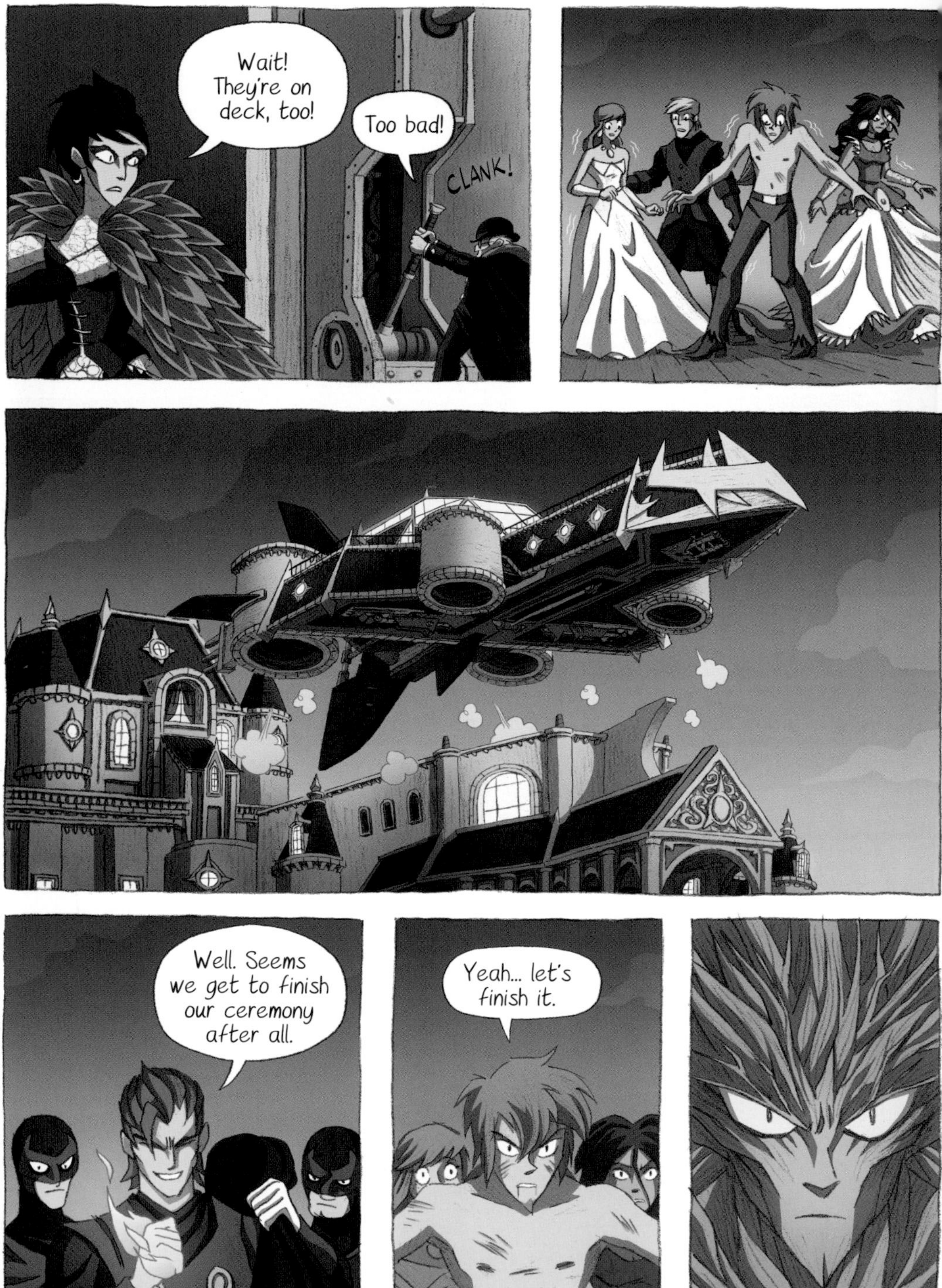
Wait! They're on deck, too!
Too bad!
CLANK!
Well. Seems we get to finish our ceremony after all.
Yeah... let's finish it.

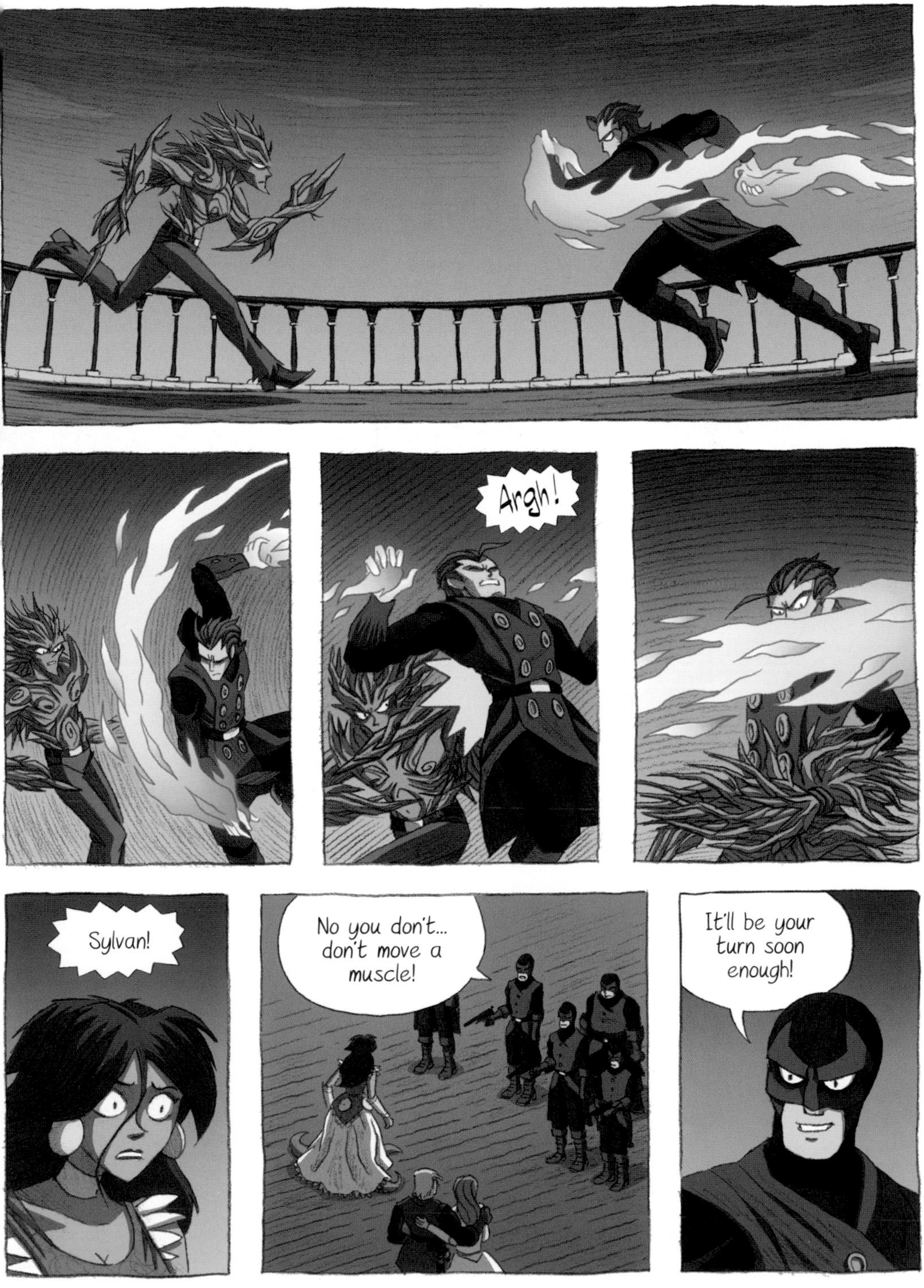
Argh!
Sylvan!
No you don't... don't move a muscle!
It'll be your turn soon enough!

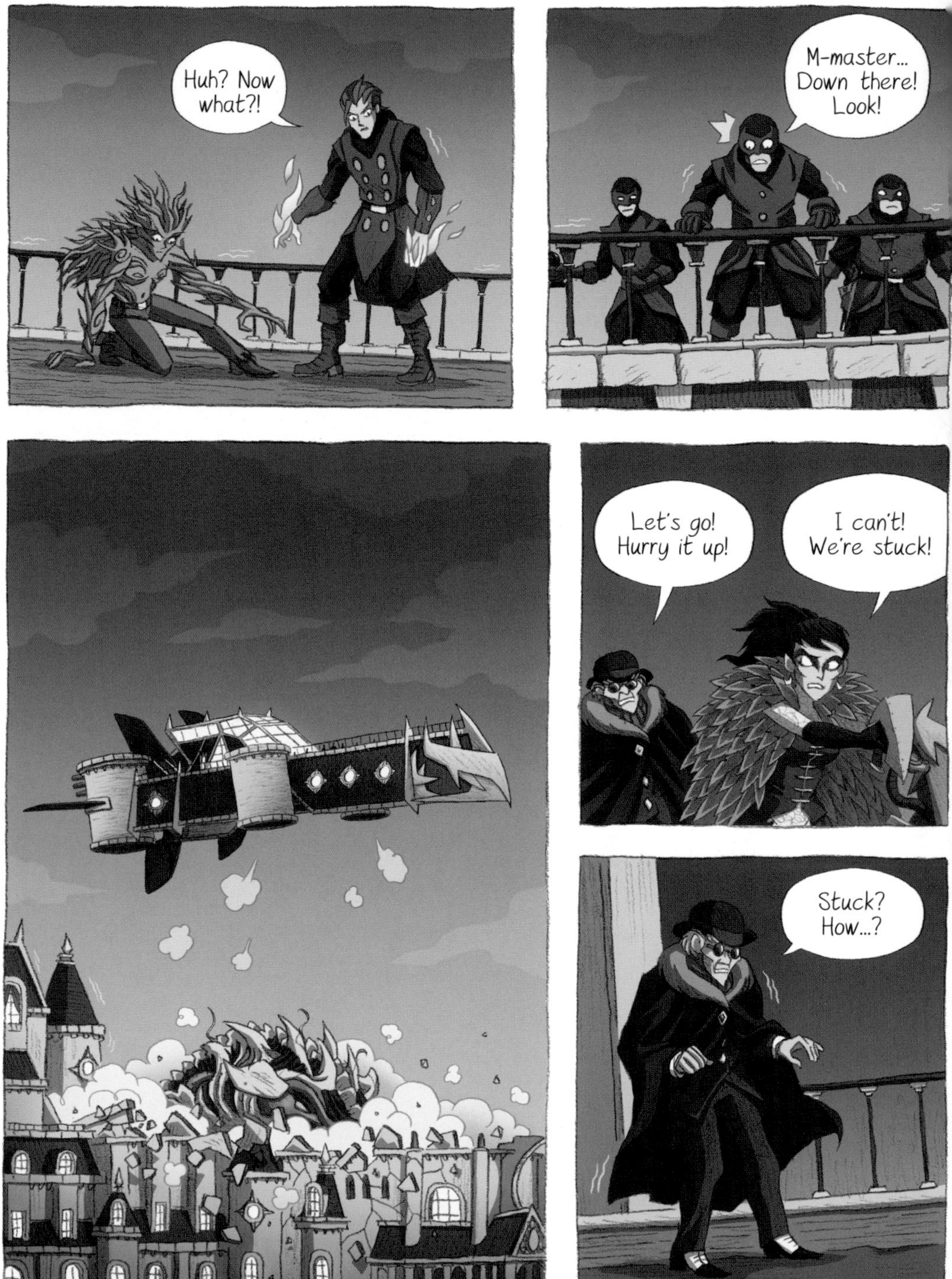

Huh? Now what?!
M-master... Down there! Look!
Let's go! Hurry it up!
I can't! We're stuck!
Stuck? How...?

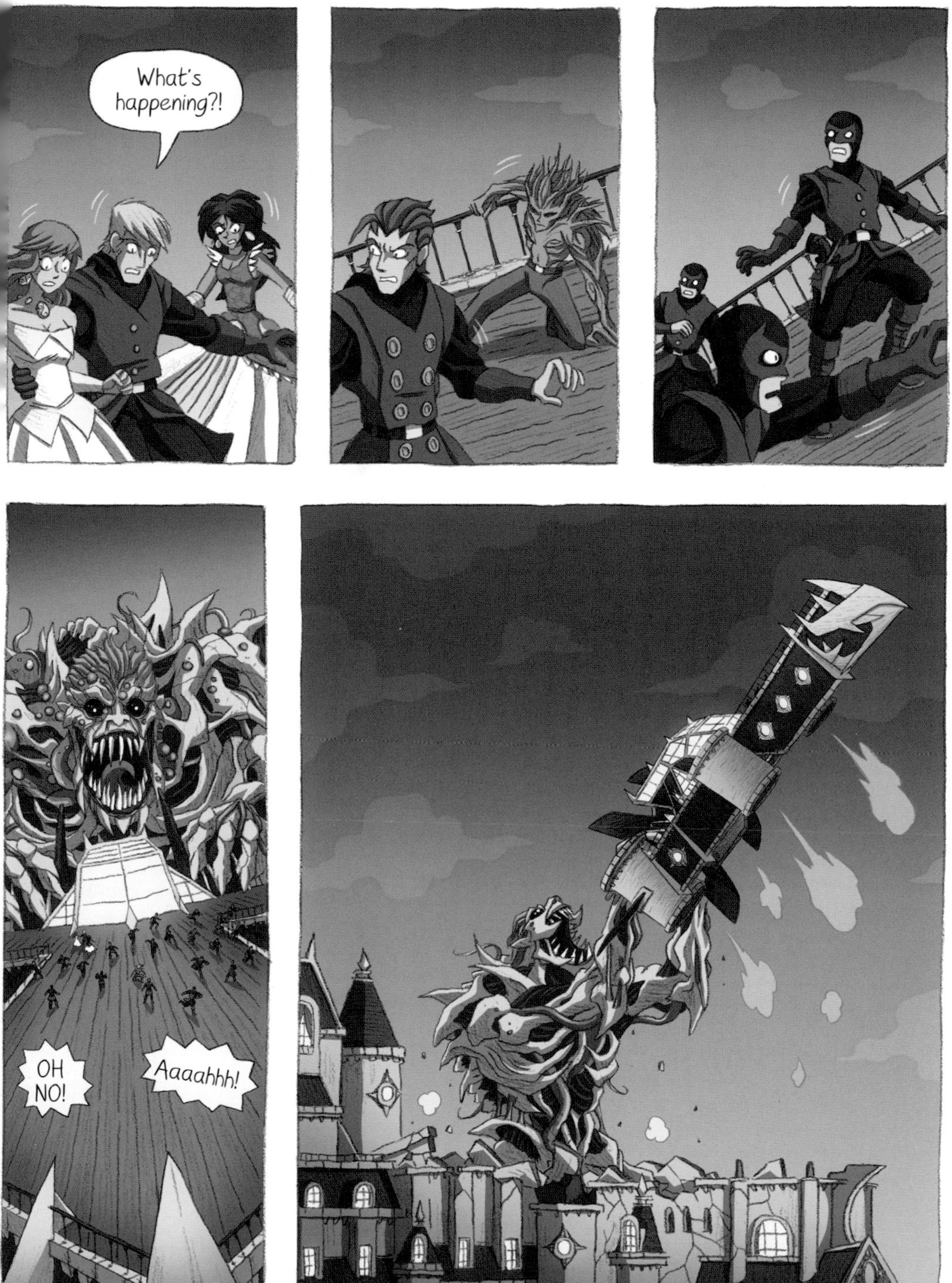
What's happening?!
OH NO!
Aaaahhh!

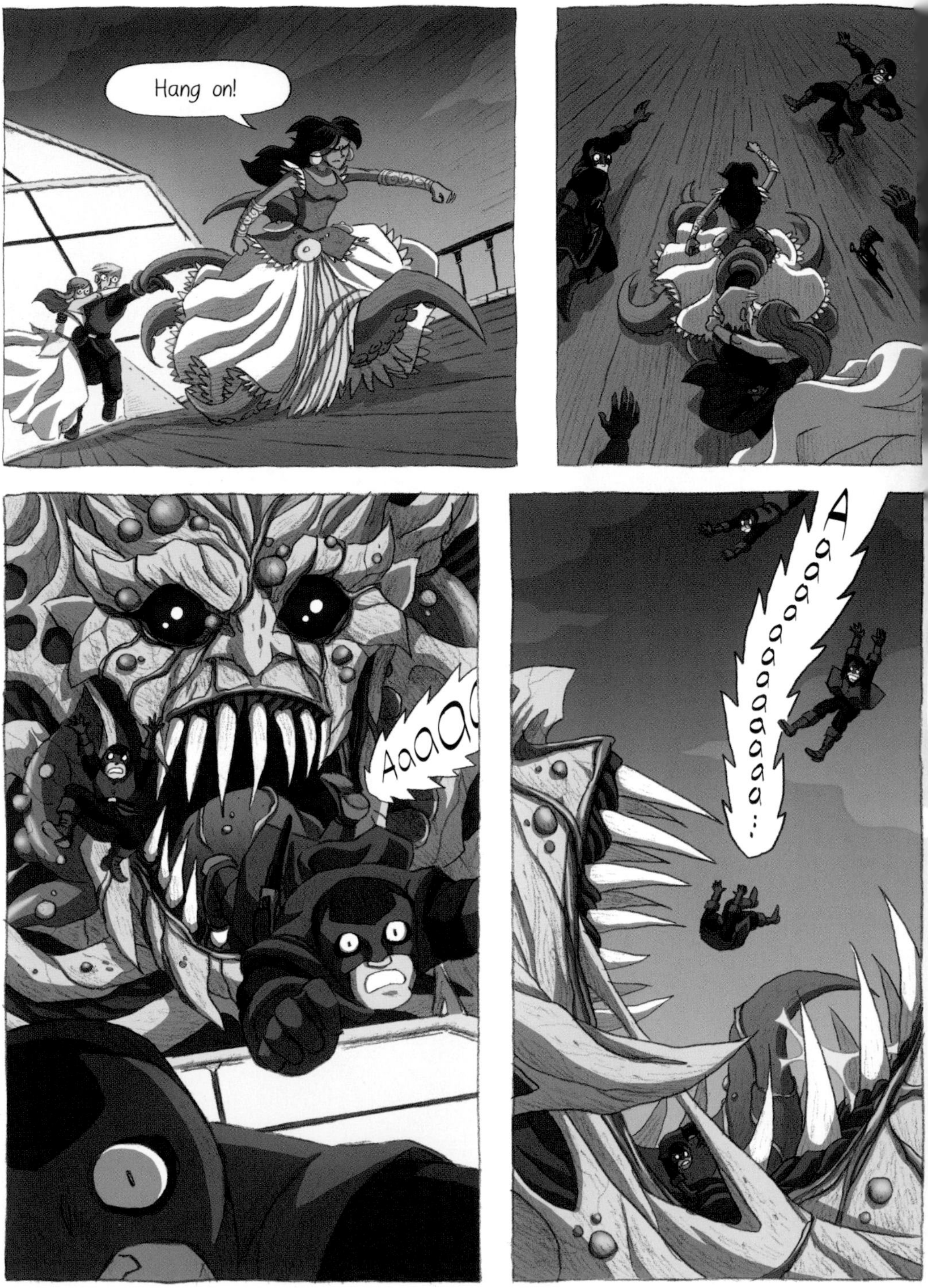

Hang on!
Aaaa
Aaaaaaaaaaaa...

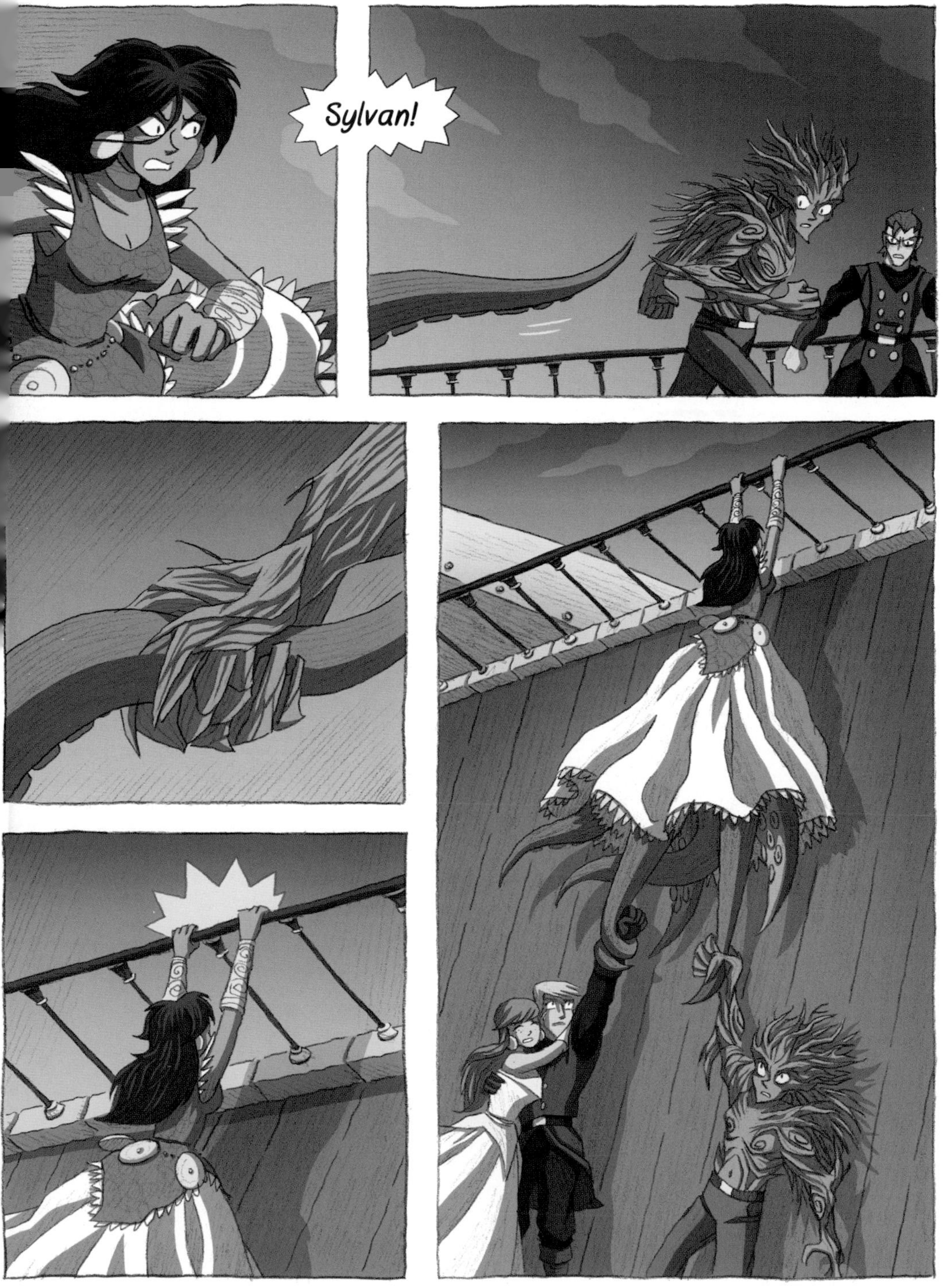
Sylvan!

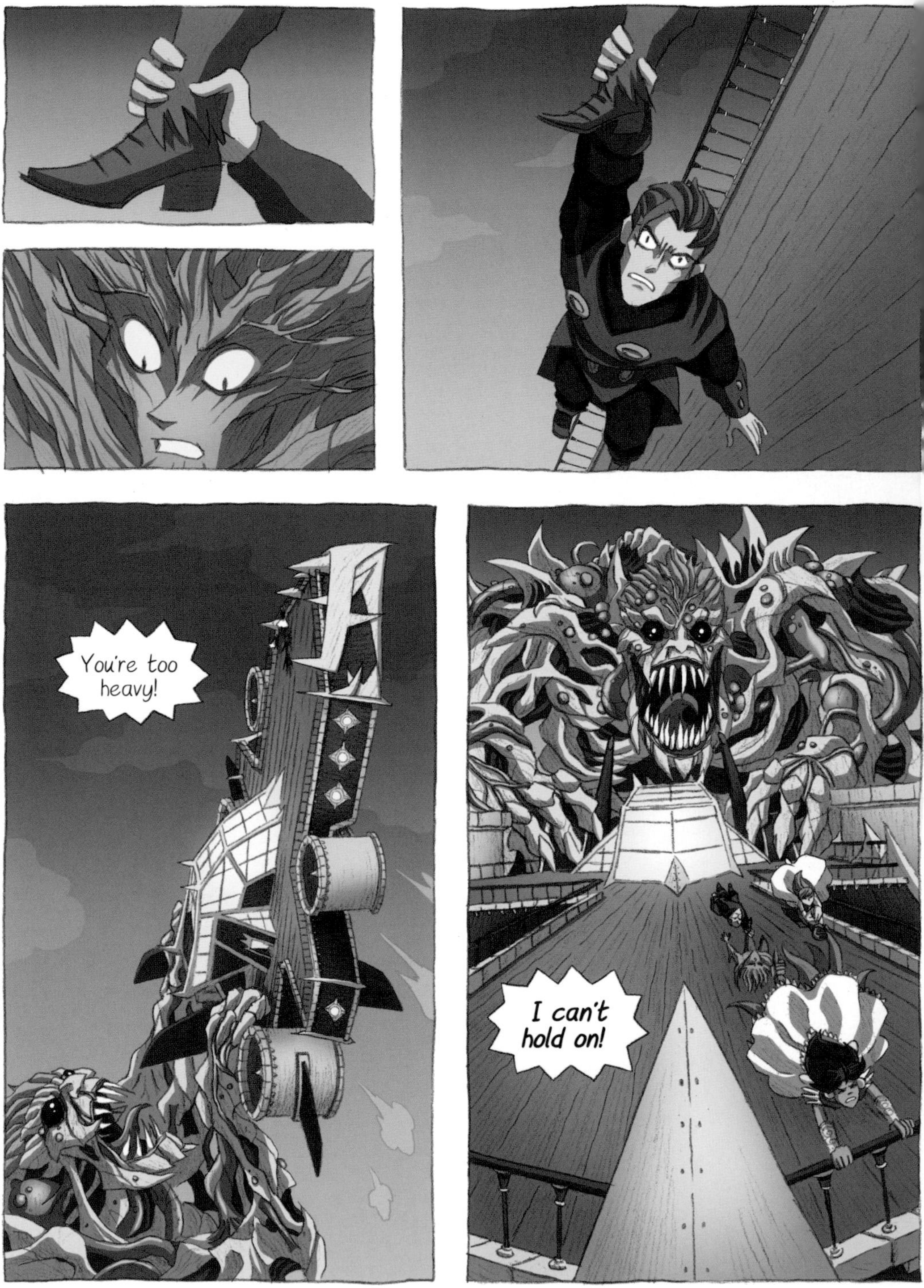
You're too heavy!
I can't hold on!

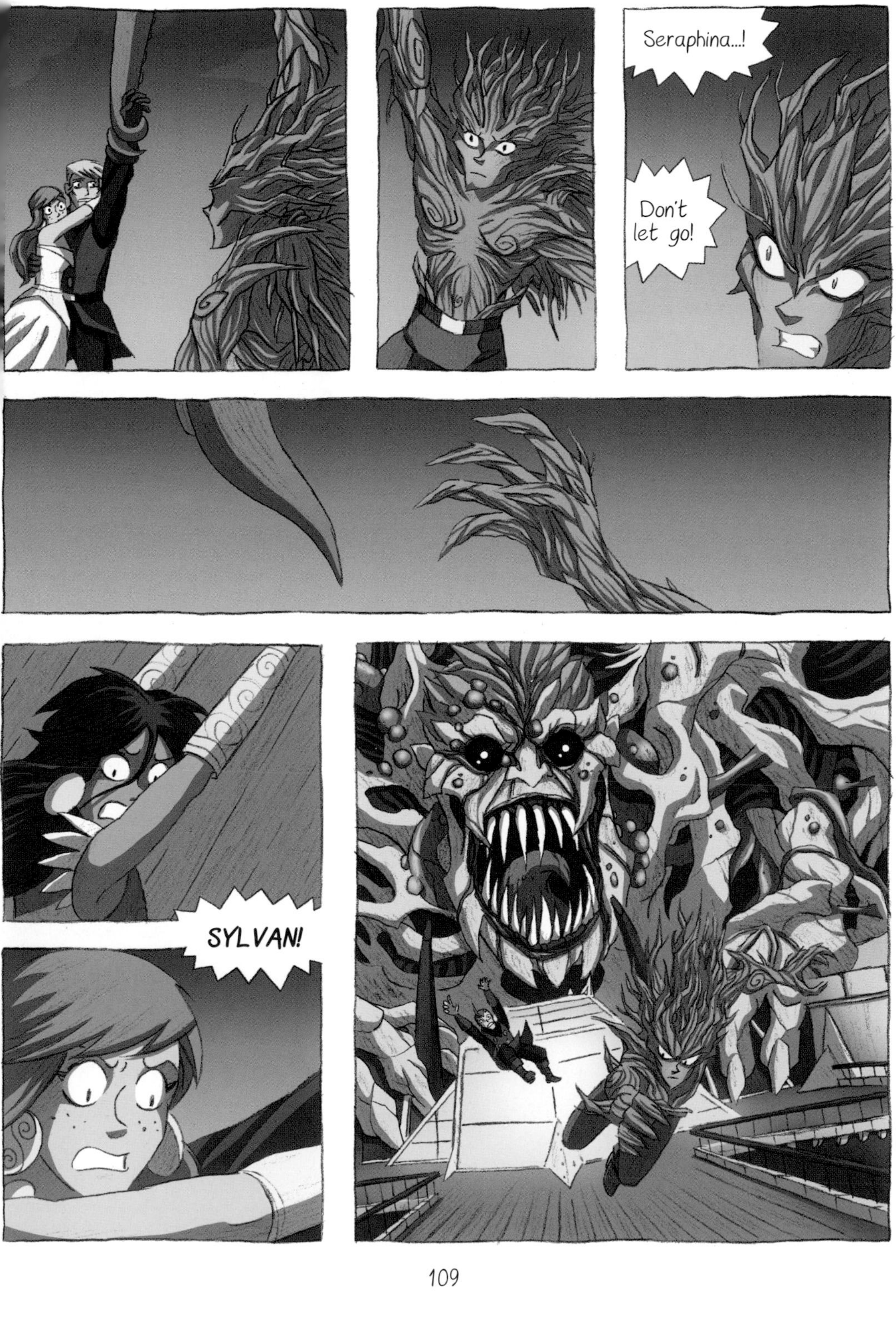
Seraphina...!
Don't let go!
SYLVAN!

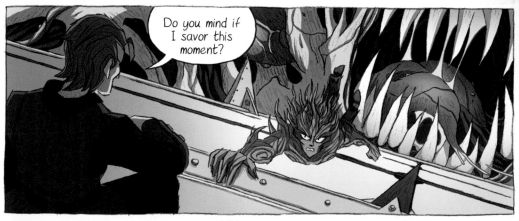

Do you mind if I savor this moment?

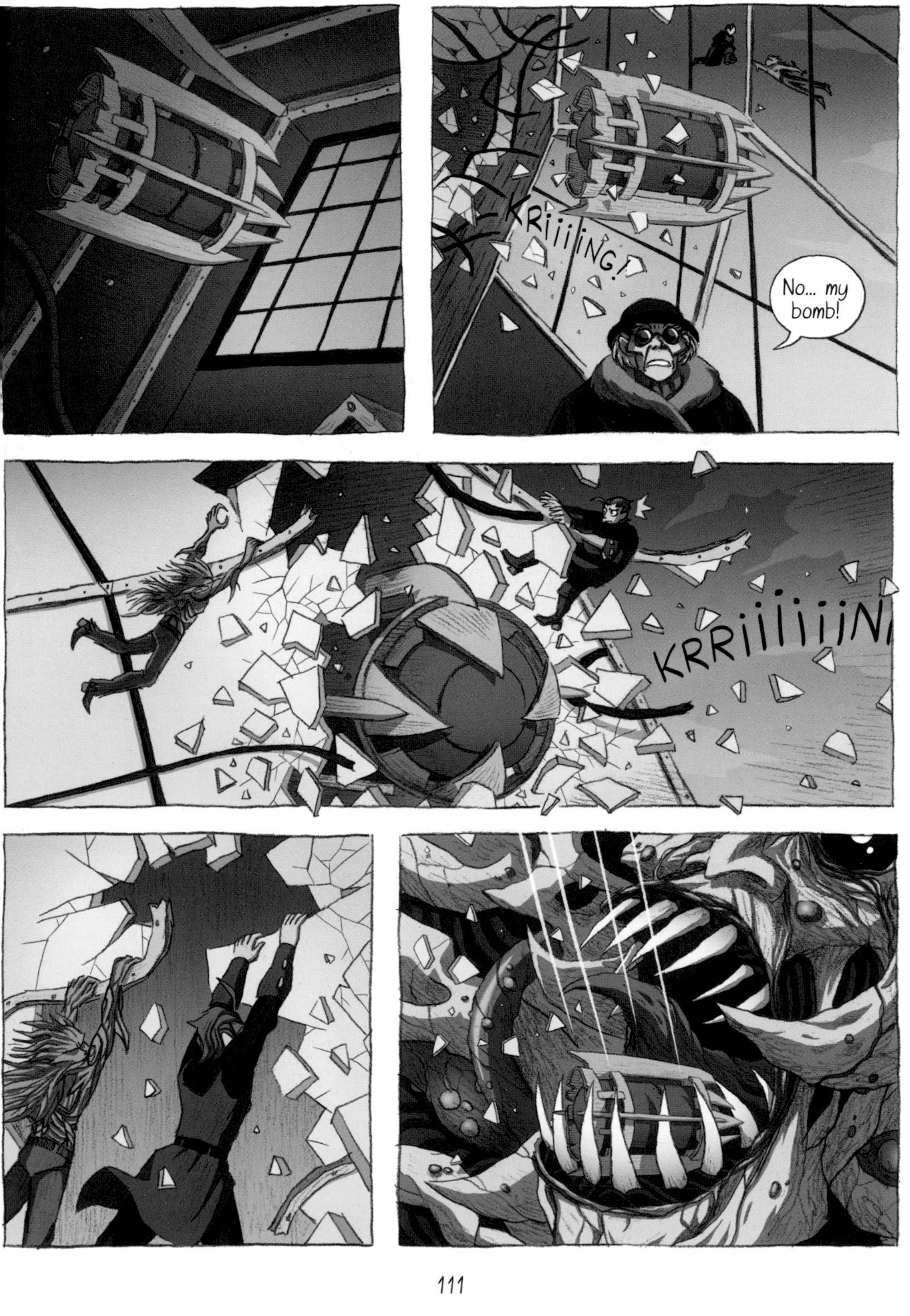
KRiiiiNG!
No... my bomb!
KRRiiiiiiN

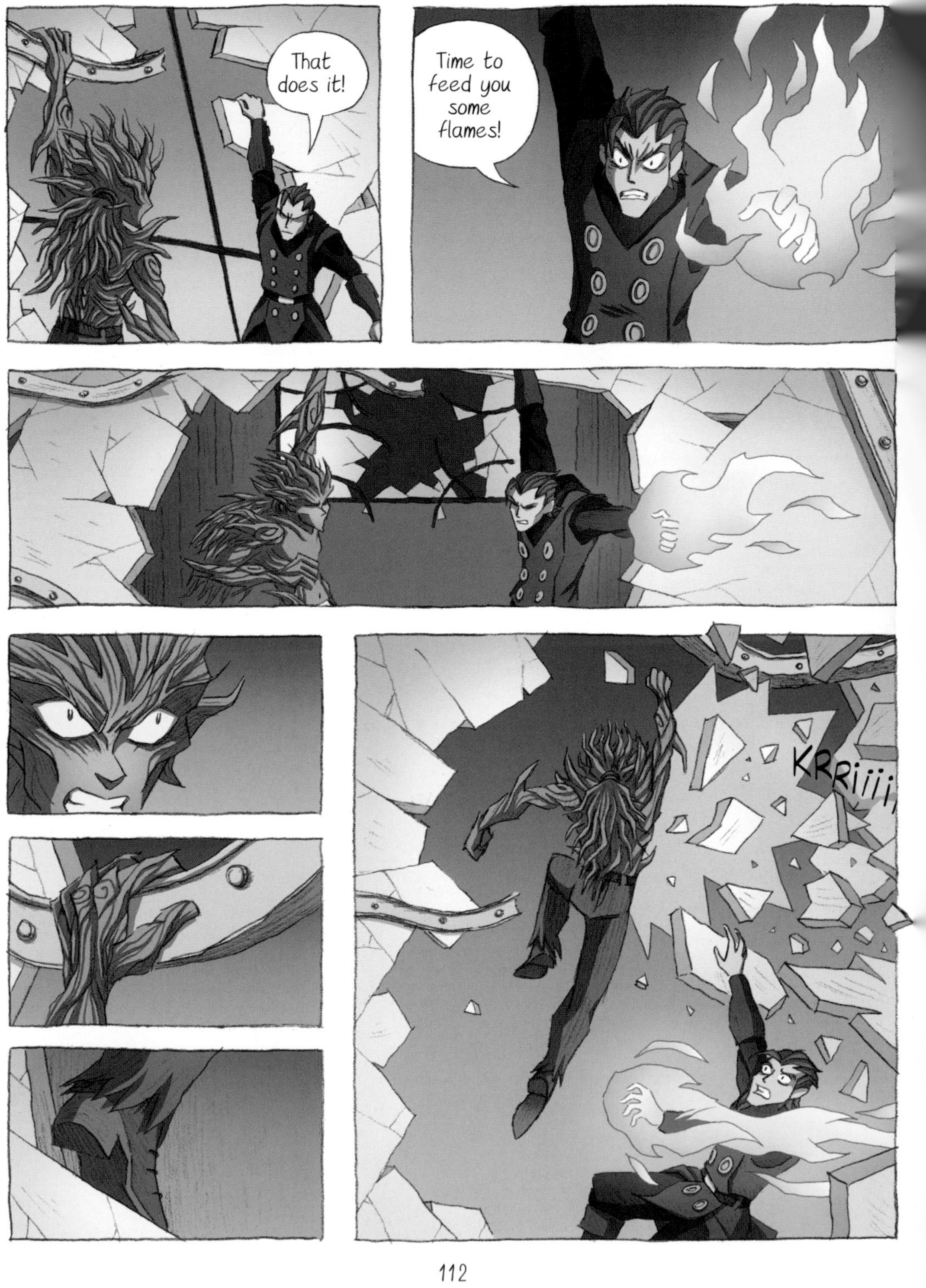
That does it!
Time to feed you some flames!
KRRiiiii

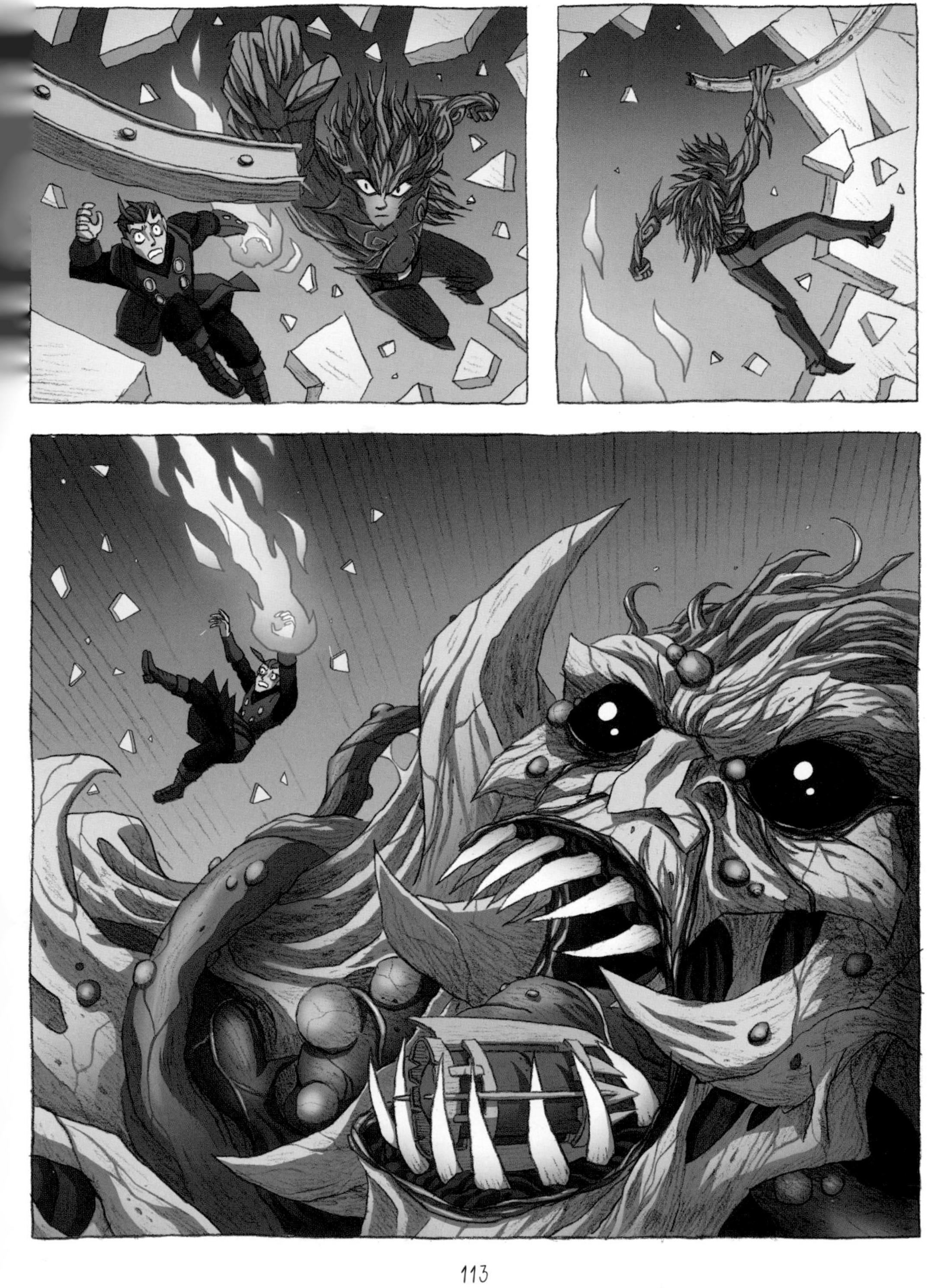

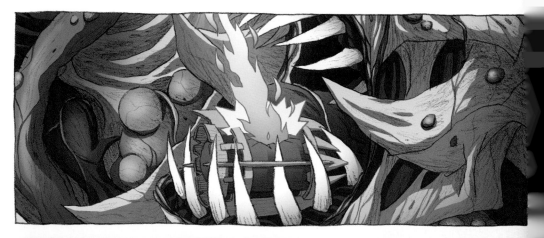

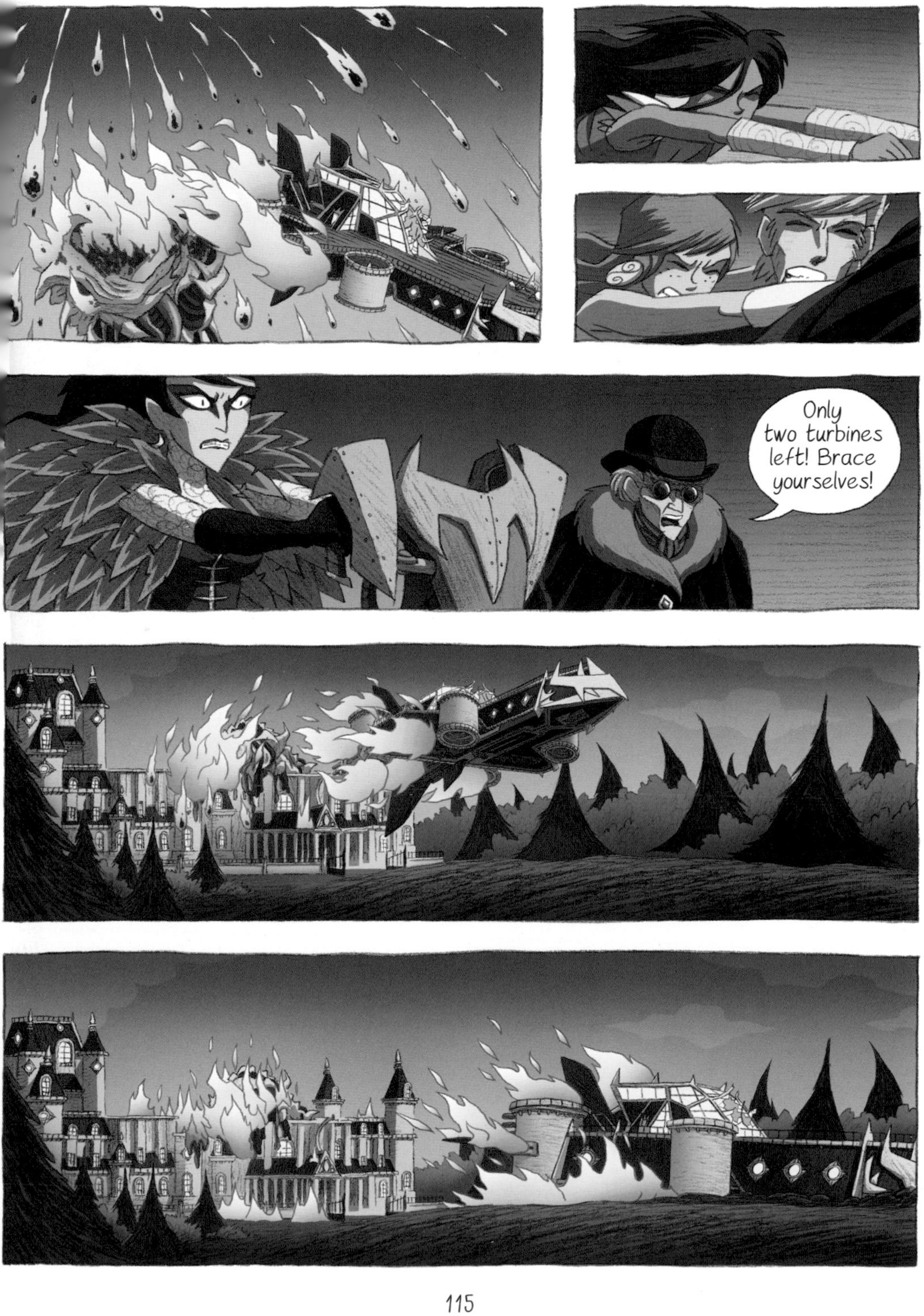
Only two turbines left! Brace yourselves!

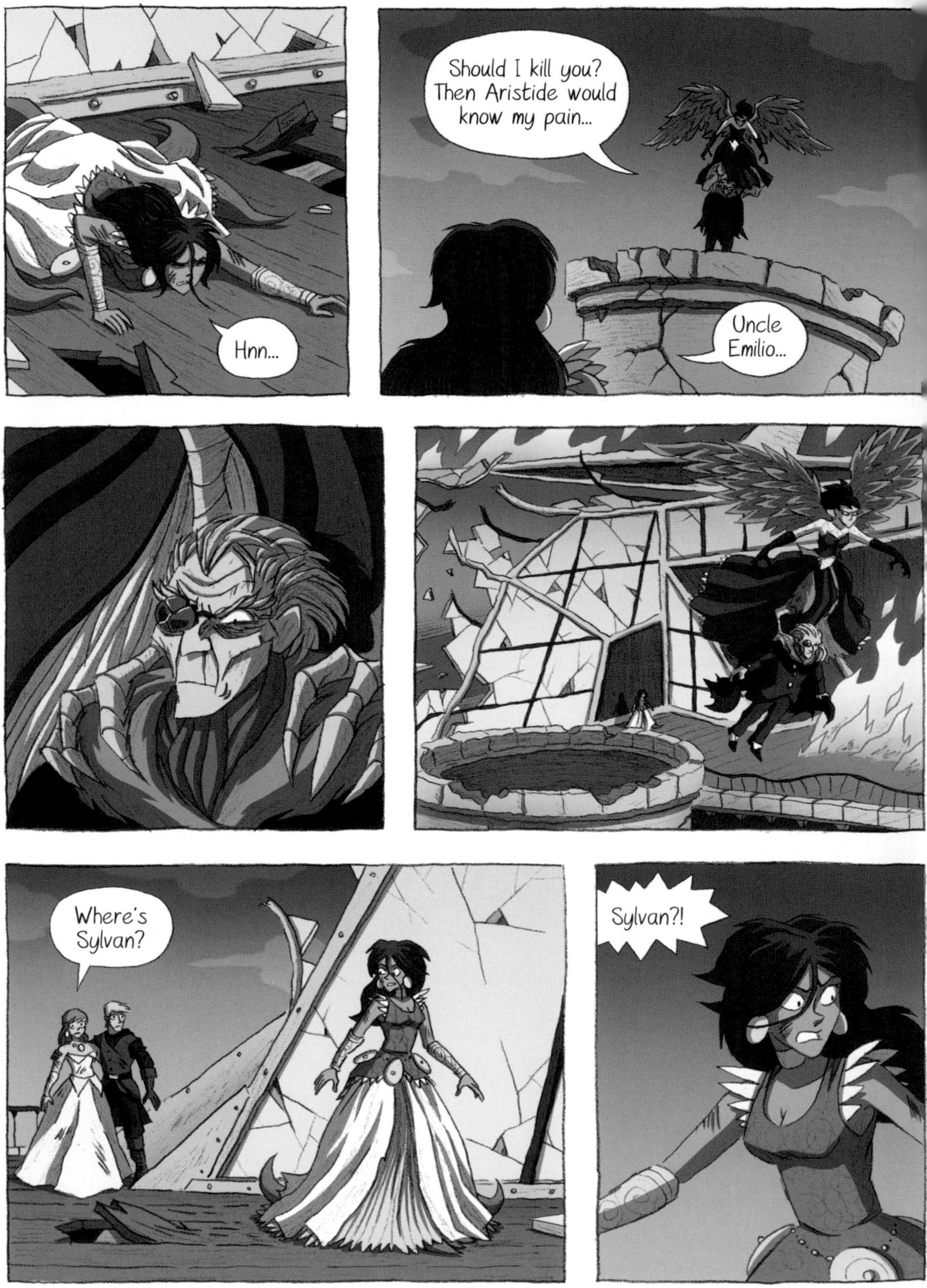
Hnn...
Should I kill you? Then Aristide would know my pain...
Uncle Emilio...
Where's Sylvan?
Sylvan?!

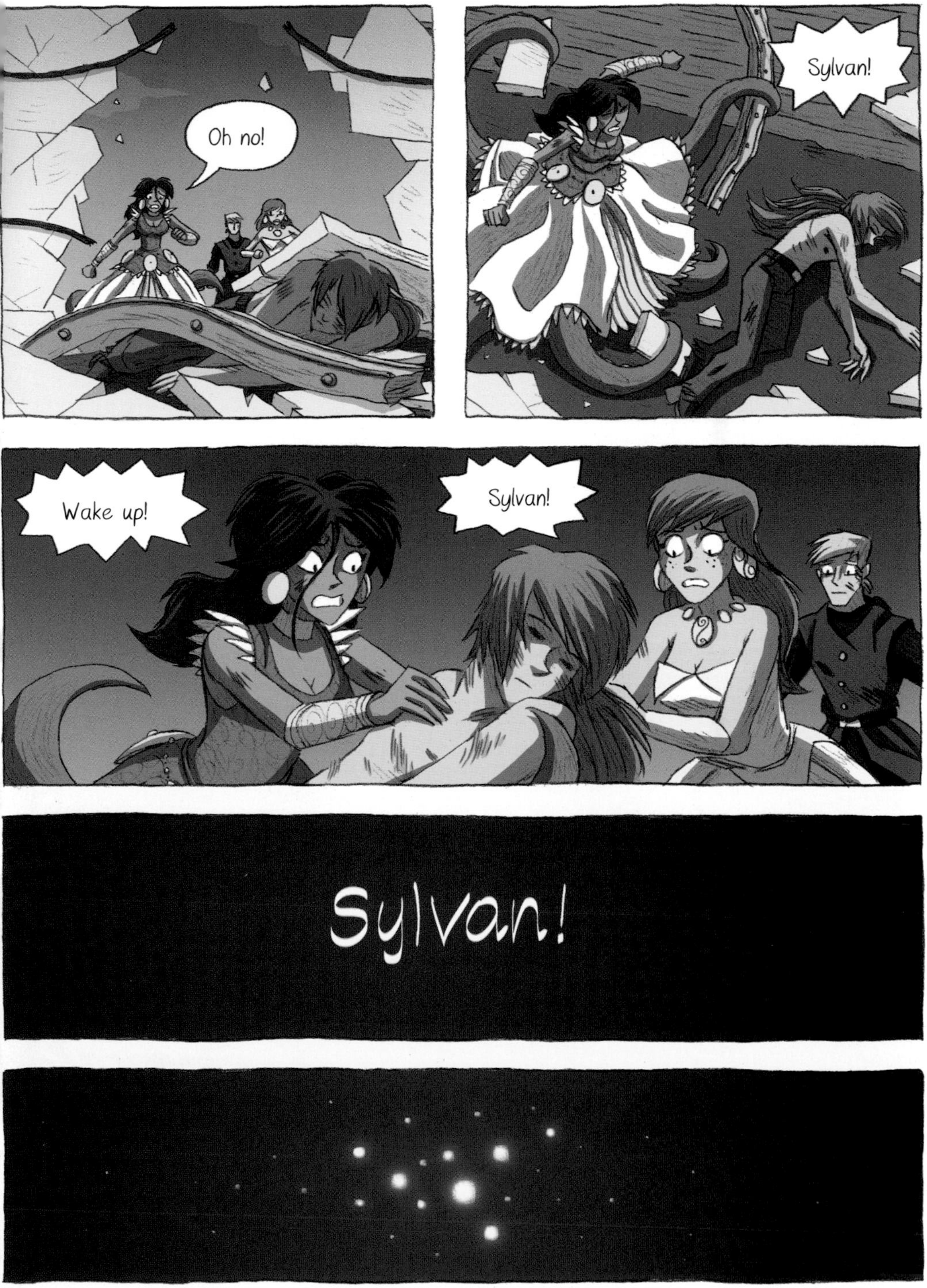
Oh no!
Sylvan!
Wake up!
Sylvan!
Sylvan!

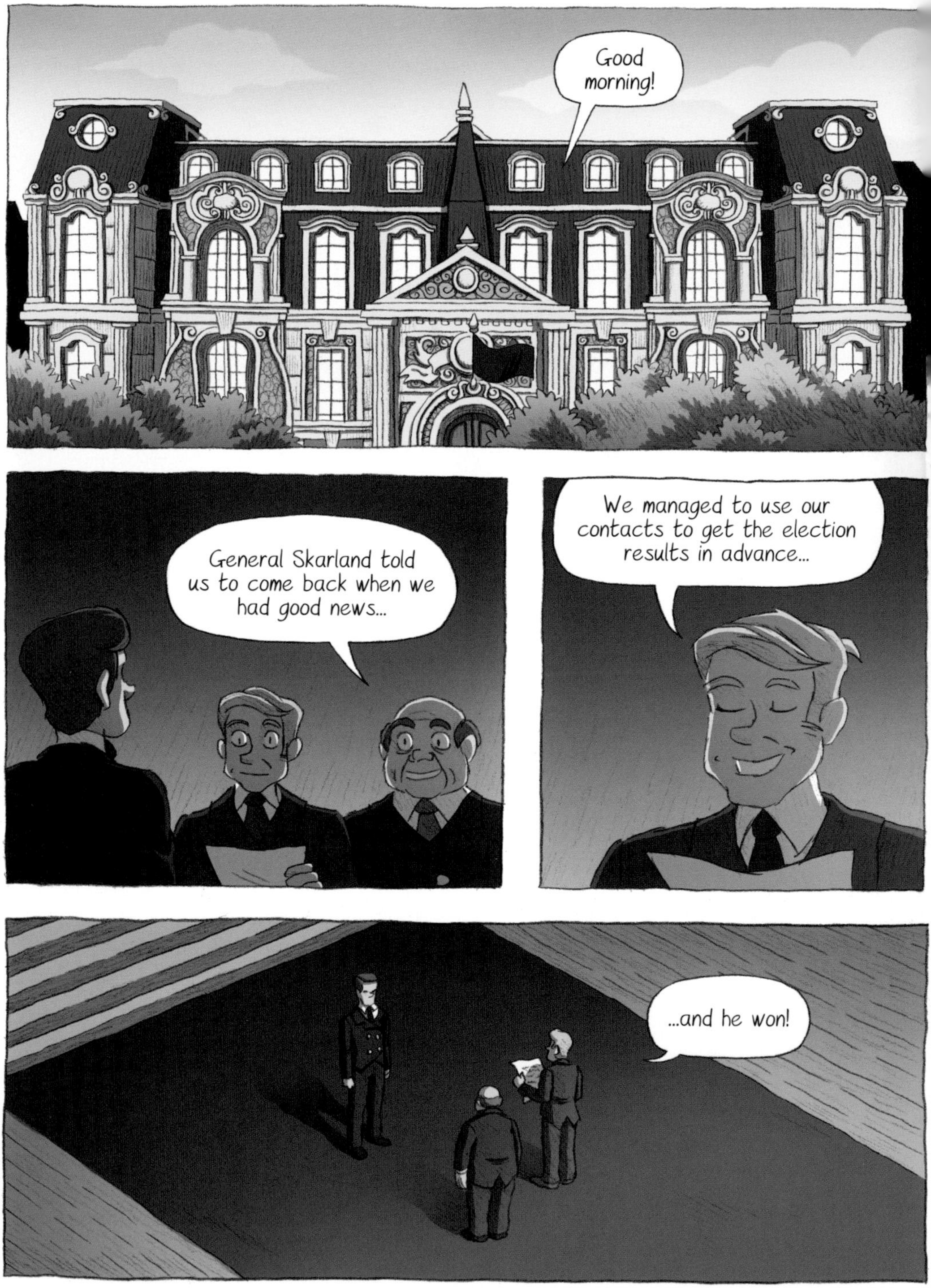
Good morning!
General Skarland told us to come back when we had good news...
We managed to use our contacts to get the election results in advance...
...and he won!

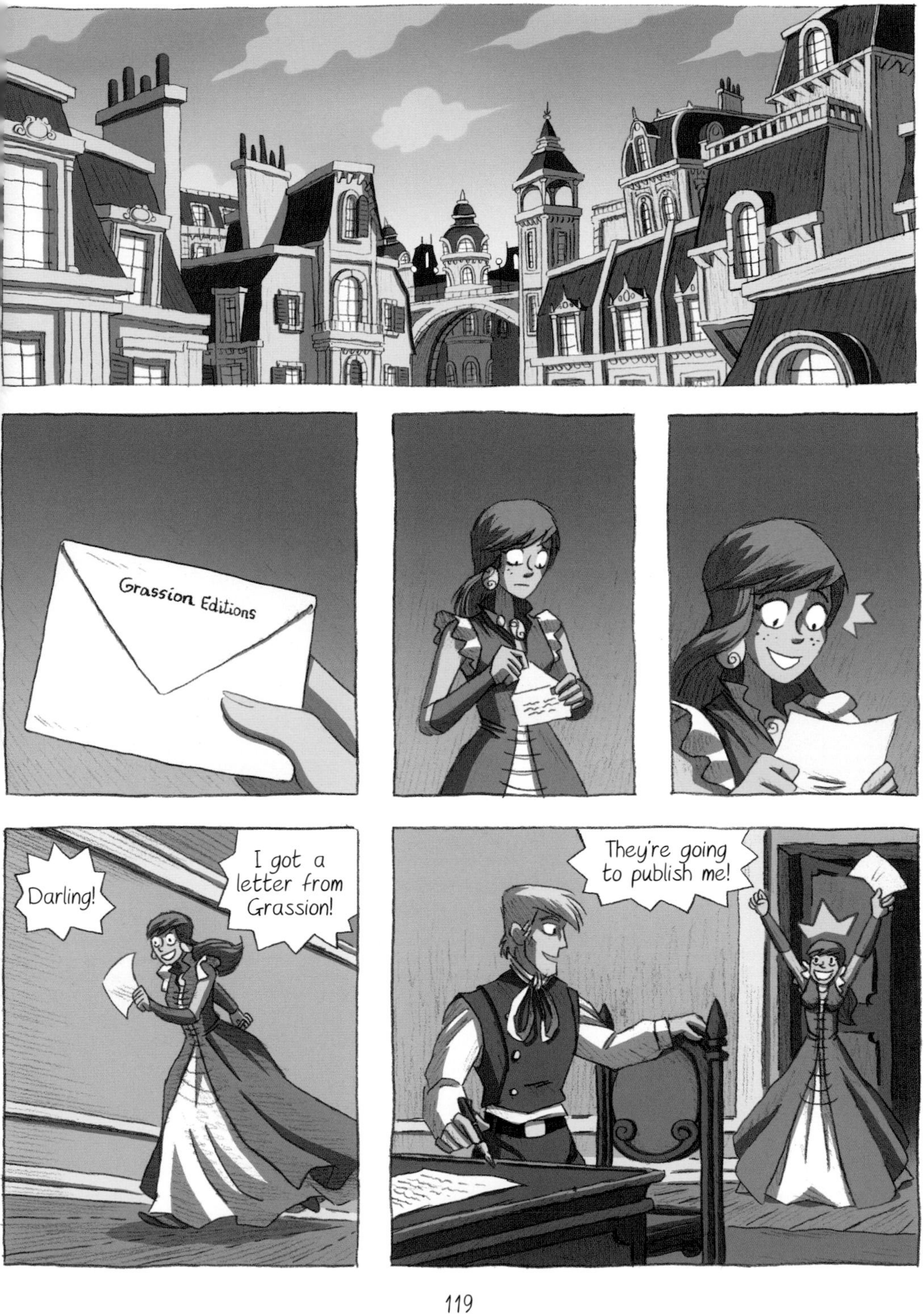
Grassion Editions
Darling!
I got a letter from Grassion!
They're going to publish me!

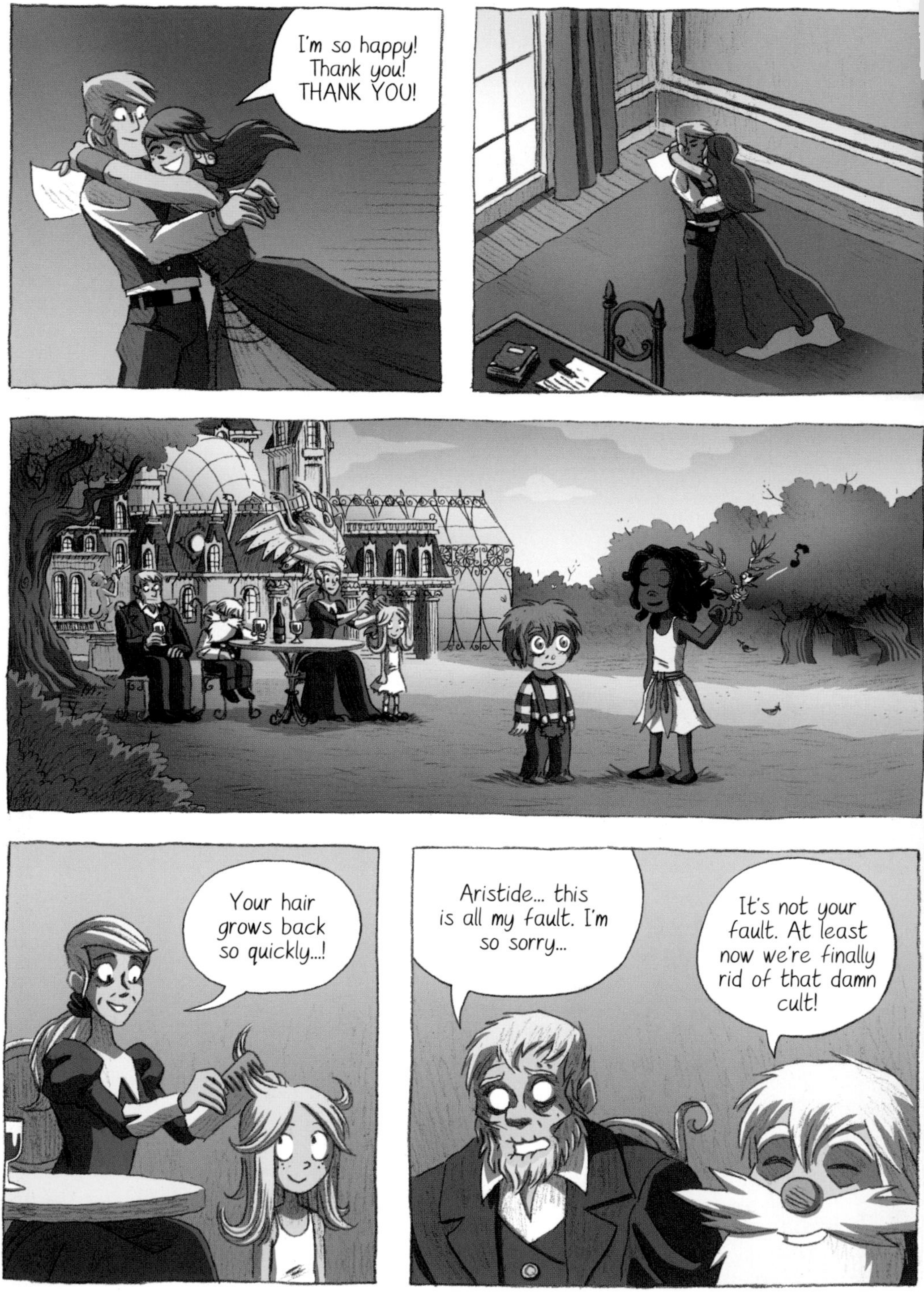
I'm so happy! Thank you! THANK YOU!
Your hair grows back so quickly...!
Aristide... this is all my fault. I'm so sorry...
It's not your fault. At least now we're finally rid of that damn cult!

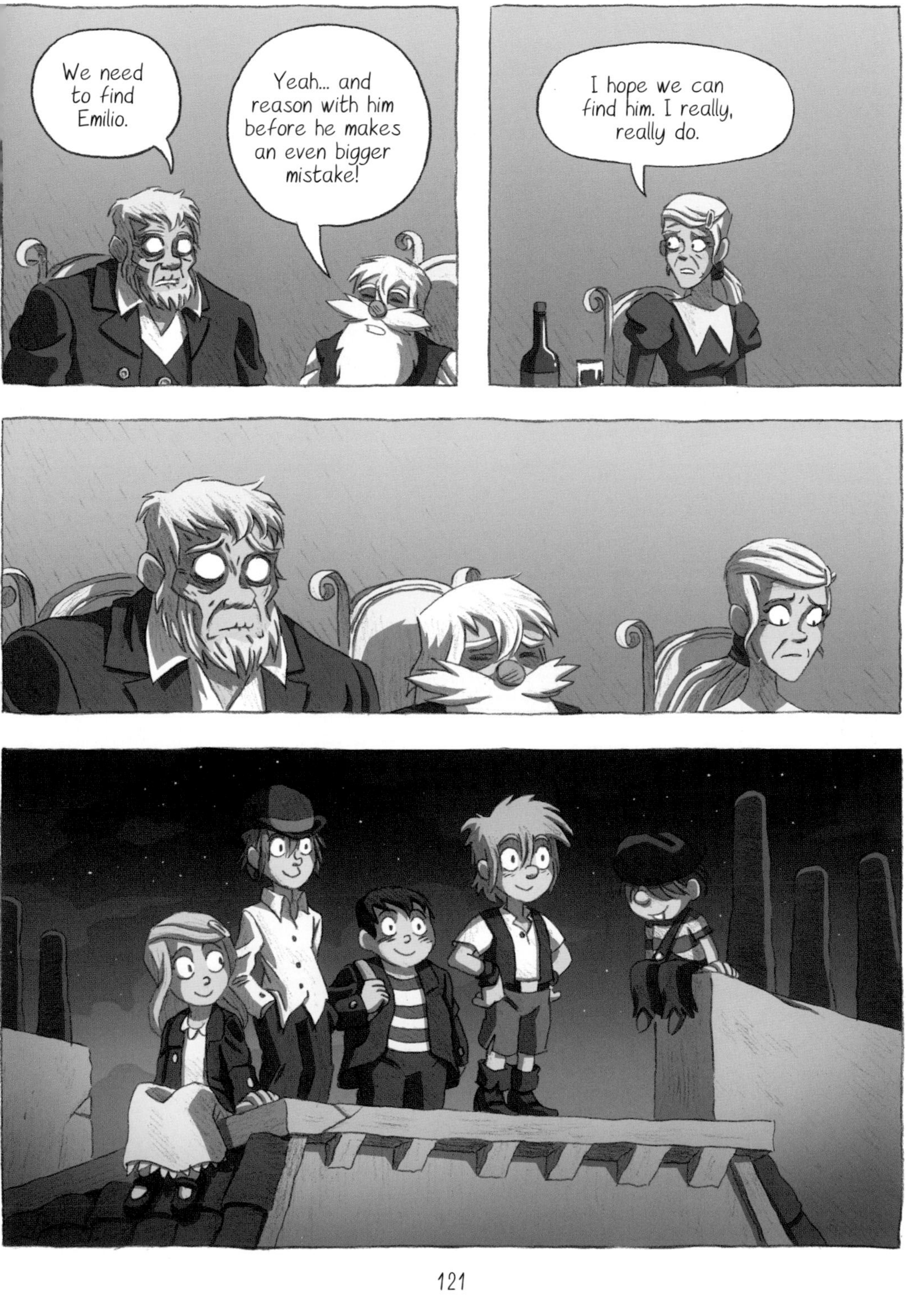
We need to find Emilio.
Yeah... and reason with him before he makes an even bigger mistake!
I hope we can find him. I really, really do.

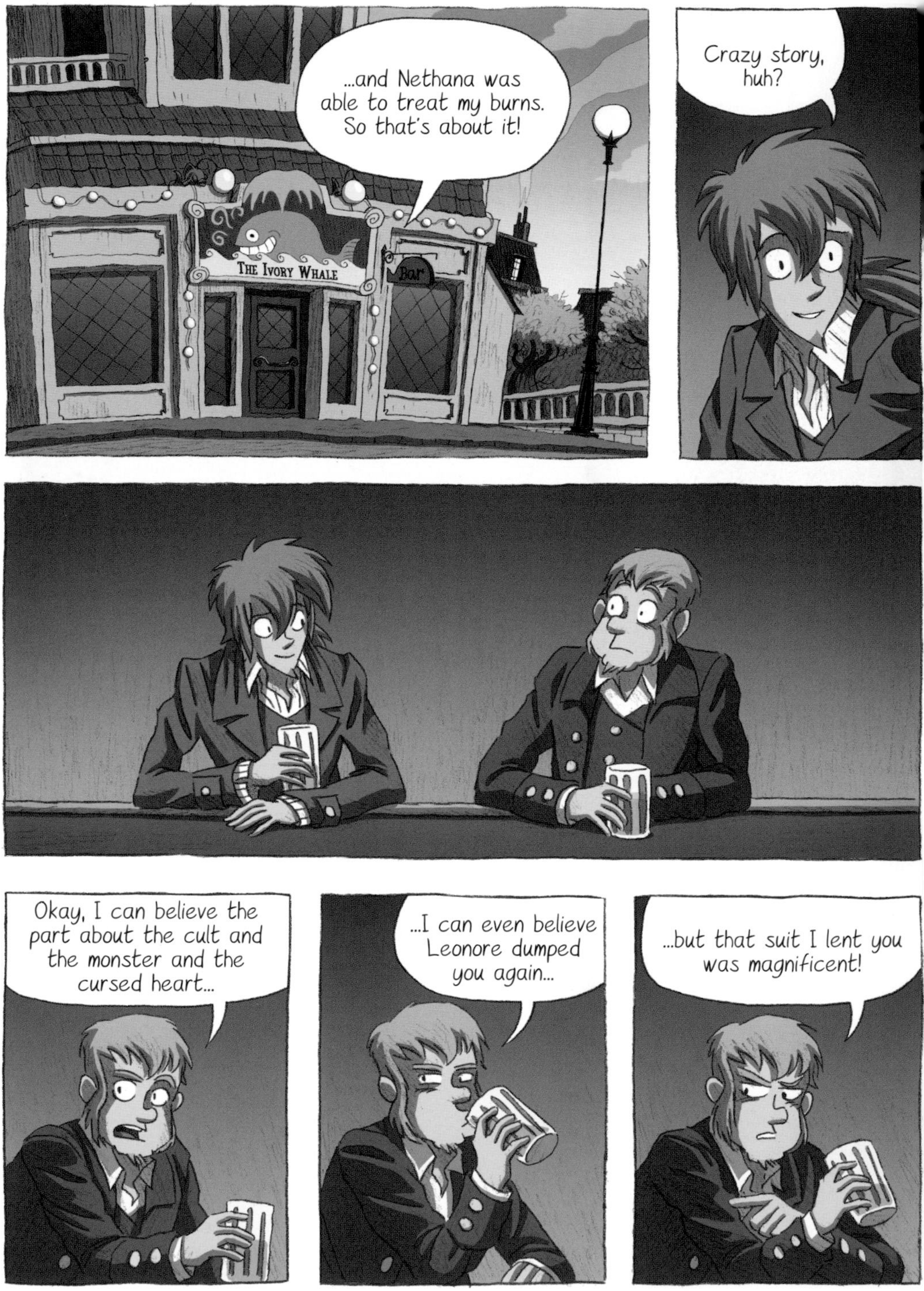
...and Nethana was able to treat my burns. So that's about it!
THE IVORY WHALE
Bar
Crazy story, huh?
Okay, I can believe the part about the cult and the monster and the cursed heart...
...I can even believe Leonore dumped you again...
...but that suit I lent you was magnificent!

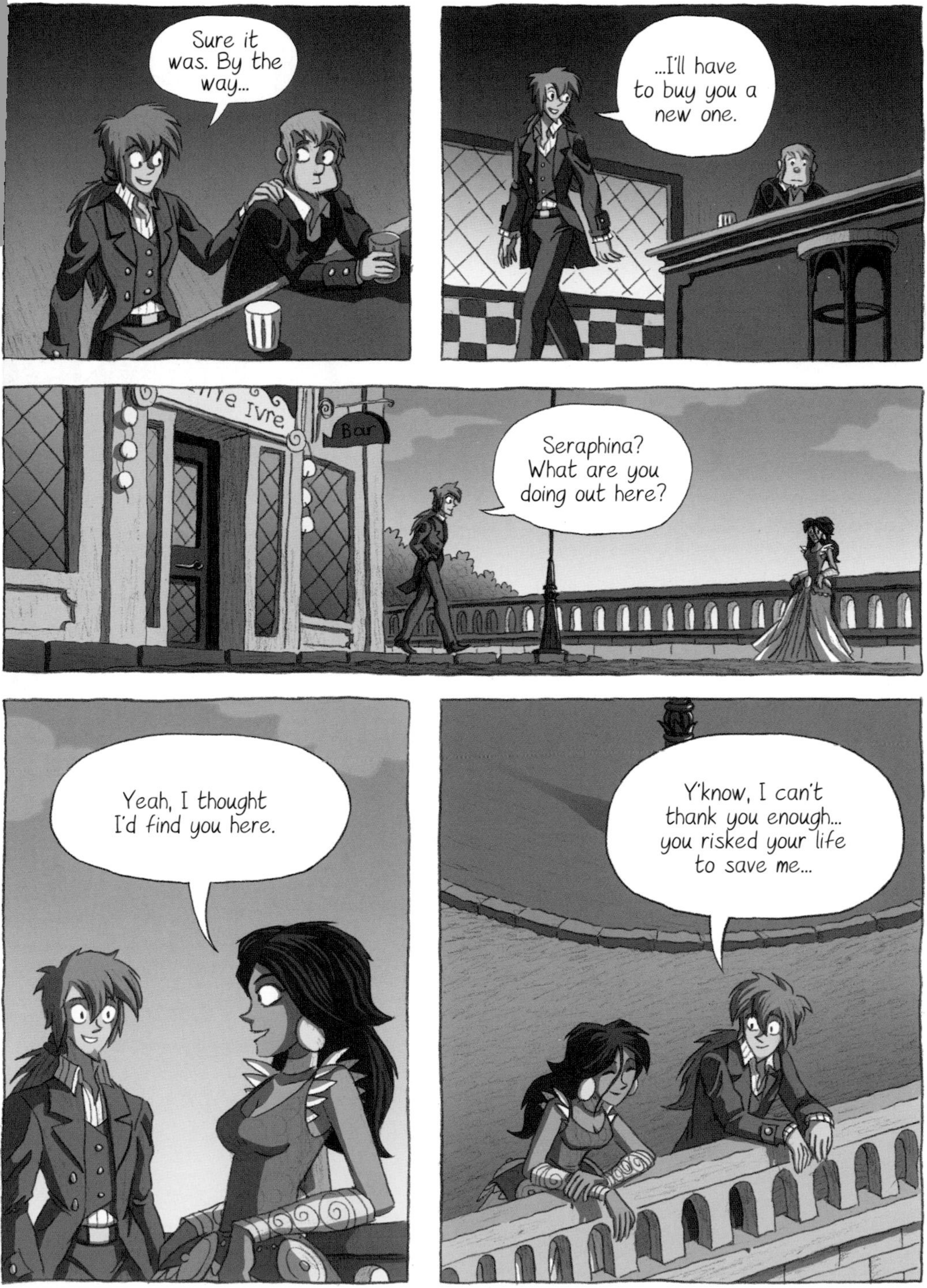
Sure it was. By the way...
...I'll have to buy you a new one.
Ivre
Bar
Seraphina? What are you doing out here?
Yeah, I thought I'd find you here.
Y'know, I can't thank you enough... you risked your life to save me...

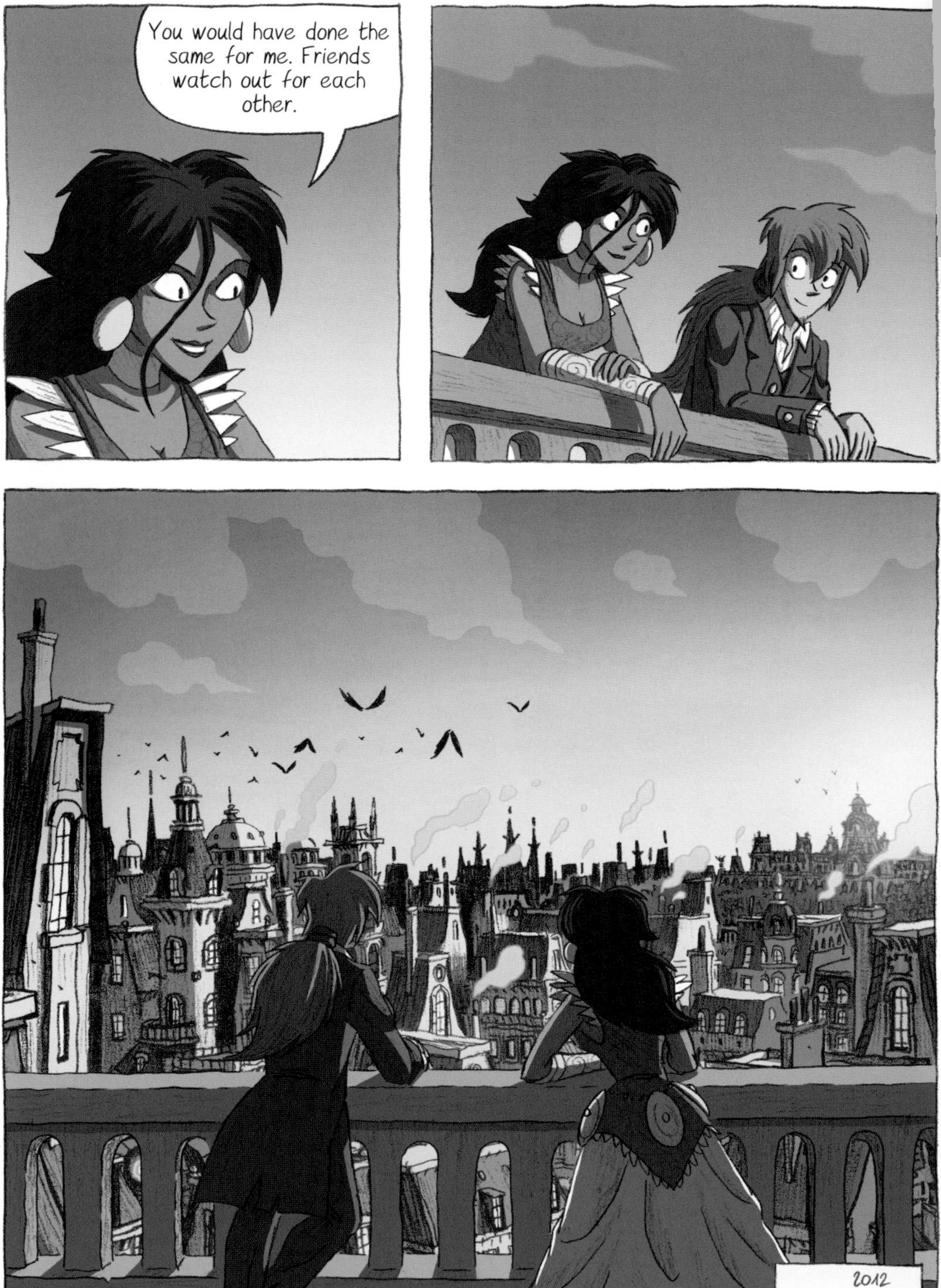
You would have done the same for me. Friends watch out for each other.
2012
Karim Friha

Seraphina, by Muchu

Seraphina bathing

ABOUT THE AUTHOR

 Karim Friha was born in Maisons-Laffitte, France, in 1980. As a child, he took a liking to comics with the Franco-Belgian classics, most notably *Asterix* and *Gaston Lagaffe*. After receiving his bachelors degree in science, he studied math but ended up drawing far more than anything else, enjoying the history of art more than trigonometry. While he became passionate about the artistic period of the eighteenth and nineteenth centuries, particularly the works of Voltaire and Victor Hugo, that didn't keep him from enjoying *The Simpsons*, *Calvin and Hobbes*, the works of Tim Burton, *Batman*, and a whole host of other superhero stories. Eventually, his art allowed him to work on kids' magazines and several animated films. *Rise of the Zelphire* is his first graphic novel series, showcasing his great talent for both storytelling and sequential art. It was an official selection of the 2010 Angoulême International Comics Festival and has been translated into several languages since.

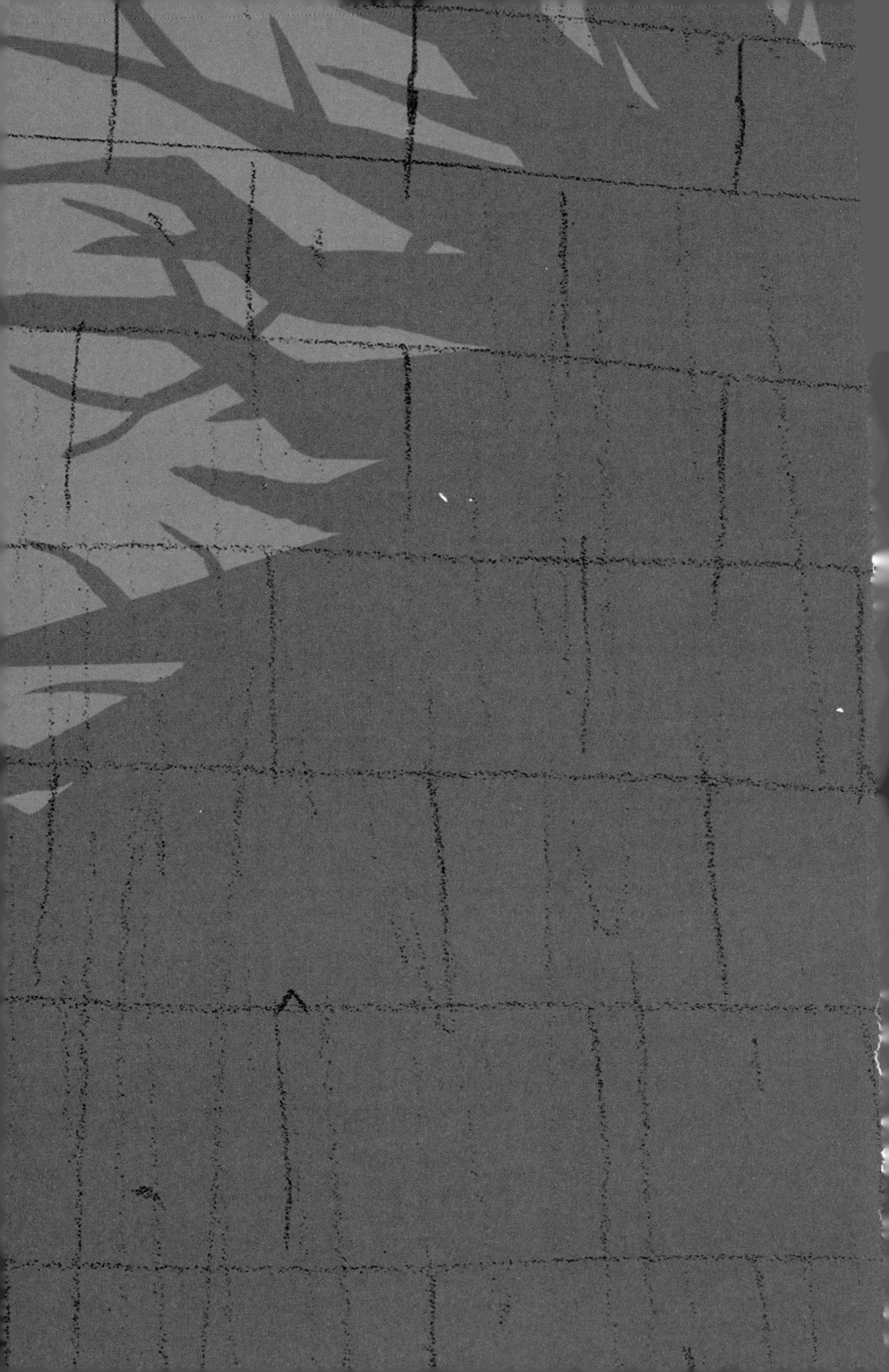